SMALL Change

DOMESTIC POLICY UNDER THE CLINTON PRESIDENCY

DAVID STOESZ
Virginia Commonwealth University

Longman Publishers USA

Small Change: Domestic Policy under the Clinton Presidency

Copyright © 1996 by Longman Publishers USA.
All rights reserved.
No part of this publication may be reproduced,
stored in a retrieval system, or transmitted
in any form or by any means, electronic, mechanical,
photocopying, recording, or otherwise,
without the prior permission of the publisher.

Longman, 10 Bank Street, White Plains, N.Y. 10606

Associated companies:
Longman Group Ltd., London
Longman Cheshire Pty., Melbourne
Longman Paul Pty., Auckland
Copp Clark Longman Ltd., Toronto

Acquisitions editor: George T. Hoffman
Assistant editor: Hillary Henderson
Production editor: Linda Moser
Cover design: Tom Phon
Production supervisor: Richard Bretan
Compositor: ExecuStaff

Library of Congress Cataloging-in-Publication Data
Stoesz, David.
    Small change : domestic policy under the Clinton presidency / by David Stoesz.
        p.   cm.
    Includes bibliographical references and index.
    ISBN 08013-1515-8
    1. United States—Social policy—1993- 2. United States—Economic policy—1993- 3. United States—Politics and government—1993-
    I. Title.
HN59.2.S76 1996
361.6'1'0973—dc20   95-11002
                                                                                CIP

1 2 3 4 5 6 7 8 9 10-MA-9998979695

For Lizzie, Carl, and Mattie—the next generation.

Contents

Preface   ix

CHAPTER 1   **PARADIGM PROMISED**   1

    Competing Visions of Social Policy   *2*
    The Welfare State on Autopilot   *6*
    Invasion of the ConWonks: Hyphenating Ideology I   *11*
    Rex Reagan   *13*
    Hyphenating Ideology II: Neoliberalism   *15*
    The "New Paradigm"   *18*
    Ideological Regression: Paleoliberalism   *19*
    A Decade of Transition   *22*
        Commerce versus Commonweal 23, Hypermobility versus Dualism 23, Restructuring versus Bureaucracy 23, Human Capital versus Entitlements 24

CHAPTER 2   **HEALTH CARE: FALSE PROFITS**   29

    Medicare   *30*
    Medicaid   *33*
    The Rise of Corporate Health Care   *33*
    Catastrophic Health Insurance   *35*
    Prelude to Health Care Reform   *36*
    The Health Security Act   *39*

Postmortem on Health Care Reform *41*
The Next Health Care Policy Agenda *44*
  Invest in Prevention 45, Tax For-Profit Health Providers 47,
  Federally Charter a Consumer-Controlled HMO 48

CHAPTER 3 WELFARE: POOR POLICY 57

"Welfare" *59*
Poverty *60*
Conservative Welfare Reform *63*
Welfare-to-Work *65*
"The End of Welfare As We Know It" *69*
The Next Welfare Reform Agenda *73*
  Child Support Assurance 75, Creation of Individual Development Accounts 77, Deconstruction of Welfare Bureaucracies 78

CHAPTER 4 URBAN POLICY: MAINSTREAMING THE UNDERCLASS 85

An Urban Diaspora *87*
The Reagan Revolution *90*
The Rise of the Underclass *92*
Plumping the Overclass *94*
The Inner City Besieged *96*
  Gang Violence 96, Homelessness 99
The Clinton Urban Policy *102*
The Next Urban Policy Agenda *105*
  Disperse Public Housing 106, Establish Youth Enterprise Zones 107, Forge Urban Compacts 108

CHAPTER 5 EDUCATION: SLOUCHING TOWARD THE TWENTY-FIRST CENTURY 117

A History of American Education *119*
"A Rising Tide of Mediocrity" *122*
A Decade of Experimentation *124*
The School Choice Debate *127*
America 2000 *129*
Whither Higher Education? *131*
The Next Agenda in Education Policy *133*
  School-Based Human Services 134, Preferred School Choice 136, Apprentice Warranties 138, Universities in the Public Interest 140

CHAPTER 6 **IMMIGRATION: THE CLOSING OF THE
AMERICAN DREAM   149**

    The European Migrant Waves   *150*
    Early Immigration Statutes   *153*
    The Immigration Reform and Control Act   *155*
    "Birds of Passage"   *158*
    Immigration and Social Welfare   *159*
    The Next Immigration Policy Agenda   *162*
      *A Rolling Amnesty Date 163, A Guest-Worker Program 164,
      Negotiate a NAFTA Side-Agreement on Immigrant Labor 165*

CHAPTER 7 **SOCIAL SECURITY: SHOWDOWN
AT GEEZER GULCH   173**

    The Origins of Social Security   *174*
    An Expanding Entitlement   *177*
    The Burgeoning Surplus   *179*
    The Entitlement Crisis   *183*
    The Next Agenda for Social Security   *188*
      *Lift the Cap on Taxable Income 189, Make the Withholding Tax
      Progressive 190, Allow Workers to Designate a Portion of
      Withholding 190, Create a Generational Investment Fund 190*

CHAPTER 8 **PARADIGM LOST   195**

    The "New Democrats"   *197*
    White House Follies   *198*
    The Clinton Record   *200*
    Small Change   *202*
      *Health 203, Welfare 204, Urban Policy 204, Education 205,
      Immigration 206, Social Security 206*
    Seismic Shock: The 1994 Midterm Elections   *207*
    Beyond the Politics of Retrenchment   *211*
      *From Commonweal to Commerce 211, From Dualism to
      Hypermobility 212, From Bureaucracy to Restructuring 212, From
      Entitlements to Human Capital 213*

Index   223

About the Author   228

Preface

Well I'm accustomed to a smoother ride.
Maybe I'm a dog that's lost its bite.
I don't expect to be treated like a fool
   no more.
I don't expect to sleep the night.
Some people say a lie is just a lie,
But I say the cross is in the ball park.
Why deny the obvious child?

Paul Simon[1]

Every generation is confronted with the challenge of resolving the social issues of the day. The result of their labors is never complete, nor is it definitive. When done well, it reveals a template or set of rules that seem to offer direction for social policy. Successful presidents fashion their domestic initiatives by drawing from social and intellectual momentum as it evolves. Thus, distinctive presidencies, such as Johnson and his "Great Society" or Reagan and his "New Federalism," attain an enduring coherence. With great presidents, a legislative legacy provides a foundation upon which future generations can build. Nevertheless, all edifices decay over time; none is immune from the corrosion accompanying alterations of culture. Eventually, even the most durable of foundations must be reworked, and the course of domestic policy takes new direction.

The thesis of *Small Change* is that the United States is at such a threshold: The traditional solutions to political, economic, and social dynamics of domestic policy have been relegated to the dustbin. The next generation is thus faced with a series of extraordinarily difficult problems involving health, welfare, education, cities, immigration, and retirement—but with fewer public resources to solve them. But this is *not* to say they are insuperable. "When the going gets weird," observed Hunter Thompson, "the weird turn pro." Mostly, we need imagination and gumption.

In order to generate discussion about policy options, I have briefly summarized by own ideas on how to proceed. They may not be politically correct in terms of ideological convention. Many liberals will balk at my support of school choice for poor families; many conservatives will gag at my endorsement of making Social Security withholding more progressive. Good. As I argue in the first chapter, too often the public interest has been subverted by public officials using historical metaphor or ideological polemic to dodge their responsibility. Given our polity, smoke and mirrors will continue to characterize discussion of domestic policy until an informed public puts a stop to it by demanding that public officials perform commensurate with their salaries. Ultimately, the quality of domestic policy in a democracy is only as good as the knowledge held by its citizens.

Toward that end, I invite readers to call. That's right, pick up the phone; call the author. Book format suggests a permanence that belies the true origin of publications such as this. Everything that follows is the result of reading, discussing, and deliberating about social affairs. In the final analysis, a book is little more than formalizing a lot of conversation. If so inclined, you too can be part of the dialogue. I'm in the phone book. Two requests: call before 10 P.M. (my time), and pronounce my name correctly—Stoesz rhymes with "ace." You may also contact me by E-mail. My E-mail address is dstoesz@vcu.edu.

Second, students can enter the "Social Policy Sweepstakes," a semi-annual competition for new ideas in public policy. To enter, submit your idea on plain paper, typed double-spaced, no more than five pages of text, a bibliography limited to ten sources, and a stamped self-addressed envelope with proper postage. On the cover page, provide a title, your name and address, the discipline you are studying, and your institutional affiliation. At the end of each semester, I will select a winner who will receive a cash award in an amount to be determined by me. Submissions should be sent to me at Virginia Commonwealth University. The deadlines for receipt of submissions are May 15 and December 15. I reserve the right not to designate a winner if submissions are unsatisfactory.

I wish to express gratitude to several people who contributed to *Small Change*. The following individuals reviewed the manuscript and provided helpful suggestions: Tom Roy, University of Montana; Philip Jackson, University of Cincinnati; Todd Rofuth, Southern Connecticut State University; Katharine V. Byers, Indiana University; Richard Hoefer, University of Texas—Arlington; John M. Herrick, Michigan State University; and Dolores Finger Wright, Delaware State University. Among the professors who provoked the germinal thoughts that are elaborated here, I recognize June Hopps, Norman Chance, Ben Kleinberg, and Harry Chaiklin. During the writing of the book, Howard Karger provided essential doses of encouragement as well as caution. Mark Lusk put me up in an office at Boise State University that afforded an expansive view of my first autumn in almost a decade, and he captured my attention in more engaging discussions than I can count. San Diego State University provided the sabbatical leave during which this was written, and Dolores Wozniak, the Dean of the College of Health and Human Service, provided timely, and I suspect, unintended support. The astute observations of Paul Stoesz improved the manuscript immeasurably, as did the comments of colleagues who reviewed early drafts: Steve Savas, Jim Pinkerton, Will Marshall, and the staff at Longman—Roth Wilkofsky, Pam Gordon, Owen Lancer, and George Hoffman—executed the manuscript expeditiously and professionally.

To all of you, thanks!

David Stoesz

NOTE

1. Paul Simon, "The Obvious Child," *The Rhythm of the Saints* (Warner Brothers, 1990).

chapter 1

Paradigm Promised

Man always seeks to rationalize his necessities—and, whenever possible, to glorify them.

H.L. Mencken[1]

1995: Bill Clinton is approaching the end of his first term as president, and his social policy agenda is due for an accounting. Are disadvantaged Americans—minorities, women, and the poor—better off in 1996 than they were four years before? Has the nation prospered as a result of the administration's economic stewardship? Will the president be able to overcome the electoral reversal of 1994 and revitalize "new Democrat" thinking in preparation for the 1996 elections? Invariably, the answers to such questions will fill the editorial columns of newspapers. Appointees within the administration will undoubtedly recount the accomplishments of their respective agencies. The president will explain—once again—that his has been the "most effective" first term within recent memory.

Such presidential reassurances notwithstanding, the Clinton administration experienced a precipitous decline in credibility. The media's initial tendency to indulge the administration during the early months of the Clinton presidency left Republicans uncertain about how to respond to a centrist Democrat. Initially, the party out of power oscillated between petty whining about alleged improprieties—Hillary Clinton's windfall in livestock futures comes to mind—to evisceration of Democratic policy initiatives—the surgical strike against Clinton's economic stimulus package under the direction of Bob Dole, the dark prince of American politics, and his sidekick, Newt Gingrich, as an example.

But by the end of the 103rd Congress, it became strikingly clear that the Clinton administration had to contend with more substantial problems than

Republican obstructionism. The White House passed a budget by the slimmest of margins, skated to victory in passage of the North American Free Trade Agreement (NAFTA), struggled to convince intransigent Democrats to release a crime bill from committee, only to take a drubbing in the defeat of its health care reform initiative. By the end of his first two years in office, Bill Clinton had seen little of his "new Democrat" agenda become law; Congress had approved a small National Service Program, but health care and campaign reform were dead, and welfare reform had been postponed. As if to aggravate matters, two books appeared—*The Agenda* by Bob Woodward[2] and *On the Edge* by Elizabeth Drew[3]—portraying the Clinton White House in less than flattering terms. Then, to underscore the tenuousness of the Clinton administration, Republicans swept to victory in the 1994 midterm election, gaining control of Congress for the first time in forty years.

Suddenly, the policy momentum seemed to pass from the president to the new Speaker of the House, Newt Gingrich, whose ten-point "Contract with America" was retrospectively credited with the Republican electoral triumph. As pundits dissected the entrails of the conservative Congressional takeover, however, the implications of the Contract with America were not at all clear. Does the Grand Old Party offer a confident rendering of the nation's future—or is it serving up warmed-over Reaganism? Will the Contract be the death knell of the American welfare state, as Gingrich has promised, or will it galvanize liberals to reassert the hegemony in domestic policy that they had enjoyed for the half-century following the passage of the Social Security Act in 1935? If for Gingrich welfare reform translates into orphanages, can welfare colonies in the Arctic be far behind? Ironically, if Gingrich is able to enact the Contract with America, traditional liberals may find themselves pining for the 1980s when a more benign conservative served as president.

COMPETING VISIONS OF SOCIAL POLICY

Untangling domestic policy in an open, democratic-capitalistic society such as ours is not simple. Government programs intrude on markets and vice versa; public policy advances in fits and starts; often programs sharing a common target, but evolving within different agencies, are not coordinated with one another; elected officials distort legislative intent and program outcomes for political advantage. If the sheer mass of material necessary for understanding the substance of any given policy area is not intimidating enough, the frequent changes in policy are enough to drive the most seasoned analyst daffy on occasion.

Conceptually, much of the current debate in domestic policy revolves around a powerful dynamic that incorporates economic, social, and political features: the understanding of social programs as being public utilities or market commodities. Since the earliest period of the industrial era, the Left has preferred that social programs be understood as public utilities: Certain activities are a common good needed by everyone. Because of the importance of social programs, the Left has argued that social programs should be removed from the market and either provided directly by government or, if they are contracted out, supervised closely by public officials. The public utility assumption held by the Left has led to the expectation that, for example, health should be the province of the public sector, much as education has been. A contrasting view advanced by the Right is that social programs, as they have evolved during the industrial era, are administered by inflexible and wasteful governmental bureaucracies. It is far better, argue conservatives, to subject such activities to the rigor of the marketplace. Market reformers suggest that, if social programs are run humanely, the beneficiaries will receive goods and services more efficiently and responsively than when such programs fell under the control of government bureaucrats. The primary characteristics of each assumption are indicated in Table 1.1.

These conceptualizations generate considerable heat when contrasted by proponents from opposing ends of the ideological continuum. The Left contends that the Right overlooks the downside of markets: The poor are often neglected, services tend to ignore citizens with multiple and chronic problems, and so forth. The Right argues that the Left insists that the poor obtain services from a second-rate public sector, one that not even leftists would elect if given a choice. Whereas research can help differentiate which solution might be better under certain conditions, studies evolve from assumptions, and the basic premises of studies often suggest that researchers implicitly favor one concept over another. As a result, it is not uncommon for studies to be employed by different camps to demonstrate the superiority of one orientation over the other. All too frequently, debate about preferences in program options degenerates into statistical battles where the primary concern appears to be methodological sophistry instead of what might be in the public interest.

Because of its very complexity, metaphor is often used to assess transitions in social policy. The metaphor frequently invoked by liberals is "the pendulum." The pendulum theory has two virtues: It is simple—and it has been employed by historian Arthur Schlesinger, Jr. Schlesinger, a doyen of American historiography, established a reputation for his recounting of the last epoch in liberal Americana, beginning with the presidency of John Fitzgerald Kennedy.

TABLE 1.1 Conceptualizations of social programs

Attribute	Public Utility	Market Commodity
Auspice	Governmental	Private
Dominant norm	Equality	Equity
Benefit archetype	Entitlements as rights	Benefits conditioned on productivity
Standard of benefits	Uniform nationwide	Vary regionally
Role of citizen	Recipient	Consumer
Method of finance	Compulsory taxes	Elected contributions

Later, smarting from the successes enjoyed by the Reagan administration in the early 1980s, Schlesinger suggested that ideological cycles occurred in thirty-year intervals. Drawing on the New Deal of the mid-1930s and the Great Society of the mid-1960s, Schlesinger prophesied the election of the next unapologetically liberal president in the early 1990s.[4] An obvious question is begged by Schlesinger's scenario: Is Bill Clinton liberal? The answer is "no"—though this answer warrants elaboration.[5]

If a liberal president advocates major social welfare entitlements available to Americans as a right of citizenship, provided by the national government, and financed through progressive taxes, then Bill Clinton has a different ideological pedigree.[6] In many respects, Clinton's illiberal inclinations have already been demonstrated. Toward the end of the 1980s, prominent mainstream Democrats created the Democratic Leadership Council (DLC) to pull the party away from the liberal interest groups that the Reaganauts had exploited so successfully. Two of the founders of the DLC were Bill Clinton and Al Gore.[7] Moreover, Clinton's legislative track record raises doubts about any liberal orientation to social policy, most notably his ramming the North American Free Trade Agreement (NAFTA) through Congress. Of course, there is more to the administration's legislative agenda than NAFTA—indeed, much of that is the subject of this book.

Still, many academic liberals have insisted that Bill Clinton *is* liberal, an assessment due, perhaps, more to their frustrations during the Reagan/Bush era and a longing for a Kennedyesque Camelot than an accurate reading of current reality. Dyed-in-the-wool liberals do exist, of course—Edward Kennedy, Jesse Jackson, and Barbara Mikulski are examples. But, as the 1994 Republican electoral victory demonstrated, the classic Democratic liberal seems to be an endangered species, a breed that may go the way of liberals within the Republican party—they are extinct. And this says a lot about the pendulum theory of American politics. Classical liberalism—the sort that presaged the New Deal and the War on Poverty—will return to dominate American politics for the same reason that music emanates from metronomes.

Conservatives have used a different metaphor to project their ideology onto the future: tides of history. The ideological surfer in this case is Milton Friedman, who—with the assistance of his wife, Rose—has posited three epochs following the Enlightenment: the rise of laissez-faire during the nineteenth century (the Adam Smith tide); the rise of the welfare state during the twentieth century (the Fabian [Marxist] tide); and the resurgence of free markets during the next century (the Hayek tide). In naming the next tide after Frederich Hayek, the Friedmans recognize a philosopher, little known to liberals, who not only foretold the demise of state socialism, Communism, but also predicted the globalization of capitalism.[8] Now, of this conservative rendering of human affairs, one thing must be admitted: It helps to be on the right side of history.

Beyond that, the "tide" metaphor is not particularly informative. From an international perspective, the expansion and exploitation of world markets does seem apropos with Nike sneakers showing up in Nairobi and McDonalds opening in Moscow, but it offers little consolation for the tragedies in Bosnia, Rwanda, or Guatemala. In the cold war, the first world throttled the second world, leaving many nations of the third world in smoldering debris. The expansion of international capitalism has implications for domestic affairs as well, but the results have been disputed. Metropolitan areas that have strategically positioned themselves to exploit emerging foreign markets—such as Miami and Los Angeles—will prosper, conservatives have claimed. But this will occur for the same reason that American cities prominent during industrialization, such as Detroit and Philadelphia, now comprise the "rustbowl." The consequence of global markets is that capital and jobs have flowed out of the United States, leaving behind abandoned plants, unemployed workers, and fiscally stricken cities—a painful observation cultivated by liberals and the Left.[9] Only recently have the commercial sectors of older northeastern cities rebounded.

The biggest problems with the tide metaphor, however, are related to scope and time. Regarding the former, the analogy draws our attention outward, away from domestic concerns over which we would like to have some control and toward foreign inevitabilities by which we are apparently held captive. Regarding the latter, the time scale is so long-range as to make any individual and most groups (save, perhaps, the American Association of Retired Persons and the National Rifle Association) irrelevant. For the same reason that John Maynard Keynes quipped, "In the long run, we are all dead," Tulsa is not Taiwan.

The tendency of liberals and conservatives to resort to metaphor in discussions of domestic issues avoids the substantial difficulties facing the nation, if not contributes to a general dishonesty and expediency of motive—the means of public policy (getting into office) eclipsing the ends (solving social problems). The deterioration of our social circumstance has undoubtedly come to the attention of most Americans—in ways they probably would have rather avoided. For too many too often, the United States has become a nation in which predation, violence, and dejection overcome opportunity, tranquillity, and hope. Consider two illustrations.

In the mid-1960s, Claude Brown published *Manchild in the Promised Land,* his then-celebrated autobiographical account of growing up in gang-ridden Harlem. With the help of youth workers, his own perseverance, and good luck, Brown left the streets, went to college, and eventually became an attorney.[10] In the mid-1980s, the *New York Times Magazine* commissioned Brown to write about New York gangs. Returning to the streets with which he was so familiar from 20 years before, Brown was astonished at the casual violence of gang members, much of it seemingly random.[11] Put another way, Senator Daniel Patrick Moynihan has argued that Americans have become desensitized to a degree of mayhem that would have been incomprehensible not so long ago. To make the point, he notes that when a handful of thugs were mowed down in a Chicago garage during the Depression, every major newspaper covered the St. Valentine's Day "massacre" in banner headlines. Today, Moynihan observes that a greater number of homicides happen each weekend in major American cities, and the news rarely makes the front page.[12]

Since the creation of Head Start during the War on Poverty, the condition of children—particularly poor, minority children—has become a matter of public policy. Yet, the general well-being of American children has lagged. In a popular book on the subject, Sylvia Ann Hewlett noted that, "Although the United States ranks No. 2 worldwide in per capita income, this country does not even make it into the top ten on any significant indicator of child welfare."[13] If evidence suggesting that American children suffer from institutional neglect is troubling, what are we to make of data indicating that our children are being brutalized, even killed? Child abuse has been a focus for social policy for some time, of course, certainly since passage of the Child Abuse Prevention and Treatment Act of 1974. In the intervening years, substantial funds and activity have been directed at remediating child abuse, but with little success. Just how ineffectual Americans have been in this regard has been demonstrated by data comparing child homicide rates in the United States with those in other industrialized nations. By the mid-1980s, the most recent period for which data are available, the child homicide rate in the United States was over twice what it was in the next most lethal country for children, Australia. Moreover, the rate of homicide for three subgroups of American children—babies, infants, and children—all increased between the mid-1970s and the mid-1980s. Whereas most industrialized nations experienced a reduction in the rate of child homicides or at least held the rate constant, rates in the United States increased dramatically.[14]

The evidence on youth gangs and abused children indicates that our collective efforts have failed in the essential feature of any culture: the nurture and socialization of the young. From this perspective, it is difficult to imagine a more debilitating social condition. Certainly, we are leagues away from the quaint references to "social diseases" in *West Side Story*. Yet because it is so extensive, such social deterioration invites broad and bipartisan intervention. Insofar as these activities demonstrate the irrelevance of traditional understandings of social problems justified by referents to liberalism and conservatism, they build the case for a new orientation to social policy—a new paradigm, in the words of advisors to President Bush; a "third way" in the words of Bush's successor, Bill Clinton. The extent to which domestic policy under Bill Clinton's presidency breaks new ideological ground depends in part on the historical record, the subject to which we now turn.

THE WELFARE STATE ON AUTOPILOT

The American welfare state was introduced by way of Franklin Delano Roosevelt's Social Security Act of 1935, a bold, if somewhat tardy, response to the Great Depression that had dogged the nation since 1929. The Social Security Act is hailed by liberals as the cornerstone of the progressive legislation that was to unfold during the next 50 years (see Chapter 7). Among the aides shepherding the Social Security Act through Congress was Harry Hopkins, the director of the Federal Emergency Relief Administration (FERA), an umbrella of New Deal jobs programs. In addition to his administrative talents, Hopkins was a first-class political operator, recognizing the electoral gains possible through New Deal social programs. Hopkins's shorthand for this was "tax, tax; spend, spend; elect, elect." He advocated taxing the rich so that government would have revenues for social programs for workers and the poor, who would express their gratitude by voting Democratic. Hopkins was right. In one of the more shrewd observations in modern American politics, Hopkins foresaw the liberal-Democratic combine that was to dominate domestic policy in the United States for a half-century.

Political facility notwithstanding, the Social Security Act was anything but elegant legislation. It consisted of two different types of programs: social insurance, including Social Security and Unemployment Compensation; and public assistance, what are now known as Aid to Families with Dependent Children (AFDC) and Supplemental Security Income (SSI). The social insurance programs were primarily self-financing and paid benefits to anyone who met the eligibility criteria. The public assistance programs were financed through general revenues and paid benefits only to the poor, who often had to meet additional requirements to receive benefits. With the exception of Social Security, the remaining programs at the time[15] were operated by the states, meaning that for each program there were more than fifty variations. Under these circumstances, it is not surprising that most anyone with the audacity to try to fathom the intricacies of such a mis-arrangement of programs would be seen walking away, head shaking, muttering something about the "welfare mess."

Despite the bureaucratic convolutions it generated, the Social Security Act performed famously. Most Americans who had worked had contributed to Social Security, and they were grateful to receive benefits at retirement in amounts far beyond what they had contributed. American workers who had been laid off were eligible for Unemployment Compensation for thirteen weeks or longer, depending on how high the unemployment rate was in their area. Virtually all of the early beneficiaries of these social insurance programs were workers who had experienced the Great Depression, and when it came time to express their gratitude they voted as Harry Hopkins had bet they would—Democratic. Little need be said of the public assistance programs included in the Social Security Act, because before the War on Poverty the programs for the poor were so small, consuming less than one percent of the Gross Domestic Product. But the public assistance programs, managed by the states, were extraordinarily punitive, so much so that few, save the most stricken, received benefits. Compared to the publicly popular social insurance programs, the highly stigmatized public assistance programs were fiscal asterisks in the emerging American welfare state.

In its early period, few analysts paid much attention to one characteristic of both the social insurance and public assistance programs articulated in the Social Security Act—they were all entitlements. Indeed, the fact that anyone who met the eligibility criteria would receive benefits seemed inconsequential so long as the nation's economy was robust and candidates were elected who supported the Social Security Act. By the late 1970s, however, the fact that virtually all social programs were entitlements raised major concern. As long as the American economy expanded sufficiently to meet the revenue demands of social programs, entitlements were relatively innocuous, but as an enormous budget deficit grew (due to increased military expenditures and falling revenues resulting from tax cuts), the inexorable growth of entitlements moved to center stage. As Figure 1.1 indicates, social entitlements—both social insurance and public assistance programs—experienced substantial increases after the 1950s.

The percentages of Gross Domestic Product that various social welfare programs represent are indicated in Tables 1.2 and 1.3.

Assuming the growth vector during the 1960s and 1970s, social entitlements were poised to consume as much as half of the Gross Domestic Product by the millennium. As early as 1975, social entitlements were consuming more than half of all federal expenditures, exceeding 57 percent in 1980.[16]

Social entitlements became a political issue because they seemed fiscally insatiable, and also because containing them was so problematic. Only one social entitlement had been contained before the 1980s, and that was social services that were provided through Title XX. In a Machiavellian move to cut the number of social workers employed nationwide by welfare departments, President Nixon had successfully separated financial management from social service provision to AFDC clients in the early 1970s. Prior to this, the number of social workers automatically increased with the number of AFDC families. AFDC caseworkers provided two services to families: social services and grant management. With the "separation of services," AFDC remained an open-ended entitlement, but revenues funded by Title XX for social services were capped at $2.5 billion

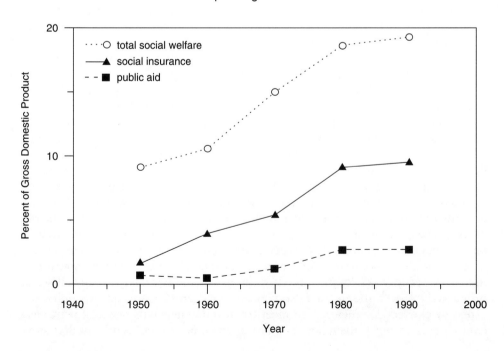

FIGURE 1.1 Social welfare spending

TABLE 1.2 Gross domestic product and social welfare expenditures under public programs, fiscal years 1950–1990 (amounts in millions of dollars)

Item	1950	1960	1970	1980	1990
Gross Domestic Product	$266,800	506,700	985,800	2,664,500	5,459,500
Total Social Welfare	23,508	52,293	145,555	492,714	1,045,372
Social Insurance	4,947	19,307	54,691	229,754	510,616
Public Aid	2,496	4,101	16,444	72,703	145,602
Health Care	2,064	4,464	9,606	27,263	62,428
Veterans	6,866	5,479	9,078	21,466	30,916
Education	6,674	17,626	50,846	121,050	258,385
Housing	15	177	701	6,879	17,918
Other Social Welfare	448	1,139	4,145	13,599	17,918

Adapted from Social Security Administration, *Annual Statistical Summary 1993* (Washington, DC: US GPO, 1993), Table 3.A1.

TABLE 1.3 Gross domestic product and social welfare expenditures under public programs, fiscal years 1950–1990 (as percent of gross domestic product)

Item	1950	1960	1970	1980	1990
Gross Domestic Product	100.0	100.0	100.0	100.0	100.0
Total Social Welfare	8.8	10.3	14.7	18.6	19.1
Social Insurance	1.8	3.8	5.5	8.7	9.4
Public Aid	.9	.8	1.7	2.7	2.7
Health Care	.8	.9	1.0	1.0	1.1
Veterans	2.6	1.1	.9	.8	.6
Education	2.5	3.5	5.2	4.6	4.7
Housing	(1)	(1)	(1)	.3	.4
Other Social Welfare	.2	.2	.4	.5	.3

(1) Less than 0.05 percent.

Adapted from Social Security Administration, *Annual Statistical Summary 1993* (Washington, DC: US GPO, 1993), Table 3.A1.

annually. This meant that state and local government would receive a fixed amount for a range of social services provided to the poor. As the 1970s hinted, and the 1980s demonstrated, this was a Faustian bargain for human service professionals if ever there was one. To compound matters, in 1981 the Reagan administration transformed Title XX into a social services block grant and in the process reduced appropriations 25 percent. Coupled with the cap, this cut left local public welfare agencies struggling to provide protection to abused children, day care to working parents, and in-home health care to the homebound, among other services. By the end of the 1980s, several metropolitan welfare departments had been the subject of news exposés featuring abused children who had died after they had been reported to, and were receiving services from, hard-pressed public welfare agencies.[17] If the Title XX Social Services Block Grant was any indication, solving the social entitlement problem by capping allocation was not an acceptable option—at least for liberal-minded social program advocates.

Yet, capping allocation is precisely what Newt Gingrich proposed for welfare reform through the Personal Responsibility Act. This part of the "Contract with America" would radically alter welfare by instituting several changes simultaneously: (1) Dozens of categorical programs for poor families would be consolidated into a few block grants; (2) these block grants would be devolved to the states with minimal federal constraints; (3) in the process, the block grants for welfare would be cut 20 percent; and (4) future federal funding for welfare would be capped. The experience with Title XX suggested that state and local government would not make up the federal shortfall in funding, leaving poor families in even more dire straits. The likelihood, as many liberal social advocates have pointed out, was not that more families would feel motivated to get off of welfare (as conservatives have insisted), but they would find themselves on the streets, instead.

Even though an entitlement issue loomed in the future, voter enthusiasm for social programs during the post–World War II era was so strong that even conservative Republicans supported them. In fact, the largest expansion of programs created through the Social Security Act occurred during the presidency of Richard Nixon. During the postwar era, the American economy ballooned, in part because the industrial base of what were to be the nation's competitors later in the century had been destroyed. Economic growth led to major public works projects, such as the Tennessee Valley Authority and the Interstate Highway System, contributing to a national pride and optimism that was unprecedented. The social programs created during the New Deal simply rode a cresting wave of postwar prosperity.[18]

A second expansion of the American welfare state occurred during the mid-1960s with Lyndon Johnson's War on Poverty. Seemingly intractable poverty in Appalachia had been brought to John Kennedy's attention during his presidential campaign, a feature of American culture that Michael Harrington's *The Other American*[19] portrayed as extensive in urban as well as rural areas. The civil rights movement in the South and the riots of the mid-1960s underscored the political marginalization of African Americans.[20] The social programs of the War on Poverty were, in large measure, President Johnson's attempt to appease increasingly militant African-American leaders. Many of the programs established under the Economic Opportunity Act of 1964 were targeted for the minority poor of which African Americans featured disproportionately. Coupled with other initiatives of the period, the Great Society bolstered the public assistance programs that had been given short shrift in the Social Security Act.[21] Among the poverty programs enacted in the mid-1960s were Head Start, the Community Action Program, Job Corps, Food Stamps, Medicaid, and the Elementary and Secondary Education Act.[22]

The expansion of programs for the poor during the Great Society provided important benefits to minorities.[23] The civil rights movement served to acquaint many of the minority poor with their benefit rights, and legal decisions thwarted attempts by states to curtail access to program benefits by devices such as residency requirements. As a result, public assistance programs expanded significantly during the 1960s, though their growth slowed during the following decade. Although the domestic policy agenda focused on poverty, social insurance programs grew even more than those that served the poor. Richard Nixon's attempt to use the momentum of the social insurance programs to reform public assistance by enacting a guaranteed annual income for all poor families was aborted when the chairman of the Senate Finance Committee, Russell Long, stood firmly in opposition to what he perceived as welfarism run amok. Ineffective in domestic policy reforms, Jimmy Carter oversaw a continuing expansion of existing social programs.

During the 1970s, then, liberal advocates of social programs preoccupied themselves with consolidating policies that had evolved during the New Deal and Great Society. Neglect of the minority poor during the New Deal was addressed by the initiatives of the War on Poverty, and welfare advocates looked on approvingly as the new poverty programs, such as Head Start, Job Corps, and Medicaid, helped accelerate the upward mobility of poor minority families. Overall, their larger vision was unchanged: the creation of a welfare state on a par with those of northern Europe. Virtually every welfare scholar of the period thought this was a desirable, if not inevitable, end to the liberal project. To be sure, several intellectuals from the Left argued that the liberally inspired welfare state in the United States did not go far enough in creating equality by redistributing income. Leftist academics indicted the political economy of the United States for a class structure that denied opportunity for the poor and disadvantaged populations. At best, Frances Fox Piven and Richard Cloward argued that relief programs expanded and contracted in cycles related to unemployment and resultant civil disorder.[24] William Ryan theorized that antisocial behaviors of the poor were attributable to a dysfunctional economic system that had to produce social programs in order to control poor deviants.[25] Indeed, navel gazing by the Left had become so focused that, on the eve of the 1980 presidential election, a prominent left intellectual, the late Irving Howe, charged that Ronald Reagan's candidacy was an "over-heated reaction to the welfare state" and predicted his loss would "prove to be the last gasp of the American right."[26]

INVASION OF THE CONWONKS: HYPHENATING IDEOLOGY I[27]

Given such poor judgment, it is not surprising that liberals and the Left would blame Ronald Reagan for the trauma of the 1980s; but cracks were evident in the foundation of the American welfare state well before then. Late in the 1970s, Henry Aaron, a senior fellow at the liberal Brookings Institution, was expressing reservations about social programs consuming increasingly larger portions of the nation's economic largesse.[28] This concern reverberated with other liberal academics who had second thoughts about the social and economic consequences of unchecked liberalism in social policy. As their numbers grew, this coterie of intellectuals became known as "neoconservatives." During the period, a joke making the rounds in Washington had it that "a neoconservative was a liberal who had been mugged by reality." The neoconservatives were an elusive group, not formally constituted nor aligned with any particular organization, but their membership posed a strategic threat to liberal social policy advocates—as former liberals, neoconservatives knew the ins-and-outs, the nuances, and most important, the financing of social programs. For example, at the time a commonly identified neoconservative was Daniel Patrick Moynihan, former professor and domestic policy advisor to President Nixon, elected to the Senate in 1976—a formidable adversary, indeed.[29]

Quite irrespective of the ideological infidelity of some liberal intellectuals, conservatives were already well on their way to subverting liberal hegemony in domestic affairs. During the early 1970s, conservative political scientist and editor Irving Kristol had made a cogent comment in response to the unhappiness business executives had expressed about the liberal direction of public policy. Kristol observed correctly that much of the intellectual groundwork for social policy was done at liberal policy institutes. "Why," he asked rhetorically, "if you don't like what's coming out of the liberal think tanks, don't you set up your own?" Chief executive officers of America's major corporations responded with a vengeance, writing checks directly, or diverting funds indirectly through foundations, to a new intellectual infrastructure of conservative policy institutes.[30]

Conservative think tanks thrived. The first beneficiary was the American Enterprise Institute for Public Policy Research (AEI). In 1970, AEI was a small, Chamber of Commerce clone with a budget of $800,000. By 1978, its budget had swollen to $5 million, only to expand to $11.7 million in 1982.[31] Shortly after the inauguration of Ronald Reagan, AEI's then-president William Baroody, Jr., stated the ambitious objective of the Institute:

> The public philosophy that has guided American policy for decades is undergoing change. For more than four decades, the philosophy of Franklin Delano Roosevelt's New Deal prevailed, in essence calling upon government to do whatever individual men and women could not do for themselves.
>
> Today we see growing signs of a new public philosophy, one that still seeks to meet fundamental human needs, but to meet them through a better balance between the public and private sectors of society.
>
> The American Enterprise Institute has been at the forefront of this change. Many of today's policy initiatives are building on intellectual foundations partly laid down by the Institute.[32]

By the time the 1980 presidential campaign was heating up, AEI had 30 scholars and fellows in residence (earning $30,000 to $50,000 a year), 77 adjunct scholars, and 250 professors associated with the Institute nationwide. AEI's senior staff and board members represented a *Who's Who* of the nation's conservative business and political elite.

The Heritage Foundation assumed leadership of the conservative crusade in public policy when AEI appeared to move too close to the ideological center. Started up with a $250,000 grant from the Coors family in 1973, the Heritage budget equaled that of AEI within a decade. By the time the Reagan administration was in place, Heritage had out-gunned AEI, having placed more than 35 staff in upper-level positions in the executive branch.[33] Notable among Heritage personnel of the period was Burton Pines, whose *Back to Basics* had become required reading for the "traditionalist movement." Pines acknowledged the pivotal role that think tanks had played in the rapid evolution of conservatism in the United States. Including the Hoover Institution of Stanford in the campaign, Pines likened their work to a crusade: "Together, Hoover, AEI and Heritage can today deploy formidable armies on the battlefield of ideas—forces which traditionalist movements previously lacked."[34]

REX REAGAN

The conservative mission of the 1980s was threefold: (1) to put an end to liberal hegemony in federal affairs; (2) to the extent possible, reroute public policy through the private sector, and (3) preclude the prospect of any resurgence in social entitlements. In these, the conservatives were enormously successful. Ronald Reagan won the presidency in 1980, and Republicans seized a majority in the Senate—in the process beating several well-known liberal Democrats. Faced with a popular president and an adversarial Senate, the House of Representatives assumed a more compliant pose. Democrats were so bewildered by the Reagan legislative assault that when the administration's new director of the Office of Management and the Budget, David Stockman, "cooked" the numbers in Congressional testimony affirming the soundness of the President's fateful 1981 Omnibus Budget Reconciliation Act (OBRA), the House leadership was completely hoodwinked.

By 1983, the Draconian consequences of the 1981 OBRA were clear. Some 408,000 families were terminated from AFDC; another 299,000 had their benefits reduced. Among the casualties were the working poor. Thirty-five percent of adults who persisted in working while on AFDC, despite the punitive way in which their income was subtracted from their aid, were removed from the program. In addition to cuts exacted on AFDC, 1981 OBRA consolidated many categorical programs into block grants, in the process reducing appropriations. When this procedure was applied to the Title XX program, the long-term consequence was a 50 percent loss of revenue.[35]

Through the print and electronic media, ConWonks (conservative policy wonks) paraded a number of reform ideas before the public. In the early 1980s, a common theme was privatization, and ConWonks suggested turning just about every governmental function, except defense, over to the corporate sector.

Gradually, their comprehension of social programs improved until any ConWonk think tank worth its salt had cobbled together a platform on welfare reform. A theme running through most of these position statements featured a requirement that in order to receive benefits, welfare recipients engage in some productive activity, such as work—up to that point, a four-letter word for liberals. At the insistence of the Reagan administration, there were experiments in encouraging public assistance recipients to work. Some were moderately successful. Eventually, efforts put into welfare-to-work initiatives paid off; the concept was to be central to the administration's welfare reform, the Family Support Act of 1988.

The ultimate conservative triumph was indirect, however. Extrapolating the fiscal implications of Reagan budgeting, Senator Daniel Patrick Moynihan recognized that the magnitude of interest payments on the deficit would effectively preclude any future social entitlements until the end of the century.[36] In 1979—toward the end of the Carter presidency—the budget deficit stood at $40.2 billion, 1.2 percent of the Gross National Product (GNP). During Reagan's first term, the deficit skyrocketed so that by 1983 it was $207.8 billion, 6.3 percent of the GNP. By the end of the 1980s, interest on the debt, over $150 billion per year, was the third largest item on the federal budget, exceeded only by defense spending and Social Security.[37]

To any seasoned observer, the Reagan record represented the conservatives' rout of liberals in domestic affairs. Conservatives rewrote tax policy providing substantial gains to the wealthy at the expense of the poor.[38] Questions about the future structure of Social Security were addressed by creating a bipartisan commission that dodged major issues about solvency of the program, deferring them to the next generation.[39] Welfare reform vis-à-vis the Family Support Act of 1988 appropriated a paltry $3.34 billion over five years for workfare, representing about half of what AFDC families had lost to inflation since 1970.[40] Surely, the unkindest cut of all was the fate of Catastrophic Health Insurance. The Medicare Catastrophic Coverage Act of 1988 was honed by the twin necessities of Reagan austerity and liberal desperation to produce *anything* remotely positive in social policy. It insured 32 million Americans against bankruptcy from health care costs by imposing a progressive tax on the elderly rich, yet it was met with a firestorm that scorched even veteran liberal policy advocates. Congress repealed the Act the following year due to the intense pressure brought by elderly lobbying organizations, such as Save Our Security and the American Association of Retired Persons (AARP).[41]

Yet, despite this, conservative successes betrayed a profound failure. For all the political capital they were able to bring to stem a liberal flood that had been running against them for a half-century, conservatives were unable to conceptualize a surrogate for the liberal, governmental welfare state.[42] This was not because there were no possibilities. Conservatives emphasized monetary policy that would generate jobs, a strategy that enjoyed success after the recession of the early 1980s. And new job opportunities could have been wedded to *employment* benefits, thus reinforcing the work ethic and productivity. Historically, considerable social welfare has been provided to American workers through benefit plans associated with employment. Yet the Reagan administration took no action to extend such benefits to the working poor. As social need increased due to federal funding rescissions, private nonprofit agencies stepped forward and provided services. During the 1980s, total philanthropic contributions increased from $48.55 billion to $111.89 billion, 240 percent; and contributions for health and human services increased from $10.25 billion to $21.72 billion, 211 percent.[43] Yet, only a limited and late appeal to voluntarism was to emerge to this prospect: President Bush's "thousand points of light." Even hard-headed conservatives went to the trouble of learning about poverty. Jack Kemp, having promoted Enterprise Zones as a Congressman during the Reagan administration, eagerly accepted President Bush's offer to run the Department of Housing and Urban Development, and as a result earned the sobriquet "bleeding-heart conservative." Kemp's interest in "empowerment" of the poor would eventually lead to the founding of a think tank ("Empower America") to accelerate the political and economic mobility of the minority poor.

But the Reaganites seemed incapable of harnessing these opportunities in order to present a coherent alternative to the much-despised liberal welfare state. Charging Democrats and liberals with immorality and welfare dependency, the Reagan presidency effectively pulled a tattered rug from under the poor. With no alternative to compensate for the federal divestiture of its social responsibility, the 1980s became an era of excess—Savings and Loan flim-flam artists, matched by the self-destruction of a growing underclass. Indeed, the disparity in income of the rich and poor, the growing presence of drugs in blighted neighborhoods, and the stagnant earnings of working families offered grist for any savvy ideological entrepreneur from the Left. Given the pounding that liberals received during the 1980s, one would expect the Left to respond with vitriol and indignation. Surprisingly, the most astute critique of the Reagan era was written by a Nixon Republican, Kevin Phillips.[44]

HYPHENATING IDEOLOGY II: NEOLIBERALISM

Given the inept response to Reaganism, it is not a surprise that it took the Democratic party two wake-up calls to get the message that liberal designs in domestic policy were no longer popular. The first call came in 1984 when Walter Mondale lost the presidential campaign. This election occurred in the downdraft of what had been the worst recession since the Great Depression, yet Mondale lost by a landslide. The second call came in 1988 when Michael Dukakis lost the presidential campaign. The 1988 election occurred as the federal budget deficit spiraled out of control. Republican candidate George Bush admitted suffering from "the vision thing" and confirmed it by picking Dan Quayle as a running mate. Yet Dukakis also lost by a landslide.

Finally, a small group of Democrats woke up, smelled the coffee, and created neoliberalism. The impetus for a major ideological shift within the Democratic party may have come from the drubbing liberals were receiving from conservatives (neo- and otherwise), but the idea of "neoliberalism" was articulated by Charles Peters, the irascible editor of the *Washington Monthly*. As a former appointee in the Kennedy administration, Peters yearned for the days when the Democratic party forged domestic policy that attracted the support of the disenfranchised and throttled Republicans in the process. In nailing the neoliberal credo to the door of the Democratic party, Peters put into motion forces that would eventually lead to the inauguration of Bill Clinton. "We still believe in liberty and justice and a fair chance for all, in mercy for the afflicted, and help for the down and out," Peters wrote with characteristic candor, "but we no longer automatically favor unions and big government or oppose the military and big business."[45] With respect to poverty programs, Peters suggested junking social insurance programs.

> We want to eliminate duplication and apply a means-test to these programs. As a practical matter the country can't afford to spend money on people who don't need it. . . . [A]s liberal idealists, we don't think the well-off should be getting money from those programs anyway—every cent we can afford should go to helping those in real need. Social Security for those totally dependent on it is miserably inadequate, as is welfare in many states.[46]

That Peters would choose to savage Social Security, the very foundation of the American welfare state, spoke volumes about how low liberalism had sunk. Ominously, his remarks began to resonate with younger workers and baby boomers accustomed to hearing that Social Security would be broke by the time they retired.

Legislatively, the major tenets of liberalism provided less and less confidence in guiding domestic policy. For much of the century, domestic policy had been formulated around four liberal premises.

1. *National Economic Planning*—Liberals long held that capitalism caused uneven economic development, and for that reason the federal government could spread prosperity more evenly by planning. Through economic planning the federal government would "socialize" capitalism, ameliorating its dislocating tendencies. During the Reagan/Bush era, the planning capacity of the federal government, limited as it had become, was neutralized; instead the virtues of capitalism were trumpeted. (Much to the chagrin of the left wing of the Democratic party, Bill Clinton embraced NAFTA, continuing the legacy of laissez-faire.)
2. *Universal Benefits as a Right of Citizenship*—Advanced welfare states assure citizens of essential commodities, such as income, employment, health, housing, and social services. To date, the only commodity assured to citizens of the United States has been education; all other benefits have additional requirements for eligibility. In a comprehensive

assessment of the social development of 107 nations, Richard Estes ranked the United States nineteenth. Of social benefits, three entitlements have dominated the liberal agenda.
   a. *Full Employment*—Despite passage over a decade ago of the Humphrey-Hawkins Full Employment Act, which set official unemployment at a fractional level, three to four percent, unemployment remains higher. Federal programs, such as the Job Training and Partnership Act, cut previous benefits to workers and subsequently has had a negligible influence on unemployment.
   b. *National Health Care*—Throughout the 1980s, health coverage diminished, leaving 38 million Americans without insurance. A small number of states experimented with reform plans, but with mixed results. The Massachusetts attempt to insure all residents was a casualty to state fiscal problems, and Oregon fielded a plan to insure all residents by rationing health care to the poor. Only geographically isolated Hawaii had extended health care to most state residents. (Liberals enjoyed a brief, if misplaced, enthusiasm for health reform before Clinton's ill-fated Health Security Act died in Congress.)
   c. *A Guaranteed Annual Income*—Assuring an income floor for all Americans has not received serious attention since the Family Assistance Plan was scrapped during the Nixon administration.
3. *Income Redistribution by a Progressive Tax Structure*—Tax policy during the 1980s favored the rich at the expense of the poor and middle class, resulting in the greatest spread in income since the federal government began compiling such data in 1947. Discrepancies in assets held by the rich and the poor far exceeded those regarding income. (Elements of the Clinton economic package reversed the upward redistribution in income, but only slightly.)
4. *Reductions in Defense Spending*—The 1980s witnessed the largest military buildup in peace time. Efforts by liberals to claim defense reductions and transfer these to social programs failed. Following the 1990 Gramm-Rudman budget compromise, all such savings are being earmarked for deficit reduction. (Clinton's first response to the Republican election sweep of 1994 was the announcement of a $25 billion appropriation to the Pentagon.)

Increasing irrelevance of liberal domestic policy led several prominent Democrats—Paul Tsongas, Richard Gephardt, Sam Nunn, and Bill Bradley—to found the Democratic Leadership Council (DLC) to pull the party to the Right. The DLC hired Al From as its political director and soon established a think tank, the Progressive Policy Institute (PPI), under the direction of Will Marshall. The DLC scored a major victory when the 1992 Democratic party ticket featured two founders of the organization: Bill Clinton and Al Gore. After a decade of frustration, Democrats had found the key to the White House.

THE "NEW PARADIGM"

Independent of the 1992 presidential campaign, a small, but well-positioned group of intellectuals interpreted the ideological shift underway in structural terms. Representing conservatives as well as liberals, and Republicans as well as Democrats, this group read the hyphenated ideologies that were emerging during the 1980s as an indication that the traditional constellation of values underlying the political parties was antiquated. They saw the sum of all prefixes that had become attached to conservatism and liberalism as a prelude to the evolution of a "new paradigm" of American social policy.

One liberal in the new paradigm group was David Osborne, a policy analyst who had followed six governors during the 1980s to determine their solutions to the substantial transfer of program responsibility from the federal government to the states. This devolution was predicated on the willingness of states to raise taxes in order to shoulder the social burden that the Reagan administration wanted to shirk. A lingering recession and the deindustrialization of the older industrial states left them with few options as the federal government back-pedaled. Many states convulsed fiscally, and several teetered on the brink of bankruptcy. So, when Osborne presented a short-list of principles that governors had used to address the problems dumped on them by Washington, he secured a loyal, if limited, readership. Significantly, Osborne discerned a pattern to the fiscal and policy chaos with which the governors had struggled, one that had radical implications. "The traditional liberal and conservative ideologies that competed within the New Deal paradigm [have] simply outlived their usefulness," Osborne observed. "They evolved in response to the industrial age, and that era is over."[47]

Osborne's counterpart on the Right was James Pinkerton, domestic advisor to President Bush. In remarks before the Illinois New Paradigm Society, Pinkerton noted with some exasperation that "the federal government alone spends $150 billion a year fighting poverty. That's $5,000 for every poor person in this country. Someone suggested we just give them the money and let them start their own war on poverty!" But, Pinkerton conceded, this is unlikely considering the transformation that poverty has undergone during the years since the War on Poverty. "The poverty of the underclass is qualitatively different from what we have seen before. The new problems are violence, teen pregnancy, and drugs," he said. "Hundreds of billions of dollars later, we have figured out that these kinds of problems can not be remedied by the same old bureaucratic approaches."[48]

Seizing the opportunity, Pinkerton invited select liberal and conservative representatives to the White House to confer on the New Paradigm. Among those who followed Pinkerton's philosophical drift was Mickey Kaus, a brash New York attorney who had moved to Washington to examine what had become the debris of progressive politics. In Kaus's introduction to Pinkerton and the new paradigm, Kaus acknowledged that David Osborne had first coined the term "new paradigm," but it was Pinkerton who used the idea to transform himself from a gawky political hack into someone *Mademoiselle* actually put on its list of "the greatest lovers of the Western world." I remember going to a Christmas party in 1989 and finding myself in a corner, talking policy with this giraffe-like man who seemed to wear his trousers up around his navel. He was funny and openminded—at the time he was pushing an idealistic plan to give underclass kids jobs planting trees. Soon I was attending his "paradigm" meetings.[49]

Kaus's *The End of Equality*, in which he argued that old-fashioned "money liberalism" be replaced by a more current "civic liberalism," owed substantial debt to Pinkerton's "New Paradigm Society."[50]

In no time, the new paradigm thesis was central to contemporary political analysis. David Osborne teamed up with Ted Gaebler to write *Reinventing Government*, a manifesto on revitalizing local governance that called for a new generation of solutions.[51] In his bestseller *Why Americans Hate Politics*, E.J. Dionne attributed the stalemate in domestic policy to adherence to antiquated recitations of liberalism and conservatism.[52] The director of the Progressive Policy Institute, Will Marshall, exploited the ideological opening stating that "the dominant ideas of both U.S. parties have outlived their time," and offered a "new social contract" in their stead.[53] Following his election to the presidency, Bill Clinton put the new paradigm to use in outlining his economic program. Clinton deftly divided government spending into two categories: consumption and investment. *Consumption*—unproductive expenditures such as welfare and price supports—was "bad"; *Investment*—productive expenditures such as education and research—was "good." New programs could be justified, the president-elect indicated, if they contributed to the formation of human capital. Back in Washington, James Pinkerton was cleaning out his desk, anticipating an appointment to the conservative Manhattan Institute. "What I've said all along is that the 1992 election would be won by the party that best understood that there was a new paradigm and adapted to it," he said. Reflecting on his inability to highlight the idea within the Bush administration, Pinkerton conceded, "Clearly, we failed."[54]

IDEOLOGICAL REGRESSION: PALEOLIBERALISM

If Pinkerton was dismayed about the fate of the new paradigm, the Left was apoplectic. Having watched the liberal superstructure for public policy implode during the 1980s, the Left was instantly skeptical of anything suggestive of a new agenda for social policy. The case was stated best by Max Sawicky of the leftist Economic Policy Institute. Sawicky recast "new paradigm" as "NEWP" and then proceeded to align it with Reaganism. Sawicky claimed that the primary features of NEWP were markets, decentralization, choice, empowerment, and pragmatism. Added together, NEWP was nothing more than a disguised attempt on the part of conservatives to further deny social program benefits to workers and the poor.[55] Ironically, markets, decentralization, choice, empowerment, and pragmatism are also the primary methods by which the professional middle class receives essential goods and services, while registering its preferences through the polity. Sawicky's apparatchik rebuttal to the new paradigm indicated that, in matters of public policy, the American Left continued to insist that recipients of social welfare receive benefits through an arrangement that was unacceptable to most Americans—namely, government welfare agencies.

Rather than reject the new paradigm outright, more reasoned liberals manned the ramparts and continued to defend a besieged American welfare state. There was some basis for this. Despite conservative victories of the Reagan/Bush era and the DLC's pull of the Democratic party to the Right, few programs had been eliminated, and opinion polls indicated that the public supported social programs. Liberalism remained the fulcrum for leveraging domestic policy, they argued, quick to point out that most of the American welfare state was intact despite the conservative offensive of the 1980s. Evidence to this effect can be found in Table 1.1 above. Total social welfare expenditures did increase during the 1980s. A closer examination, however, reveals cracks in the liberal ideological edifice. Clearly, social insurance allocations were not slowed during the Reagan/Bush era, but this was not the case for public assistance programs. The growth of poverty programs halted during the 1980s, a period in which they should have expanded due to a substantial increase in the number of poor people. Thus, social insurance programs that served workers fared well, but poverty programs were battered during the decade. Because poverty is not equally distributed throughout the population, the groups bearing the brunt of federal cuts in poverty programs were the most vulnerable: the young, the old, the infirm, women, and racial minorities.

To be sure, public sentiment tended to favor social programs—at least until the 1994 Republican Congressional victories suggested otherwise. This was demonstrated in a rather remarkable project undertaken by Fay Cook and Edith Barrett who sampled over a thousand Americans and select members of the House of Representatives during the late 1980s. Well into the second Reagan term, the public supported social programs, although somewhat differently. As Table 1.4 indicates, support for social insurance (Social Security and Medicare) was stronger than for public assistance (AFDC and Food Stamps).

Respondents from the public and the House of Representatives tended to favor increasing benefits for social insurance programs, but preferred to hold the line on expansion of public assistance programs. "The picture painted by these data is hardly what one would have expected given the so-called crisis rhetoric of the 1980s," concluded Cook and Barrett, "when opponents of social welfare argued to the federal administration that social welfare programs had lost their legitimacy in the eyes of the public."[56]

From another perspective, however, the results of the Cook and Barrett study are less sanguine. The public is decidedly unwilling to increase benefits for AFDC and Food Stamp recipients, a troubling finding since these are two

TABLE 1.4 Public support for increasing, maintaining, or decreasing benefits for four social welfare programs

	Percent of respondents saying programs should be:		
	Increased	*Maintained*	*Decreased*
Medicare	67.6	29.9	2.5
Social Security	56.7	40.0	3.3
Aid to Families with Dependent Children	32.6	51.9	15.5
Food Stamps	24.6	51.0	24.4

Adapted from Fay Cook and Edith Barrett, *Support for the American Welfare State* (New York: Columbia University Press, 1992), p. 62.

programs that were most pommeled during the Reagan administration. That most Americans favor the status quo for programs as inadequate as AFDC and Food Stamps is hardly cause for celebration. Congressional support for social welfare is more problematic. To their credit, Cook and Barrett intended to survey both houses of Congress, but Senators refused to participate. This makes their Congressional findings suspect for two reasons. First, the Senate from 1980 to 1986 was controlled by Republicans who, by all indications, had a decidedly negative perception of government social programs. Second, the House was controlled by Democrats who have tended to—guess what?—favor social programs.

A more doctrinaire approach to the plight of the American welfare state was presented by Ted Marmor, Jerry Mashaw, and Philip Harvey. In one of the surprisingly few defenses of public social programs issued at the end of the Reagan/Bush era, Marmor, Mashaw, and Harvey conceded that the United States had an inadequate configuration of social programs, but insisted that liberal ideology that evolved during the New Deal remained the best hope for evolving new programs. Ideological legacy intact, Marmor and his associates admitted that the public was anything but enthusiastic about public social programs. "The public has made it clear that it does not wish to roll back the clock, but the welfare state shows no signs of experiencing a renaissance either," they admit. "Public confidence in the durability of welfare state institutions remains low."[57] Running on empty, the welfare state was showing all the indications of grinding to a halt. This was underscored by the battering Democratic liberals experienced at the hands of conservative Republicans in the 1994 election.

Liberal intransigence about the welfare state as an organizing construct for social programs—paleoliberalism—is understandable in light of the punishing 1980s. Certainly, the poor took a beating by policies begun with the Reagan administration and continued by President Bush. As a result, the prospects for African Americans, Latinos, women, and the disabled plummeted. Traditional liberals must also be implicated in this result because they were adhering to an antiquated vision of the public good—the governmental welfare state. American liberals favored a welfare state that was a burdensome bureaucracy lacking the support of the tax-paying public. And welfare clients became increasingly vocal in their complaints about program shortcomings.

Consider this: In 1994, the maximum AFDC grant for a family of three was $366 per month, an amount that had declined in its real purchasing value by 47 percent since 1970 due to inflation.[58] In other words, by the early 1990s the primary income for poor, often minority mothers was worth only about half of its value a generation earlier. Despite the bitter existence of poor families on public assistance, neither the public nor a Democratic House of Representatives indicated much willingness to increase benefits to them.

Liberals responded to public disenchantment with welfare by putting their heads in the sand. The Right moved into the policy void, fashioning ever more plausible solutions to the problems of the poor. Conservatives were rightly and roundly ridiculed for trying to label catsup a vegetable in order to minimize expenditures for the School Lunch Program during the early years of the Reagan administration. But their learning curve turned sharply upward. Later suggestions by Jack Kemp to empower the poor by allowing them to purchase their public housing units were well received by residents in the nation's public housing gulags. Similar conservative reforms suggested allowing the poor the opportunity to choose the schools that their children could attend, further empowering them. Where were the liberals during the unfolding of these bold initiatives? If Newt Gingrich's "Contract with America" that featured so prominently in the 1994 Republican takeover of Congress is any indication, liberals were watching from the sidelines, apparently baffled.

A DECADE OF TRANSITION

The conservatives seemed unable to exploit the domestic policy opening of Reagan's first term, and the traditional liberals seemed unwilling to take a hard look at their half-century of hegemony in domestic policy. This left the prospect of a new policy agenda squarely on the shoulders of Bill Clinton. As a Democratic *nominee,* Clinton had toyed with that possibility, identifying himself as a "new Democrat," seeking to legislate a "new covenant," as evidence of a "third way" in American politics. *President* Clinton, on the other hand, proved less willing to address such grand paradigmatic intentions, and a much-enamored media was willing—at least initially—to let him get away with elliptical references to "change."

To the extent the administration tackles the challenges to be encountered as the nation enters the next century, Clinton and company will have to deal with four dynamics: commerce versus commonweal, hypermobility versus dualism, restructuring versus bureaucracy, and human capital versus entitlements.

Commerce versus Commonweal

This dynamic relates to the acceleration of capitalism evident in the last two decades. Corporations are no longer satisfied to exploit new markets; when possible, they strategically create them. Items that would not have been considered subject to market forces a generation ago, such as health care, have been "commodified," a development that the Clintons confronted abruptly in their failed attempt at health reform. Further, global markets require diplomatic initiatives to keep capital fluid while at the same time retaining the value of labor. The globalization of capitalism has brought about the stateless corporation, effectively requiring government to develop adaptive, as opposed to adversarial, relations with commerce.

The centrifugal forces associated with this stage of capitalism clearly hurt certain communities. Many older industrial communities have experienced the escape of capital, industrial capacity, and finally workers. National governments have scrambled to piece together protective syndicates, such as the European Economic Community and the international collaboration created by NAFTA. The primary question posed by this dynamic is, how can government ensure a sense of community to citizens?

Hypermobility versus Dualism

The proliferation of global capitalism has a pronounced effect on workers. On the one hand, labor has many more opportunities than had been available during the industrial era. Today's employees can expect to have a work history reflecting a series of occupations, or multiple occupational activities at the same time. Technology allows workers to be more productive, both independently and creatively, than had been possible a generation ago. Mobility is enhanced horizontally and vertically with workers able to relocate and assume more or less administrative responsibility than before. This flux in the labor market has affected middle-class professionals as much as it has migrant workers.

This contrasts with the dualism of the industrial era, marked by relatively rigid class positions determined by formal education, gender, and race. When coupled to the dynamic above—commerce versus commonweal—the contrast becomes stark. Centers of international capital, such as London, Miami, and Los Angeles, have communities of extraordinary cultural variation and wealth side-by-side with an unskilled, working-aged population that is virtually redundant. The central question posed by this dynamic is, how can opportunity be modulated in order to ensure essentials while at the same time avoid excess?

Restructuring versus Bureaucracy

The large organizational edifices generated during the industrial era have been under intense pressure to downsize. Both corporate and governmental sectors have found it necessary to create smaller, less costly, more flexible, and socially responsive organizational forms. Government has been slower to restructure despite taxpayer reluctance to continue subsidizing inflexible and unresponsive agencies. Still, local experiments in restructuring health and education reflect this trend.

Restructuring requires government to decide which mandated services will be provided by public employees and which will be contracted out, or privatized. Restructuring has occurred during a period when federal and many state governments have been in fiscal straits, and this has provided powerful incentives for them to try to shift responsibility onto one another. Often lost in the shuffle are citizens dependent on public services and employees who had been protected by civil service and/or collective bargaining agreements. A fundamental question presented by this dynamic is, how can the competing interests of the taxpayers, government employees, and service consumers be balanced while at the same time providing mandated services?

Human Capital versus Entitlements

During the industrial era more progressive nations justified universal health and welfare benefits as basic rights of citizens. Such unconditional entitlements have come to pose enormous fiscal problems for government. Federal and state government budgets are increasingly consumed by entitlements that progressively push discretionary programs out of the budget. When entitlements are disproportionately assured to the aged and discretionary programs used to aid the young are crowded out, a generation gap develops, clearly evident in the future of Social Security.

A postindustrial context requires more strategic investments in human capital than that afforded by unconditional entitlements. Government in partnership with the private sector needs to be able to target programs to specific populations in order to optimize national competitiveness. Prosperity becomes contingent on public-private accords in which social policy is used to make specific investments in human capital. The question posed by this dynamic is, how can security be assured citizens but not encumber the economy?

The dynamics described above illustrate a watershed in the evolution of American domestic affairs. Taken as a group, *commonweal, dualism, bureaucracy,* and *entitlements* are distinguishing features of the industrial era and served to shape the institution central to domestic social policy, the American welfare state. In contrast, the aggregation of *commerce, hypermobility, restructuring,* and *human capital* are distinctive features of the postindustrial era. Their articulation will constitute the sequel to the government welfare state. The implications of this extend beyond mechanistic social analysis; for the Clinton administration to forge ahead with substantive "change," it must make the transition from an industrial-era comprehension of social policy to a postmodern formulation of the public good.

Such transitions do not happen automatically. National leaders can be ineffective and lead their countries to ruin. It is sobering to recognize, for example, that pre-World War II Argentina had a level of consumption and culture that rivaled Europe. Fifty years later, the nation has yet to recover from the political and economic mistakes of the populism associated with Juan Perón. A more immediate example is the late Soviet Union. In this case, the insistence by political elites that a particular economic theory be executed caused the isolation of the nations of Eastern Europe from the West and drove them into bankruptcy. As the turmoil in the former Yugoslavia suggests, the mistakes associated with Communism may take generations to resolve.

Does a similar fate await the United States? Conceivably. It is ironic that, in a context where prospects for the nation appear to be threatened by foreign economic and political affairs, so much of our future prosperity rests with leaders who will move boldly on the domestic policy front. With increasing frequency, students of public policy are portraying the specter of deficit budgeting and entitlement spending in apocalyptic terms. Washington journalist David Broder has written that the 1990s are "the last, best chance to achieve real fiscal discipline" before the nation's economy is overcome by the economic juggernaut.[59]

To the extent Bill Clinton proves himself a leader, he will have reconciled this dilemma with the more specific policy demands of the nation in health, education, welfare, immigration, urban affairs, and public pensions. Certainly, the president has aspirations to greatness. Whether or not his administration will construct a coherent vision for leading America confidently into the next century remains to be seen.[60] The temptation, of course, is to settle for the politics of banality, those minimal policy adjustments that ensure reelection. In that eventuality, President Clinton will have succumbed to decidedly more pedestrian talents: rationalizing and glorifying necessity.

NOTES

1. H. L. Mencken, *Minority Report: H.L. Mencken's Notebooks* (New York: Knopf, 1956), p. 176.
2. Bob Woodward, *The Agenda* (New York: Simon & Schuster, 1994).
3. Elizabeth Drew, *On the Edge* (New York: Simon & Schuster, 1994).
4. Arthur Schlesinger, Jr., *The Cycles of American History* (Boston: Houghton Mifflin, 1986), p. 47.
5. For first-year assessments of Clinton's ideological orientation, see Kevin Phillips, "Clinton's Policies Have FDR Rolling in His Grave," *Los Angeles Times* (August 22, 1993), p. M-1; E. J. Dionne, Jr., "He Never Moved Left," *Washington Post National Weekly* (July 5-11, 1993), p. 28.
6. The exception may be health care reform, the nature of which is considered in a later chapter.
7. Prior to declaring his candidacy for the presidency, Clinton chaired the DLC.
8. Milton and Rose Friedman, "The Tide in the Affairs of Men," in Annelise Anderson and Dennis Bark, eds., *Thinking About America: The United States in the 1990s* (Stanford: Hoover Institution, 1988).
9. Barry Bluestone and Bennett Harrison, *The Deindustrialization of America* (New York: Basic Books, 1982).

10. Claude Brown, *Manchild in the Promised Land* (New York: Macmillan, 1965).
11. Claude Brown, "Manchild in Harlem," *New York Times Magazine* (September 16, 1984).
12. Daniel Patrick Moynihan, "Defining Deviancy Down," *American Scholar* (Winter 1993).
13. Sylvia Ann Hewlett, *When The Bough Breaks* (New York: HarperCollins, 1992), p. 14.
14. Colin Pritchard, "Re-analysing Children's Homicide and Undetermined Death Rates as an Indication of Improved Child Protection," *British Journal of Social Work* 23 (1993) 645-52.
15. What had been Aid to the Blind, Aid to the Disabled, and Old Age Assistance were initially state-operated programs, later consolidated into SSI in the early 1970s, a program operated by the federal government.
16. Neil Gilbert, Harry Specht, and Paul Terrell, *Dimensions of Social Welfare Policy* (Englewood Cliffs, NJ: Prentice Hall, 1993), p. 34.
17. Lela Costin, Howard Karger, and David Stoesz, *Child Abuse Politics* (New York: Oxford University Press, forthcoming).
18. Katherine Newman, *Declining Fortunes* (New York: Basic Books, 1993).
19. Michael Harrington, *The Other America* (New York: Penguin Books, 1962).
20. Taylor Branch, *Parting the Waters* (New York: Simon & Schuster, 1988).
21. Jill Quadagno, *The Color of Welfare* (New York: Oxford University Press, 1994).
22. With one exception, all of these programs were public assistance programs—to be eligible one had to be poor. During the Great Society, only one social insurance was added to the American welfare state: Medicare.
23. Although the use of social programs to redistribute power to the poor through Community Action Programs was quickly snuffed out.
24. Frances Fox Piven and Richard Cloward, *Regulating the Poor* (New York: Vintage, 1971).
25. William Ryan, *Blaming the Victim* (New York: Pantheon, 1971).
26. Irving Howe, *Beyond the Welfare State* (New York: Schocken Books, 1982), p. 10.
27. "ConWonk" is an abbreviation of "conservative policy wonk." A wonk is an enthusiast for an obscure area of inquiry.
28. Henry Aaron, *Politics and the Professors* (Washington, DC: Brookings Institution, 1978).
29. Karen Tumulty, "The Lost Faith of Daniel Patrick Moynihan," *Los Angeles Times Magazine* (June 18, 1994).
30. James Smith, *The Idea Brokers* (New York: Free Press, 1991), p. 170.
31. David Stoesz, "Packaging the Conservative Revolution," *Social Epistemology*, Vol. 2 No. 2 (1988).
32. William Baroody, Jr., "The President's Review," *AEI Annual Report 1981-1982* (Washington, DC: American Enterprise Institute, n.d.), p. 2.
33. See Stoesz, "Packaging the Conservative Revolution."
34. Burton Pines, *Back to Basics* (New York: William Morrow, 1982), p. 254.
35. David Stoesz and Howard Karger, *Reconstructing the American Welfare State* (Lanham, MD: Rowman and Littlefield, 1992), pp. 51-53.
36. Moynihan, *Came the Revolution* (San Diego: Harcourt Brace Jovanovich, 1988), pp. 151-60.
37. *The Economic and Budget Outlook: Fiscal Years 1991-1995* (Washington, DC: Congressional Budget Office, 1990), pp. 122, 112.
38. Sidney Blumenthal and Thomas Edsall, *The Reagan Legacy* (New York: Pantheon, 1988), pp. 42-43.

39. Stoesz and Karger, *Reconstructing*, pp. 56-57.
40. Stoesz and Karger, *Reconstructing*, pp. 59-60.
41. Stoesz and Karger, *Reconstructing*, p. 64.
42. Stuart Butler, "Power to the People," *Policy Review* (Spring 1987).
43. American Association of Fundraising Counsels, *Giving USA* (New York: American Assoc. of Fundraising Counsels, 1994), chart: "Giving by Use, 1959-93."
44. Kevin Phillips, *The Politics of Rich and Poor* (New York: Random House, 1990).
45. Charles Peters, "A New Politics," *Public Welfare* 18 (1983), p. 34.
46. Peters, *A New Politics*, p. 36.
47. David Osborne, *Laboratories of Democracy* (Boston: Harvard Business School Press, 1988), p. 321.
48. James Pinkerton, "Post-Modern Politics: The Search for a New Paradigm," remarks before the Illinois New Paradigm Society, September 16, 1991, pp. 1, 4.
49. Mickey Kaus, "Paradigm's Loss," *The New Republic* (July 27, 1992), p. 16.
50. Mickey Kaus, *The End of Equality* (New York: Basic Books, 1992).
51. The work by Osborne and Gaebler owed a substantial debt to the work on privatization that E.S. Savas had pioneered. David Osborne and Ted Gaebler, *Reinventing Government* (Reading, MA: Addison Wesley, 1992).
52. E. J. Dionne, *Why Americans Hate Politics* (New York: Simon & Schuster, 1992).
53. Will Marshall, "The Politics of Reciprocity," *The New Democrat*, Vol. 4, No. 4 (July 1992), p. 6.
54. Steven Pearlstein, "A New Paradigm for a New Administration," *The Washington Post National Weekly* (December 28, 1992-January 3, 1993), p. 20.
55. Max Sawicky, "The Poverty of the New Paradigm," (Washington, DC: Economic Policy Institute, n.d.).
56. Fay Cook and Edith Barrett, *Support for the American Welfare State* (New York: Columbia University Press, 1992), p. 163.
57. Theodore Marmor, Jerry Mashaw, and Philip Harvey, *America's Misunderstood Welfare State* (New York: Basic Books, 1990), p. 57.
58. Committee on Ways and Means, *Overview of Entitlement Programs* (Washington, DC: United States Government Printing Office, 1994), pp. 367, 377.
59. David Broder, "Good Politics, Bad Leadership," *Los Angeles Times* (February 12, 1995), p. C-7.
60. Woodward, *The Agenda*.

chapter 2

Health Care: False Profits

The solution to the health care crisis is to conscript all the doctors but, upon their acceptance to medical school, promise them all new BMWs.
Charles Peters[1]

When a nation establishes a national health plan affects *what* type of program will likely be enacted. Had the United States adopted a national health care program during the New Deal era, the result would probably have resembled the British National Health Service, a system in which the national government owns health care facilities and employs health care professionals while ensuring universal coverage for the population. The United States has an example of such government control in the Veterans Administration (VA). One of the less subtle contradictions of the American health care reform debate is that although conservatives have ardently defended Veterans Administration–style health care for veterans, they oppose for the rest of the population the adoption of health care reform that features a strong role for the federal government, calling such a system "socialized medicine." Regardless, it is unlikely that American voters would want their health care modeled after the Veterans Administration.

Had national health care reform been implemented during the era of the Great Society, the result would likely have resembled the Canadian health care program, which provides universal access to health care through the private sector, while the national government raises revenues to reimburse providers and regulates health care consumption. The United States also has experience with such a "single-payer" arrangement for health care provision—the Medicare program. Some people maintain that the easiest way to establish a national health care program would be to eliminate the age-65 requirement for receipt of Medicare.

In fact, in the discussion of health care reform during the early 1990s, Representative Pete Stark (D-California) presented such an option by suggesting the addition of a "Part C" to the Medicare program. Despite the popularity of the Medicare program among the elderly and the Clinton administration's insistence on health care reform, Stark's proposal failed to attract serious consideration.

The health care reform proposal Clinton introduced resembled neither a national health service nor a single-payer plan. Instead, the administration advocated a "managed competition" strategy in which large health care alliances would compete to subscribe members. The adoption of managed competition has its precedent in the Health Maintenance Organization Act of 1973, federal legislation that caused a tremendous expansion of health maintenance organizations (HMOs) in the United States. To Clinton, managed competition avoided the ponderous bureaucracy and enormous cost that were associated with Medicare while it took advantage of a more competitive and preventive design for health care.

Yet, by mid-1994 the administration's centerpiece of domestic policy reform, health care reform, was dead, the victim of media manipulation by health interests, White House mismanagement, and an intransigent, though Democratic, Congress. How is it possible that, under such prescient circumstance, health care reform would stall? Public opinion polls consistently indicated wide support for health care reform. In 1991, Harris Wofford won a stunning victory in a Senate campaign over Richard Thornburgh, former governor of Pennsylvania and attorney general in the Bush administration. Wofford won largely by advocating a national health care program. Prominent business leaders had pleaded for a less-costly and more rational method for providing health care for employees. Labor unions echoed the call because of "give-backs" in collective bargaining concessions and the reduction of benefits for retirees during the 1980s—health care featuring prominently in both. Surely, the president could count on a Democratic Congress to design a national health care program. Under First Lady Hillary Rodham Clinton and corporate savant Ira Magaziner, the administration had retained over 500 of the nation's top health experts to fashion a workable plan for health care reform. Yet, instead of marshaling these forces to build support for a national health care program, the reform initiative dissembled. Momentum for major health care reform dwindled during the 103rd Congress. An incoming 104th Congress controlled by Republicans meant that minor, incremental improvements were more likely.

MEDICARE

Many of the Clinton administration's travails over health care reform can be attributed to health programs established during the era of the Great Society: Medicare and Medicaid. Passed in 1965, Medicare and Medicaid were half-measures, programs that liberal policy advocates hoped would presage a universal national health care program. Beyond that, they had little in common. Medicare was cast as health insurance largely financed by a portion of the same withholding tax that funded Social Security. Medicaid, on the other hand, was a public assistance program for the poor, financed through general revenues. A sequential relationship between Medicare and Medicaid soon became evident. Because of the limited hospitalization benefits of Medicare—roughly no more than 100 days of hospitalization—many of the ill elderly who needed help in paying for long-term nursing care eventually received benefits from Medicaid. To become eligible for Medicaid, however, one had to be poor—a condition that long-term nursing care quickly induced as the infirm elderly exhausted assets paying for nursing home services. Once poor, Medicaid picked up the tab for the elderly receiving extended nursing home care. The "spend down," as this sequence was labeled, affected many of the elderly, leaving them and their heirs virtually without assets. Nevertheless, as a complement to Social Security, Medicare became a popular program among the elderly—even if hospitalization benefits were limited and deductible levels were substantial. In 1993, 39 million aged and disabled Americans were insured for hospitalization under Part A of Medicare, and 34.2 million of the aged and disabled were insured for physicians' care under Part B.[2]

In creating Medicare and Medicaid, Congress made a crucial decision, one that would bedevil the Clinton administration's attempt to enact a national health care program. In ensuring health care for the elderly and the poor, Congress had to consider whether government should commit the resources to construct and staff a VA-style health care bureaucracy or conserve public resources by reimbursing existing, private providers. Congress chose the latter, though it was not as straightforward as might be suspected. In consideration of mental health reform, also in 1965, Congress created the Community Mental Health Centers Act—the result being disastrous for the mentally ill. As federal support for mental health ebbed, state and local government proved unwilling to step in. Meanwhile, on the promise that Community Mental Health Centers (CMHCs) would provide mental health care in the community, state mental health hospitals discharged tens of thousands of patients. With the demise of CMHCs, thousands of deinstitutionalized persons across the nation were stranded in communities that had neither the willingness nor the resources for their care. To this day a substantial portion of the homeless are mentally ill individuals who were once patients in state mental health hospitals.[3]

The decision to reimburse private providers proved a powerful force in driving health care costs upward. Table 2.1 illustrates the income boost that federal programs enacted in 1965 provided to a nascent health care industry.

In order to placate medical interests concerned about governmental control of health care, Medicare was designed to reimburse private providers on a "cost-plus" basis. Thus structured, Medicare became a windfall for health providers. Physicians and hospitals were free to charge what they determined to be reasonable for care *and* add to that amount associated indirect costs. The pay-off exceeded the wildest dreams of defense contractors. In 1975, a decade after its introduction, Medicare cost $14 billion; by 1985, it was budgeted at $69.5 billion; for 1994, allocations were expected to be $164 billion.[4] From 1975

TABLE 2.1 Projections of national health expenditures

Type of Spending	1965	1980	1985	1990	1995	2000
			Billions of Dollars			
Hospital	14	102	168	256	416	671
Physician	8	42	74	126	204	316
Drugs, Nondurables	6	22	36	55	78	111
Nursing Home	2	20	34	53	87	137
All other	12	64	110	177	287	444
Total	42	250	423	666	1,072	1,679
Source of Funds	**1965**	**1980**	**1985**	**1990**	**1995**	**2000**
			Billions of Dollars			
Private	31	145	248	284	574	869
Public						
Federal	5	72	124	195	343	566
State and Local	5	33	51	87	155	244
Total	42	250	423	666	1,072	1,679
Source of Funds	**1965**	**1980**	**1985**	**1990**	**1995**	**2000**
			Percentage of Total			
Private	75.3	58.0	58.6	57.6	53.5	51.7
Public						
Federal	11.6	28.8	29.2	29.3	32.0	33.7
State and Local	13.2	13.3	12.1	13.1	14.5	14.5
Total, National	100.0	100.0	100.0	100.0	100.0	100.0

Adapted from *Projections of National Health Expenditures* (Washington, DC: Congressional Budget Office, 1992), pp. xi, xii.

to 1985, Medicare grew by an *annual* rate of 17.3 percent; for the following decade, annual expansion was to slow to a still robust 10.2 percent.[5]

Uncontrolled Medicare spending soon led to efforts to contain costs. In its first term, the Reagan administration introduced a Prospective Payment System (PPS) to replace the "cost-plus" arrangement that had been so favorable to hospitals. PPS was operationalized through the application of Diagnostic Related Group (DRG) categories for which payments would be fixed. So beginning in 1983, hospitals would know in advance precisely what the Medicare payment would be for some 487 patient care categories. DRGs effectively transferred the determination of health care costs from hospitals to Medicare. By the early 1990s, the institution of DRGs slowed Medicare growth so that it approximated the overall rise in health care costs, which continued to increase at a rate that exceeded inflation.[6] DRGs notwithstanding, an aging baby-boom generation ensured the escalation of future Medicare expenditures.

MEDICAID

Unlike Medicare, a single program administered through one federal agency, Medicaid was assigned to the states, as has been the custom with most other public assistance programs. There are 52 Medicaid programs, one for each state and Puerto Rico and the Virgin Islands. Because the federal government matches state allocations for Medicaid according to per capita income and because states can opt to supplement basic Medicaid benefits, there is considerable variation in Medicaid programs. Recipients of Aid to Families with Dependent Children (AFDC) and Supplemental Security Income (SSI) automatically become eligible for Medicaid. In 1986, Medicaid was extended to pregnant women and children under 6 years of age who were below 133 percent of the federal poverty line. In addition, legislation passed during the Bush administration ensures that any poor child born after September 30, 1983, may receive Medicaid.[7]

Other than the bureaucratic tangle that characterizes Medicaid administration, the most distinguishing feature of the program has been its growth. In 1975, Medicaid cost federal and state government $12 billion; by 1985, the cost had risen to $40.9 billion; for 1994, Medicaid allocations were projected to be $160.7 billion. During the past five years, Medicaid expenditures have increased 21.4 percent annually.[8] Most Medicaid benefits cover health care costs for the elderly, blind, or disabled as opposed to poor children. For 1991, 69.9 percent of the Medicaid caseload consisted of elderly persons, while 15.1 percent were children. In that year, Medicaid expenditures for the aged, blind, and disabled were $53.7 billion, while those for poor children totaled only $11.7 billion.[9]

An irony of the Medicaid program is that, despite rising costs, less than half of the poor in America are eligible for its benefits. For example, in 1992 only 47 percent of the poor received Medicaid.[10] The majority of Medicaid benefits were paid out to nursing homes who were caring for the aged and disabled who had exhausted Medicare benefits. Neglected altogether were working class families whose income and assets exceeded the eligibility guidelines for Medicaid. By the early 1990s, various estimates placed the size of that population at more than 39 million Americans.[11] One of the more egregious faults of the American nonsystem of health care is that many of these working Americans who had no health insurance were required to contribute monthly to the Medicare program through tax withholding to make certain that the elderly would receive health care.

THE RISE OF CORPORATE HEALTH CARE

That the government was pumping tens of billions of dollars annually into health care did not go unnoticed by financiers. Capitalizing on Medicare and Medicaid, business interests moved quickly to exploit markets in hospital management, nursing home care, and—after passage of the Health Maintenance Organization Act in 1973—HMOs. Corporate health care expanded rapidly. Virtually nonexistent before 1965, the major health service corporations had grown to multibillion dollar enterprises within two decades.

Exploitation of the health care market occurred in the best tradition of American capitalism. Consider long-term nursing care as an example. Merger mania struck the nursing home industry in 1979 when Beverly Enterprises became the largest nursing home provider by purchasing Progressive Medical Group, then the eleventh largest nursing home chain. Also in 1979, National Medical Enterprises (NME) became the third largest provider by purchasing Hillhaven, the third largest operation in the field. ARA Services, the second largest provider, grew 26 percent in 1979 by consolidating smaller operations in Indiana, Colorado, and California. Acquisitions and mergers continued, undeterred by the filing of the first antitrust action in the nursing home industry. Using its Hillhaven subsidiary, in 1984 NME acquired Flagg Industries with 12 facilities in California and seven facilities in Idaho, bringing its total holdings to 339 health care facilities, representing 42,000 beds. Not to be outdone, Beverly Enterprises acquired Beacon Hill American for $60 million, thereby retaining its top ranking.[12]

A shakedown in the hospital management industry also began in the late 1970s. In 1978 Humana doubled its size through an unfriendly takeover of American Medicorp, which was worth $450 million and represented 39 hospitals and 7,838 beds. Meanwhile, Hospital Corporation of America (HCA) purchased Hospital Affiliates, worth $650 million, for 55 owned hospitals with 8,207 beds and 102 hospital management contracts; General Care Corporation, worth $78 million, for eight hospitals and 1,294 beds; and General Health Services, worth $96 million, for six hospitals and 1,115 beds. At the same time, American Medical International (AMI) acquired Hyatt Medical Enterprises, worth $69 million, for eight owned hospitals, 907 beds, and 26 hospital management contracts and Brookwood Health Services, worth $156 million, for nine owned hospitals, 1,271 beds, and five hospital management contracts.[13]

There was another wave of acquisitions in the early 1990s.[14] Anticipating regulations and revenue accompanying health care reform, health care corporations moved to consolidate their holdings. Galen Health Care bought United Health Care Corporation, only to be acquired by Columbia Hospital Corporation, a modest firm of 13,300 employees, 22 general hospitals, and four substance abuse facilities, reporting $819 million in revenues for 1992. In 1993 Columbia shocked the health care industry by taking over industry-giant HCA. *Business Week* reported that the merger would leave Columbia with 190 hospitals and annual revenues of $10 billion.[15] Instantly, Columbia had vaulted to the front of the pack, becoming the largest of American health care corporations, some of which are listed in Table 2.2.

Apart from the gratification experienced by corporate takeover and acquisition artists, precisely how any of this contributed to the health of Americans has yet to be explained. Indeed, the effect of enormous health care corporations on the nation's well-being has been met with skepticism by many. The editor of the prestigious *New England Journal of Medicine* denounced the

TABLE 2.2 Health care corporations

Company	Holdings	Number of Employees	Revenues (in billions)
Hospital Corporation of America	99 hospitals (20,323 beds)	66,000	$5.13*
Humana	119 medical centers 35 admin. offices	8,800	4.04*
Galen Health Care	77 hospitals (17,114 beds)	40,000	4.04*
National Medical Enterprises	131 hospitals (14,691 beds)	50,423	3.76
Beverly Enterprises	838 nursing homes (89,305 beds) 44 retirement centers 6 home health agencies 4 pharmacies	93,000	2.60*
United Health Care Corporation	17 HMOs (2.4 million members)	6,500	2.47
American Medical Holdings**	35 acute care hospitals	28,200	2.23
FHP	multi-state HMO (834,000 members) 56 medical and dental facilities 2 hospitals 2 nursing homes	9,900	2.00

*Revenues for 1992, all others are for 1993.
**Formerly known as American Medical International.
SOURCE: Standard and Poors.

consequences of an insatiable "medical-industrial complex."[16] The editor of the Left-leaning *International Journal of Health Services* complained accurately that health care firms were profiting largely from public funds.[17] Finally, Pulitzer prize-winning sociologist Paul Starr concluded his history of American health care with a warning about the growing influence of the "new health conglomerates."[18]

CATASTROPHIC HEALTH INSURANCE

By the early 1990s, the prospects of health reform were inextricably tied to the policy legacy of the Great Society era. Medicare and Medicaid had become durable fixtures of the American welfare state. The aged and the poor had come to depend on them for essential health care as had physicians and hospitals for revenue. In the process, an extensive array of for-profit health care corporations had emerged. In only three decades, government-financed health care had expanded, seemingly without limits. Complementing these developments—indeed, because of them—a jerry-rigged arrangement of organizations and procedures unfolded. The result was not so much a "system" as it was a pastiche slapped together of government programs designed to target select populations of needy citizens, the buying-off of private health providers through open-ended reimbursement policies, and a good deal of financial opportunism. Inelegant as the result was—particularly when put up against the health care systems of European nations—American health care programs flourished. To the seasoned policy observer, more than economic gain was at play, however. Each of the institutions that held a major stake in health care—physicians, hospitals, beneficiaries—would have to be placated if they were to participate in health reform.[19] In effect, by virtue of institutional elaboration each had gained a veto. Nowhere was this more evident than in Catastrophic Health Insurance.

The Medicare Catastrophic Coverage Act was designed to expand Medicare to cover extraordinary health care costs not already provided for under Part A, protecting 32 million beneficiaries. Catastrophic Health Insurance (CHI) was to have begun in 1989, with 40 percent of the revenues funded by a $48 per year increase in Part B premiums and the remaining 60 percent from a surcharge on the wealthy elderly. The surcharge topped out at $1,050 per person, an amount that only five percent of enrollees would have to pay. In many respects, CHI was the perfect complement to Medicare: It was crafted as a health insurance program, self-financing and not reliant on general revenues; it was financed by a moderately progressive tax on the wealthy; and it had the tentative endorsement of the largest lobby of the elderly, the American Association of Retired Persons (AARP). Finally, CHI was signed into law by Ronald Reagan, the most conservative president since Herbert Hoover.

From there, Catastrophic Health Insurance went downhill. Provoked by an elderly advocacy group, the National Committee to Preserve Social Security and Medicare, anxious pensioners flooded Congress with complaints about CHI.[20] Largely imaginary, worries of the aged focused on the financing of CHI. Many assumed that the maximum surcharge applied to all enrollees. Attempts to correct misperceptions collapsed in the deluge of mail arriving daily in Washington. Finding itself amidst a rising tide, even AARP reconsidered its endorsement of CHI. Eventually, Congress repealed CHI the year after it had been enacted, the first retraction of a social insurance program in the history of the American welfare state.[21] The CHI experience resonated ominously whenever talk of health reform surfaced in Congress; never again would the implications of program cost and constituent wrath be taken for granted.[22]

PRELUDE TO HEALTH CARE REFORM

Although the creation of a national health program had been a staple of the American Left since the Progressive era, recent momentum can be traced to a more staid influence: the *New England Journal of Medicine*. Under its former editor, Arnold Relman, the *Journal* published a series of articles during the mid-1980s promoting the discussion of health care reform.[23] Relman's initiative culminated in 1989 with the publication of two rival models of health care reform, a "single-payer" option and one promoting a new concept: "managed competition." In presenting these models in considerable detail, Relman deliberately avoided presenting a national health service model that would have been anathema to physicians. Relman artfully dodged the prospect of too much government involvement in health care. In summing up the virtues of the single-payer and managed competition options, Relman observed that "neither one represents the socialization of health care, because the government would not own or operate health care facilities or employ physicians."[24]

Writing in the *New England Journal of Medicine* on behalf of an extensive panel of physicians, David Himmelstein and Steffie Woolhandler advanced the single-payer solution to the American health care crisis. The most prominent feature of the Himmelstein and Woolhandler formulation was universal coverage. Each citizen would be provided with a national health card granting the cardholder access to health care. In order to reorient the current health care market toward a broader, public purpose, Himmelstein and Woolhandler proposed the elimination of commercial health insurance and the use of operating funds for profit. By eliminating corporate activity, American health care could be made more rational, they argued, resulting in substantial savings. These would be put toward making health care more accessible by extending coverage to all citizens, eliminating copayments and deductibles, and prohibiting selective enrollment policies. Health care costs would be restrained by "global budgets" within which hospitals and clinics would have to function, requiring them to be more prudent in using expensive diagnostic equipment, undertaking unnecessary surgical procedures, and paying excessive salaries to health care providers and administrators. Funding of the reform Himmelstein and Woolhandler proposed would be derived from a progressive tax on income and a tax on employers earmarked for national health care. All payments, whether for physician care or physical plant expansion, would be reviewed and authorized by a national health board.[25]

Essentially, what Himmelstein and Woolhandler proposed replicated the Canadian model of health care in the United States. Their strategy called for treating health care as a public utility instead of a market. In an earlier article, Himmelstein and Woolhandler calculated that the institution of a single-payer, national health insurance program would realize savings of $29.2 billion.[26] Their proposal also reassured physicians, such as Relman, that the medical-industrial complex would be contained, leaving the practice of medicine and the administration of health care in the hands of physicians. The Himmelstein and Woolhandler model rationalized a haphazard, capricious, and unfair arrangement of health care; in the process, it extended health care to everyone.

It also flew in the face of a dynamic and expanding for-profit health industry that was not about to be sent packing by a handful of idealistic physicians. For CEOs of major health care corporations and health insurance companies, the constraints imposed by the single-payer model were analogous to the Federal Highway Administration dictating a budget from which Chrysler, Ford, and Chevrolet would have to manufacture automobiles. Eventually, the medical-industrial complex would do whatever was necessary to kill the single-payer option to health reform.

The second option to health reform, "managed competition," was proposed by two health economists, Alain Enthoven and Richard Kronick. Conceding that health care in the United States was "a paradox of excess and deprivation," Enthoven and Kronick deliberately distanced their plan from universal health insurance.

> Universal health insurance has not attracted overwhelming support in this country. Those who favor it should consider carefully the sources of opposition and seek to avoid designing a plan with features so objectionable to large numbers of American people or key interest groups that the plan would not be considered seriously in the political process. The idea of universal health insurance raises fears of socialized medicine or total dependence on the government for payment, of radical change or the disruption of satisfactory existing arrangements, of large-scale redistribution of income, or of excessive regulatory coercion.[27]

In contrast to single-payer advocates suggesting the elimination or restraint of the private sector, the managed competition option Enthoven and Kronick proposed used the marketplace to reform health care. Market dynamics, they argued, could be employed to give greater choice to consumers and to increase competition, thereby lowering costs. Rather than outlaw the for-profit sector in health care, Enthoven and Kronick proposed managed competition as a way of maximizing public benefit.

The key to managed competition was the creation of "public sponsors" who would be responsible for enrolling the uninsured in a basic health insurance program. Employers would be required to insure all full-time workers and pay an 8 percent payroll tax on the first $22,500 of wages for each uninsured worker, the proceeds of which would go to a pool from which insurance would be obtained. As they are now, larger employers would be motivated to obtain health care from the provider offering the most economical and beneficial plan, whether that be through health insurance or an HMO. In order to minimize frivolous usage, a $250 deductible and 20-percent copayment would be standard.

Managed competition called for virtually no restructuring of health care. Medicare and Medicaid would be left unchanged. Commercial insurance and health care would be encouraged to compete for enrollees. Care of the uninsured would be paid for by imposing a health withholding tax on employers for those workers uninsured, limiting tax deductions for excessive health benefits, and requiring the states to share in the cost of the program. The total cost of the program was $12.8 billion, or about $2,400 per family—a realistic cost considering limits imposed by the federal deficit.[28]

The Enthoven and Kronick proposal for health reform was classic incrementalism, the least necessary adjustment to achieve an objective. Out of concern for feasibility, Enthoven and Kronick left intact existing programs, such as Medicare and Medicaid. The Enthoven and Kronick employer mandate to insure all full-time workers appealed directly to the corporate health sector, which stood to gain a great deal by enrolling and serving the millions of Americans currently without insurance. The cost of their program was to be shared by employers who were penalized for uninsured workers and employees who had excessive health benefits, the value of which would be taxed. If this was health reform, it was health reform–lite. Particularly when compared to the single-payer plan proposed by Himmelstein and Woolhandler, the benefits and advantages of the Enthoven and Kronick managed competition proposal were to health reform what virtual reality was to reality—for the most part illusory.

THE HEALTH SECURITY ACT

Soon after assuming office, President Clinton began working on the primary legislative proposal of his domestic policy—national health reform. Although Hillary Rodham Clinton was designated publicly to head the initiative, the machinations were assigned to Ira Magaziner. A corporate whiz kid, Magaziner's reputation was built on two accomplishments. A cofounder of the Telesis corporate consulting group, Magaziner was hobnobbing in the inner circles of international capital well before he turned forty. Subsequently, he organized an ambitious industrial policy to revitalize Rhode Island's flagging businesses. Voters, however, could not be persuaded to adopt Magaziner's formulation of "industrial policy" and rejected the plan by a four-to-one margin.

Magaziner was a workaholic whose passion for detailed planning was notorious.[29] In characteristic corporate style, he approached health care reform as he would any industry. The objective was to forge the most comprehensive, state-of-the-art approach. Magaziner's mission in the complex undertaking was to capture the strategic high ground and leave the mopping up to supplemental legislation. "You can never get 100 percent of what you want from the policy process," Magaziner observed. "But if you get 70 percent, you can get the other 30 percent [later] if you build in the right kinds of mechanisms."[30] Soon, Magaziner had some 500 of the nation's health experts commuting daily to the Old Executive Office Building across the street from the White House, discussing and arbitrating the major and minor facets of the nation's health crisis. At its peak, the effort consisted of 15 committees and 34 working groups operating concurrently.[31] Prominent among the participants were Alain Enthoven and Richard Kronick.[32]

The president's health care reform process was not without controversy. In order to avoid the influence of interest groups, the groups Magaziner had convened operated secretly; even their membership was kept secret. Eventually, a court decision forced Hillary Rodham Clinton to divulge the nature of the process and its participants, but by then much of the groundwork had been laid. In early April 1993, key participants strategically leaked to reporters major provisions that had evolved. The centerpiece of health reform would be regional "health alliances" that ensured at least a minimal health care package to everyone. In larger metropolitan areas, several alliances would compete for members. Alliances would also recruit physicians to care for patient-members. Health care providers would offer health care according to specific qualifications, such as price, as a condition to participating.[33]

It was a nonevent when the White House finally outlined its health reform initiative at a news conference. The absence of significant controversy over the plan was taken as an indication that the administration was on the right track. What the administration favored was an HMO-centered health reform that incorporated the private sector. This amounted to managed competition, the health care reform option that was most agreeable to the emerging corporate health sector. Still, significant issues such as cost had not been worked out. Without the resolution of financing questions, the outline was incomplete, and principle interests would reserve comment.

Bill Clinton formally announced his approach to health care reform on September 23, 1993, thinking it was sufficiently in advance for passage by the sitting Congress. The president called for a Health Security Act (HSA) that ensured universal coverage for all citizens and legal residents. People would subscribe to a regional health alliance that would offer a basic package of health benefits. Alliances would compete for members and negotiate payments to providers, keeping costs down. To minimize federal costs, employers would have to pay 80 percent of workers' premium costs, their employees paying the remainder. As a final method to contain rising health costs, the president's initiative called for the creation of a seven-member panel to set the annual budgets for health alliances, modify the basic benefit, and evaluate quality of health care. Medicare would remain untouched. "By drawing on market-oriented strategies favored by some Republicans and Conservative Democrats," a reporter observed, "Clinton's blueprint is designed to capitalize on bipartisan sentiment that the time has come to tackle one of the most sensitive and complex problems facing the country."[34] Magaziner had planned thoroughly—the Health Security Act ran to 1,342 pages.

Once the financing was finally divulged, the special interests targeted for most of the concessions in the president's plan moved into action. Smaller health insurers incapable of launching health alliances understood they were being maneuvered out of the industry and took to the airways. Immediately, the Health Insurance Association of America (HIAA) broadcast $2 million worth of "Harry and Louise" ads, attacking the president's Health Security Act as rationing health care under socialized medicine.[35] Within days of the ad's play, HIAA claimed that over 40,000 callers had phoned the 800-number televised in the ad to register their concerns about health reform.[36] On the Congressional front, small business lobbyists argued that the costs of the "employer mandate"—that businesses must provide health insurance to workers—would bankrupt thousands.

Michael Bromberg, director of the Federation of American Health Systems representing the interests of 1,400 for-profit hospitals, announced preference for the less-restrictive health care reform proposal that was advanced by Representative Jim Cooper (D-Tennessee). Bromberg threatened Hillary Rodham Clinton with an adversarial campaign if the administration did not adjust its plan to accommodate his group, and the threat was not hollow. Bromberg's Federation routinely contributed $250,000 to the campaigns of strategically placed Senate and House candidates.[37] Within weeks, dozens of lobbyists, ranging from pharmaceutical companies to tobacco companies to restaurants and labor unions, besieged Congress. Anticipating the 1994 elections, health industry interest groups contributed $26 million to Congressional campaigns.[38] Health care reform was the biggest domestic policy initiative before Congress in decades, and its provisions would not go unchallenged by interested parties. Observers put the total price tag on influence-peddling around the Health Security Act at $100 million.[39]

Momentarily on the defensive, the Clinton administration sought a political strategy to complement the esoteric planning process that had been undertaken a year earlier. Magaziner was replaced by Harold Ickes, a skilled and seasoned Democratic political advisor.[40] Hillary Rodham Clinton appeared in a series of national teleconferences, adroitly fielding audience questions about health reform. In a timely report, the Congressional Budget Office (CBO) calculated that, while the Health Security Act would impose small costs upon enactment, the long-term savings were substantial—by the year 2000, national health expenditures would fall $30 billion; by 2004, they would fall a whopping $150 billion (7 percent).[41] Arthur Flemming and Elliot Richardson, former cabinet secretaries under presidents Eisenhower and Nixon, respectively, announced their support of the employer mandate embodied in the Clinton reform package, noting that it paralleled the position taken by President Nixon.[42] Exploiting evidence that the uninsured were spread almost evenly across income groups,[43] President Clinton claimed that health care reform was primarily a middle-class issue.[44]

POSTMORTEM ON HEALTH CARE REFORM

Despite the administration's campaign for health care reform, Congress proved reluctant to endorse so "radical" a proposal. Several competing health care reform plans surfaced, all of which offered less reform than the Health Security Act.[45] The sole exception was a single-payer proposal presented by Paul Wellstone (D-Minnesota) and Jim McDermott (D-Washington), but Clinton had already written off a Canadian-style reform proposal. As reform proposals proliferated, public support wavered. A *Los Angeles Times* poll revealed that two-thirds of respondents "would not be angry if Congress cannot pass a comprehensive plan [in 1994]."[46] The *Wall Street Journal* reported that, although 71 percent of the public favor health care reform, 47 percent disapproved of the Clinton plan—a somewhat better showing than the 61 percent who disapproved of Congressional muddling in health care.[47] By July 1994, only 39 percent of physicians thought major health care reform was necessary, down 25 percentage points from a year earlier.[48] In an apparent turnaround, Alain Enthoven broke with the administration and spoke out against governmental control of health care costs.[49]

Near the time of the August recess, the administration appeared to be cornered. Congressional elections were ahead, and it looked as if the Republicans would gain a few seats in the Senate and a handful in the House of Representatives, creating a more conservative Congress than that confounding the president in 1994.[50] The administration presented its proposal to Congress but found the Senate slow to act. Of the five Senate committees with jurisdiction over health, only one addressed a plan that resembled the Health Security Act—the committee chaired by Senator Edward Kennedy. A critical problem was the Senate Finance Committee chaired by Daniel Patrick Moynihan, who was convinced any plan guaranteeing universal coverage that included an employer mandate could not pass Congress.[51]

Confronted with the prospect of his Health Security Act contributing to gridlock in Congress and fearing Democratic attrition in the next Congress, President Clinton sought concessions that would make health care reform more palatable to lawmakers. His first decision was to eliminate the health care alliances that had so threatened small insurers. Fearful that anti-abortion lawmakers would scuttle the president's plan, the administration further agreed to a compromise allowing health insurers and providers to delete abortion as a health care benefit.[52] Clinton hinted that the employer mandate was also subject to negotiation, but he pledged to veto any plan that failed to incorporate universal coverage.[53] In reply, conferees considered "triggers" for the employer mandate. If, for example, 95 percent of the population were not covered by 2005, then the employer mandate would kick in, insuring those workers not covered. Such a "hard trigger" was jettisoned for a "soft trigger": If universal coverage had not been achieved by 2002, Congress would name a commission to study ways to implement universal coverage.[54] Clinton objected to the latter as so much Congressional rhetoric, but he was willing to consider the employer mandate. His Health Security Act, after all, called for universal coverage by 1998, and the hard trigger—the employer mandate—postponed that only four years.[55]

The primary features of the administration's Health Security Act had included health alliances, a national health board, a basic benefit package, an employer mandate, and global budgets, but, for all practical purposes, all that remained was universal coverage. Yet even this seemed up for grabs. On July 19, 1994, President Clinton indicated that universal coverage was negotiable. "We know we're not going to get right at 100% [coverage], but we know that you've got to get somewhere in the ballpark of 95% or upwards," he said before the annual governors' conference.[56] The next day, the president clarified the statement, insisting that the administration's objective was universal coverage, reinforcing his promise of the month before to veto any legislation short of 100 percent.[57] Behind the scenes, however, Democratic leaders in Congress struggled to redefine universal coverage so that it fell in line with cost projections. It was generally agreed that no more than 95 percent of the population could be covered without significant increase in revenues, and even then not until 2000. Stymied by the arithmetic, the White House waited, anticipating negotiation that would include universal coverage at some future date. It never came. The implicit concession by the White House on universal coverage marked the demise of the Health Security Act. What had been state-of-the-art thinking by the nation's brightest health analysts was in tatters. "The present White House stance is light-years away from the heady days of last winter, when First Lady Hillary Rodham Clinton and her health policy guru, Ira Magaziner, led a highly publicized effort to redesign the nation's medical care system from top to bottom," eulogized the *Los Angeles Times*.[58]

By early August 1994, a few weeks before Congressional adjournment, Senate Majority Leader George Mitchell presented a proposal that Congressional Democrats hoped would attract the support of moderate Republicans and resurrect health care reform. The Mitchell plan called for 95 percent coverage by early in the next century, with the failure to achieve that goal triggering an employer mandate that required employers to pay 50 percent of employees' health insurance costs. By reducing the employers' contribution from 80 percent (as it had been under the initial Clinton proposal) to 50 percent, the cost to employers fell from $55 billion to $17 billion.[59] Although the White House endorsed the Mitchell proposal, many Senate Democrats were less than enthusiastic. With a small number of Senate Republicans, they formed a bipartisan "mainstream" coalition that drafted a separate proposal that eliminated employer mandates, hoped to cover 91 percent of the population by 2002, and reduced Medicare and Medicaid $400 billion during the next decade.[60] Meanwhile, under the leadership of Bob Dole, conservative Republicans in the Senate began working on an even more limited proposal.[61]

Momentum rapidly diminished, and the White House watched as disparate groups within Congress competed in last-minute attempts to salvage health care reform. The pieces that seemed to generate consensus were insurance reform, such as prohibiting the denial of insurance because of preexisting conditions, and instituting federal subsidies so that the uninsured, particularly parents, could afford to purchase health insurance for their children. Features unlikely to be included in a bipartisan reform package included employer mandates, federal control of health care costs, and taxes on excessive health insurance plans. Health care policy analysts estimated that the Mitchell plan would cover no more than one-third of Americans currently without health insurance.[62] Faced with the likelihood that a Congressional health care reform proposal would include only insurance reform, the White House debated whether or not to veto such narrow legislation.

Disappointed health care reform advocates wondered what had gone wrong with a reform initiative that only a year before had promised to completely overhaul American health care. Many attributed the demise of health care reform to the secret meetings of Magaziner and the First Lady and their reluctance to court Congressional leaders earlier.[63] Others identified the shadowy machinations of the special interests of the medical-industrial complex.[64] "Congress is unlikely to dramatically reform the insurance industry," observed one journalist, "even as insurers mount a sweeping takeover of health care in America."[65] Whatever contributed to the failure, health care reform expired with the 103rd Congress. On September 26, 1994, Senate Majority Leader George Mitchell, the author of the only compromise plan still under consideration, conceded defeat.

The demise of the Health Security Act was discouraging for liberal health care reform advocates, but the 1994 midterm election was devastating. Often highlighting the President's health care reform proposal as big government run amok, Republicans successfully challenged the White House and won control of the Congress. Symbolically, Harris Wofford, who only two years before had won a Senate seat on the basis of the need for health care reform, was defeated by a conservative who savaged Wofford for his advocacy of health care reform. What little hope that remained for progressive health care reform died when the single-payer health proposition on the ballot in California was soundly defeated.

THE NEXT HEALTH CARE POLICY AGENDA

The demise of the Health Security Act diverted attention away from the federal government and toward the states and the private sector. Elevating the role of state government in social policy had been a primary objective in the Reagan administration's "New Federalism." As the federal government retreated from program and funding commitments, governors assumed more responsibility in addressing social problems.[66] Thus, by the time health care reform had the full concern of Washington, several states had already begun experiments in health care, much as they had seized the initiative in welfare reform.

Prior to the Clinton health care reform initiative, several states had either established or planned to adopt health care reforms that assured broad access to health care. During the 1970s, Hawaii introduced universal health care through an employer mandate. Oregon's plan to extend health coverage to the working poor by restructuring its Medicaid program was approved by the federal government. In 1992, Minnesota enacted a plan that ensured universal coverage for all state residents by 1997.[67] In these and other instances, the states became laboratories of health care reform, surpassing a gridlocked federal government. These demonstrations would set the benchmarks for future discussions of health care reform.[68]

Within the private sector, the corporatization of health care proceeded unchecked. The health maintenance market had become so lucrative that larger HMOs had more cash than they knew what to do with. The four largest HMOs were sitting on more than $1 billion each, and several midsized HMOs held more than $500 million in reserves.[69] Still unsatiated after exploiting more conventional sectors of the health care market, for-profit firms began negotiating "managed care" contracts with older providers and selling health care benefit packages to large employers at costs below what they had paid under the previous "fee-for-service" basis.[70] As employers experienced lower personnel costs because employees used less health care, the managed care market accelerated rapidly. By 1991, managed care already accounted for 47 percent of employee health benefits; three years later, it accounted for 65 percent of such benefits.[71] After managed care demonstrably reduced HMO costs, executives applied the arrangement to the pharmaceutical industry with an enthusiasm that the *Wall Street Journal* characterized as a "feeding frenzy."[72]

Meanwhile, AIDS, the "greatest communicable disease challenge of our time,"[73] continued to ravage the population in the absence of effective national leadership. Late in 1994, David Satcher, Director of the Centers for Disease Control and Prevention, declared AIDS the chief cause of death for Americans between 25 and 44. Since 1981, 400,000 Americans have contracted AIDS, and 250,000 had died from the disease.[74] Neglected by the Reagan and Bush administrations, AIDS policy had fallen largely on state public health officials. But state health officials were unprepared for an epidemic of such magnitude and were slow to take the lead in preventing further spread of AIDS. To compound matters, the Reagan administration converted health care funding to a block grant to the states and in the process cut funding 25 percent.[75]

Suddenly, public health officials were faced with less federal aid in addition to increased competition among health care programs and their constituents for public funding. Not long thereafter, the Institute of Medicine, a national advisory panel, published a disheartening critique of the performance of state health officials.[76] So chastised, public health officers assumed a more proactive stance vis-à-vis AIDS,[77] but their work continued to flag without assertive national leadership. Although President Clinton had demonstrated early interest in AIDS, the aftermath of the 1994 midterm election drew him in a different direction. To distance himself from a disease associated with homosexuals, drug abusers, and the poor, Clinton consented to a "low-key, virtually secret meeting" with six people infected with AIDS in marking World AIDS Day—the very day he announced his $25-billion grant to the Pentagon in a full-regalia ceremony in the Rose Garden.[78]

Invest in Prevention

Complementing state innovations in health care reform, public health researchers released a series of reports documenting the quite substantial value of prevention programs. Harvard's Center for Risk Analysis listed the cost-effectiveness of various preventive health measures, concluding that investments were optimal for prenatal care, childhood immunization, and drug and alcohol treatment, which yielded benefits of twelve, six, and four life-years respectively (life-year-increased longevity by program investment). In each of these instances, program benefits exceeded costs. By contrast, heart transplants yielded a benefit of only two life-years at a cost of $54,000; vinyl chloride control produced two life-years at a cost of $1,614,000.[79] Under the direction of former-HEW Secretary Joseph Califano, Columbia University's Center on Addiction and Substance Abuse reported that 32.3 percent of Medicaid hospitalization days were due to newborn/neonatal complications associated with substance abuse. Cardiovascular and respiratory diseases associated with substance abuse each accounted for 15.7 percent of Medicaid hospitalization days. When substance abuse was a secondary diagnosis for Medicaid hospitalization, the length of stay virtually doubled.[80] In collaboration with California health officials, a National Opinion Research Center study concluded that the benefit of substance abuse treatment to taxpayers was $7 for every $1 in program costs, primarily in reduced crime. When other factors were included, the cost-benefit ratio for the total society ranged between 4:1 to 2:1. "Treatment is a good investment!" proclaimed the director of California's Department of Alcohol and Drug Programs.[81]

Prevention researchers have argued for some time that the greatest return on investment is in the area of prenatal care. Writing for the Children's Defense Fund, Arloc Sherman teases out the kinds of unfortunate events that drive up social costs attributed to the lack of health care. For 1992, one in five poor children had no health insurance. For those who receive Medicaid, health care is not necessarily available because one in four pediatricians refuse to accept Medicaid. Of pregnant women who were uninsured or on Medicaid and who had not received prenatal care, 15 percent said they could not find a physician who would see them.[82] Absence of prenatal care is a primary contributing factor to low birth weight, a condition positively correlated with a number of expensive problems. Babies born below normal weights

> have a doubled risk of learning problems (learning disability, hyperactivity, emotional problems, and mental illness) and significant greater risk of neurodevelopmental problems (seizures, epilepsy, water on the brain, cerebral palsy, and mental retardation) and loss of eyesight and hearing.[83]

Studies such as these make a strong case for a universal Maternal and Child Health Program. Current efforts in this area, such as the Women, Infants, and Children Supplemental Nutrition Program (WIC) serve too low a percentage of high risk, poor women. Moreover, child immunization and substance abuse services are not included in WIC, and the administration's Vaccine's for Children program has become mired in controversy.[84] Substance abuse treatment for pregnant women is inadequate, and residential treatment for mothers with children is virtually nonexistent. A comprehensive Maternal and Child Health Program could be created by consolidating WIC with the existing Maternal and Child Health block grant. Additional funding to make services available to all pregnant women and mothers could be obtained by modest increases in taxes on cigarettes and alcohol: for example, increasing the cigarette tax to 48 cents per pack, the tax on alcoholic beverages to $16 per proof gallon, and indexing both for inflation would yield approximately $10 billion annually.[85]

Tax For-Profit Health Providers

During the health care reform debate, much was made of escalating health care costs. As a portion of the economy, health care in the United States consumed 13.4 percent of the Gross Domestic Product, more than other industrial nations, as noted in Table 2.3.

That one-seventh of the nation's productivity would be tied up with health care was considered unacceptable to many health care reform advocates who proposed fixed budgets from which providers would have to finance care. The use of "global budgets" would contain rising health care costs, they argued. During the health care reform debate, few questioned restraining health care costs.[86]

Yet this preoccupation with total health care costs is debatable. During the height of heavy manufacturing in the United States, few questioned the portion of the economy that was dedicated to automobile production. Indeed, if American automobile manufacturers had not lost substantial market share to foreign competitors, Detroit's economic success would have gone unchallenged. Twenty years after America lost the lead in automobile manufacturing, economists still anticipate the time when Detroit will be successful once again. What automobiles were to the industrial era, health care is to the postindustrial era. In a hotly competitive global economy, health care is one of the few markets in which America enjoys superiority—despite the fact that more than 17 percent of Americans have no health insurance.[87] Put another way, the United States can *over*invest in health care in the same way that Miami can have too much tourism.

Rather than focus on stifling one of the more protean sectors of the nation's economy, a more constructive approach would be to treat health care like any other commodity and tax it. Minnesota has taken this approach by applying a

TABLE 2.3 Total health expenditure as a percentage of gross domestic product and per capita health expenditures for selected countries, 1991

Country	Percent Health Expenditure	Per Capita Expenditure
Canada	10.0	$1,915
France	9.1	1,650
Germany	8.5	1,659
Japan	6.6	1,267
Spain	6.7	848
Sweden	8.6	1,443
United Kingdom	6.6	1,035
United States	13.4	2,867

SOURCE: Committee on Ways and Means, U.S. House of Representatives, *Overview of Entitlement Programs* (Washington, DC: US GPO, 1994), p. 956.

two-percent tax on health care providers in order to finance much of its universal health care initiative. Yet Minnesota is not the norm because the state prohibits for-profit health management firms from operating. A more plausible approach for the rest of the country where the commercial activities of the medical-industrial complex are flourishing would be to target for-profit health providers. But because many nonprofits have adopted commercial practices in order to be competitive, they should be taxed as well. Given the elaboration of the American health care market then, a reasonable approach would be to levy a three-percent tax on for-profit health providers and a one-percent tax on nonprofits. The revenues from a differential tax on health providers would be pooled to cover the uninsured. For children and the disabled, the state should cover 100 percent of the cost of private health insurance for a basic benefit plan. For the uninsured who are employed, the state's contribution should be determined according to a sliding scale.[88]

Instead of viewing commercial health providers solely as sources of revenue for the state health care program, consideration should also be given to innovative ways to subsidize health care. For example, HMOs should be encouraged to enroll Medicare and Medicaid beneficiaries, as has been the case in some states and with select populations. A prototype of such an HMO is United American Healthcare, a for-profit serving 200,000 members in 42 states. Started in the early 1980s by three physicians (including African-American gynecologist Julius Combs), United American focused on the health care of the minority poor, many of whom were on Medicaid, and offered such preventive health care services as childhood vaccinations and prenatal care. For 1994, United American reported annual revenues of $40 million, $6.5 million above expenses.[89] In another instance, for-profit health providers should be given the option to count costs for the uninsured as well as those above the basic benefit plan against income as a charitable contribution.

Federally Charter a Consumer-Controlled HMO

Despite their proliferation, for-profit HMOs are unlikely to be a panacea for America's health care problems. As voluntary entities, there is no assurance they will evolve where the patients are or where services are most urgently needed. In highly competitive environments, it is unlikely that commercial HMOs will be able to resist questionable practices dictated by the bottom line, such as neglecting the uninsured, avoiding multiproblem patients, and referring poor patients to other providers. Under the management of physicians and hospital administrators, the conventions of traditional medical practice tend to dominate, even when these conflict with the needs and preferences of women, ethnic groups, and other minorities.

As a solution to these problems, health care consumers have typically joined with maverick health providers in many communities to establish nonprofit HMOs. Adequate as this may seem, nonprofit HMOs have often been tentative ventures—once a health care market has demonstrated profitability, commercial

HMOs take notice and move in. The offer a for-profit HMO franchise can make to the board of a nonprofit HMO may be too good to pass up, and another acquisition is consummated. Under new management, health care consumers in a community have no guarantee that their priorities will be honored by executives of the new HMO, or, given future transactions, whether the HMO will be there at all.

The several downsides of for-profit HMOs could be addressed by Congress chartering a national HMO that would be controlled by a consumer board. On occasion, Congress makes such designations, the nation's military academies being an example. As a quasi-public entity, a federally chartered HMO would be authorized to hire medical staff, establish a range of services (some provided directly, others contracted out), and deploy preventive services, in areas such as prenatal care, substance abuse, and HIV transmission. Significantly, as a chartered entity, such an HMO could not be sold. Conditions of the charter would ensure that the HMO not engage in discriminatory practices, by prohibiting the denial of enrollment because of preexisting condition, or engage in commercial activities, by requiring that any financial surplus be invested in services or in lower premiums. Aptly structured, a federally chartered HMO would address the primary health care needs of Americans who are uninsured or who live in areas where existing health care is inadequate.

The flaw in the Clinton health care reform initiative was assuming that health was, foremost, a public utility. From this assumption, a series of issues arose as paramount if the nation was to reform health care. First, health care costs were escalating and consuming an increasing—and unacceptable—portion of the GDP. Second, any significant reform would guarantee universal coverage—100 percent of the population. Third, there needs to be some mechanism for containing the deployment of high-cost diagnostic technology. In developing an answer to these questions, the role of the federal government loomed large. As the *New Republic* editorialized after the failure of the Clinton health care reform, Magaziner and the First Lady erred in thinking "that complex social problems are amenable to totalizing, intellectual solutions, and that democracy is an obstacle to implementing them."[90]

As the administration's health care reform initiative became subject to careful scrutiny, it was evident that the Health Security Act called for the federal government to rationalize health care. Once the particulars became known (i.e., when special interests recognized that it was *their* ox that was being gored in the name of health reform), it was only a matter of time before Clinton's health care reform was, as Hillary Rodham Clinton aptly pointed out, "demonized."[91] Special interest groups deconstructed health care reform by demanding concessions that a defensive Clinton administration had to make, one after another: health care alliances were dumped to placate small health insurers; the employer mandate was jettisoned because of the objections of small business; universal coverage was sacrificed to Congressional deficit hawks. By the end of the health care reform fiasco, many wondered if the benefit of raising the issue for public debate had actually sabotaged the prospects of future health care reform.

Indeed, the real tragedy in the Clinton health care reform initiative was not that the Health Security Act failed *in toto,* but that there was no backup plan. As had been the case in 1965 when comprehensive health care reform was salvaged in the form of Medicare and Medicaid, the Clinton White House could have settled on assured health care for children or workers, either—or both—of which would have been a substantial achievement. Facing a more conservative 104th Congress, extending health care to either of these groups was highly unlikely.

It would be more accurate in a discussion of American health care to recognize that it is a market. From tummy tucks to heart transplants, health provision has become big business, and U.S. health care corporations have profited fabulously during the past two decades, often from infusions of governmental Medicare and Medicaid dollars. From a market perspective, the questions that were prompted by the Health Security Act made either little sense or appeared antithetical to an expanding health care market. In retrospect, the lessons are clear: Rather than contain an expanding health market, government should find ways to facilitate its expansion.

Commercial health insurers and providers viewed the Clinton health care reform as little more than government control of the health market, White House assurances to the contrary notwithstanding. Although Magaziner's health policy wonks labored to convince the health care industry that reform *à la Hillary* would not be injurious to it, the voting public began to have second thoughts and ultimately defected. This should have come as no surprise. After all, the majority of voters were reasonably well insured through commercial health insurance, membership in HMOs, or Medicare, and the prospect that their benefits would be sacrificed for the 17.4 percent of the nonelderly population that had no health coverage bred apprehension. Concomitantly, opponents to health reform quickly harnessed the fury of small health insurers who faced being driven out of the market by the health alliances and small businesses who were faced with paying a majority of the cost so that the Health Security Act would not include a broad income tax. These spelled the end of health care reform. While the White House held out for a last-minute deal to be negotiated by a retiring George Mitchell, health care reform had become, in the words of one federal administrator, "a corpse."[92]

Given the eventual wreckage of the Health Security Act, what are the future prospects of health care reform? Correctly targeted, such prospects are quite good. Plausible health care reform would begin by identifying the medical-industrial complex and the wealthy and powerful firms that have been constructed largely from federal health care program revenues. Government intervention in the health care market can be justified to correct the consequences of corporate rationalization of American health care: Millions are left uninsured; resources are inequitably distributed; the nation's public health care infrastructure is neglected. Perhaps the most significant manifestation of corporate rationalization of health care is "managed care," the application of business methods for rationing health care provision, a development that has caused many physicians to favor government regulation of the health care market.[93]

Treating the health care market as any other commercial activity, it is legitimate to tax its revenues at modest levels. Pooled funds derived from such taxes should be invested in the health of the population. All children should be insured with a basic health care plan; employable adults should be expected to contribute toward their health insurance premiums according to their income. Commercial health care providers should be encouraged to serve the poor and deploy resources to underserved areas. Those Americans who are not provided for by corporate health providers should be able to enroll in a federally chartered HMO.

The health care reform strategy outlined above—perhaps more accurately labeled a "health reinvestment initiative"—differs markedly from the alternatives considered during the Clinton-inspired health care debate. It will be too conservative for proponents of a Canadian-style single-payer strategy. It will be too liberal for free-marketeers who reject government having a role. Yet it is plausible, and for that reason it merits consideration. As the postindustrial era unfolds, the United States must make substantial investments in human capital, but it must make them strategically so they do not impair the nation's productivity. A health reinvestment initiative not only targets such investments, but it also contributes to America's leadership in health care and research.

NOTES

1. Charles Peters, "Symposium on Social Policy," Howard University, Washington, DC, October 1985.
2. Committee on Ways and Means, U.S. House of Representatives, *Overview of Entitlement Programs* (Washington, DC: USGPO, 1993), p. 137.
3. Howard Karger and David Stoesz, *American Social Welfare Policy*, 2d ed. (White Plains, NY: Longman, 1994), Ch. 12.
4. *Overview of Entitlement Programs*, pp. 141–42.
5. *Overview of Entitlement Programs*, p. 140.
6. *Overview of Entitlement Programs*, p. 348.
7. *Overview of Entitlement Programs*, p. 1642.
8. *Overview of Entitlement Programs*, pp. 1646–47.
9. *Overview of Entitlement Programs*, pp. 1654, 1657.
10. Committee on Ways and Means, U.S. House of Representatives, *Overview of Entitlement Programs* (Washington, DC: USGPO, 1994), p. 787.
11. Laura Summer and Isaac Shapiro, "Trends in Health Insurance Coverage, 1987 to 1993," (Washington, DC: Center on Budget and Policy Priorities, 1994), p. 1.
12. David Stoesz, "Corporate Health Care and Social Welfare," *Health and Social Work* 11, 3 (Summer 1986), pp. 166–67.
13. David Stoesz, "Corporate Welfare," *Social Work* 31, 4 (July–August 1986), p. 247.
14. James Gomez, "Building a Medical Empire," *Los Angeles Times* (July 1, 1993), p. D-1.
15. Zachary Schiller, "HCA-Columbia," *Business Week* (October 18, 1993), p. 36.

16. Arnold Relman, "The New Medical-Industrial Complex," *New England Journal of Medicine* 303 (October 23, 1980).
17. Vincente Navarro, *Medicine Under Capitalism* (New York: Prodist, 1976), p. 216.
18. Paul Starr, *The Social Transformation of American Medicine* (New York: Basic Books, 1982), p. 448.
19. Eli Ginzberg, "Health Care Reform—Why so Slow?" *New England Journal of Medicine* (May 17, 1990), pp. 1464-65.
20. Phillip Longman, "Catastrophic Follies," *New Republic* (August 21, 1989); Jacob Weisberg, "Cat Scam," *New Republic* (October 30 1989).
21. David Stoesz and Howard Karger, *Reconstructing the American Welfare State* (Lanham, MD: Rowman and Littlefield, 1992), p. 64.
22. David Broder, "Congress Cranks Up Its Health Reform Sausage-Maker," *Washington Post Weekly* (April 25-May 1, 1994), p. 10.
23. Robert Dickman et al. "An End to Patchwork Reform of Health Care," *New England Journal of Medicine* (October 22, 1987).
24. Arnold Relman, "Universal Health Insurance: Its Time Has Come," *New England Journal of Medicine* 320, 2 (January 12, 1989), p. 118.
25. David Himmelstein and Steffie Woolhandler, "A National Health Program for the United States," *New England Journal of Medicine* 320, 2 (January 12, 1989).
26. David Himmelstein and Steffie Woolhandler, "Administrative Waste in U.S. Health Care," *New England Journal of Medicine* 314, 7 (February 13, 1986), p. 442. Their projected savings from instituting a national health service model were even greater—$38.4 billion.
27. Alain Enthoven and Richard Kronick, "A Consumer-Choice Health Plan for the 1990s," *New England Journal of Medicine* 320, 1-2 (January 5 and 12, 1989), p. 31.
28. Enthoven and Kronick, p. 36.
29. Steven Pearlstein, "Magaziner's Mission," *Washington Post Weekly* (May 10-16, 1994).
30. Dana Priest, "Health Care Reform in 1,100 Easy Steps," *Washington Post Weekly* (April 26-May 2, 1993), p. 31.
31. Priest, "Health Care Reform," p. 31.
32. Shari Roan, "California's Reform Gurus," *Los Angeles Times* (September 21, 1993).
33. David Lauter, "White House Discloses Outline of Health Plan," *Los Angeles Times* (April 10, 1993).
34. Susan Duerksen, "The Clinton Plan," *San Diego Union-Tribune* (September 23, 1993), p. A-26; Jack Nelson and Edwin Chen, "Clinton Unveils Health Reform," *Los Angeles Times* (September 23, 1994), p. A-1.
35. Robin Toner, "'Harry and Louise' Ad Campaign Biggest Gun in Health Care Battle," *San Diego Union-Tribune* (April 7, 1994).
36. Sara Fritz, "Ads Are Designed to Counter Health Care Proposals," *Los Angeles Times* (May 15, 1993), p. A-16.
37. Sandra Boodman, "Health Care's Power Player," *Washington Post Weekly* (February 14-20, 1994).
38. Dana Priest, "The Slow Death of Health Reform," *Washington Post Weekly* (September 5-11, 1994), p. 11.
39. Douglas Frantz, "Lobbyists, Interest Groups Begin Costly Health Care Battle," *Los Angeles Times* (May 24, 1993).
40. Paul Richter, "Canny and Candid, Ickes Becomes Health Reform's Point Man," *Los Angeles Times* (March 9, 1994), p. A-5.

41. Congressional Budget Office, *An Analysis of the Administration's Health Proposal* (Washington, DC: author, February 1994), p. xii.
42. Arthur Flemming and Elliot Richardson, "Let the Employer Provide," *Washington Post Weekly* (June 20–26, 1994), p. 28.
43. Robert Pear, "Tough Decision on Health Care If Employers Won't Pay the Bill," *New York Times* (July 9, 1994), p. 6.
44. Ronald Brownstein, "Clinton Targets Middle Class in Bid to Sell Health Reform," *Los Angeles Times* (July 16, 1994), p. A-18.
45. Most of these were fielded by Republicans or conservative Democrats. See Karen Tumulty and Edwin Chen, "Health Reform May Reflect Bush Approach," *Los Angeles Times* (July 11, 1994); Steven Stark, "Critical Condition," *San Diego Union-Tribune* (July 3, 1994).
46. Ronald Brownstein, "Enthusiasm for Clinton's Health Reform is Waning," *Los Angeles Times* (April 21, 1994), p. A-1.
47. Gerald Seib and Hilary Stout, "Americans Still Support Reform for Health Care, But Poll Finds Zeal Waning and Fear of Change," *Wall Street Journal* (June 16, 1994), p. A-20.
48. Edwin Chen, "Doctors Back Away from Reform, Poll Finds," *Los Angeles Times* (July 14, 1994), p. A-10.
49. Edwin Chen, "Key Economist Flays Clinton Health Plan," *Los Angeles Times* (January 13, 1994), p. A-8.
50. David Broder, "Now or Never for Health Care," *Washington Post Weekly* (July 4–10, 1994), p. 4.
51. Karen Tumulty, "Key Senate Panel, in Blow to Clinton, OKs Its Health Bill," *Los Angeles Times* (July 3, 1994), p. A-1.
52. "White House Supports Abortion Compromise," *San Diego Union-Tribune* (July 18, 1994), p. A-6.
53. Stewart Powell, "Veto Pledge May Be 'Blooper of the Year'," *San Diego Union-Tribune* (July 10, 1994), p. A-11.
54. Karen Tumulty, "Compromise Health Plan Unveiled but Without Universal Coverage," *Los Angeles Times* (June 25, 1994), p. A-4.
55. Dana Priest, "Universal Disagreement on Universal Health Care," *Washington Post Weekly* (June 27–July 3, 1994), p. 12.
56. Robert Shogan and David Lauter, "President Signals He Is Flexible on Health Coverage," *Los Angeles Times* (July 20, 1994), p. A-1.
57. David Lauter, "Clinton Says He's for Full Coverage," *Los Angeles Times* (July 21, 1994), p. A-1.
58. Jack Nelson and Edwin Chen, "Final Push on Health by Clinton Due," *Los Angeles Times* (August 7, 1994), p. A-1.
59. Edwin Chen and Paul Richter, "Mitchell's Health Care Bill to Pare Employer Mandate," *Los Angeles Times* (August 2, 1994), p. A-1.
60. John Broder and Edwin Chen, "White House Sees Chances Fading for Action on Health," *Los Angeles Times* (August 25, 1994), p. A-1.
61. Steven Waldman, "Winners and Losers," *Newsweek* (July 25, 1994), p. 20.
62. Spencer Rich, "Next Step: A Modest Consensus," *Washington Post Weekly* (September 5–11, 1994), pp. 11–12.
63. Karen Tumulty and Edwin Chen, "Blame for Health Plan's Collapse Falls Everywhere," *Los Angeles Times* (August 28, 1994), p. A-1.

64. Dana Priest, "The Slow Death of Health Reform," *Washington Post Weekly* (September 5-11, 1994), p. 11.
65. David Ewing Duncan, "The Triumph of Harry and Louise," *Los Angeles Times Magazine* (September 11, 1994), p. 28.
66. David Osborne, *Laboratories of Democracy* (Cambridge, MA: Harvard Business School, 1988).
67. Robin Toner, "California Health Care Fight Focuses on State Insurance," *New York Times* (September 30, 1994), p. A-1.
68. Dan Morgan, "While Washington Fiddles, the States March On," *Washington Post Weekly* (October 10-16, 1994), p. 47.
69. George Anders, "HMOs Pile Up Billions in Cash, Try to Decide What to Do with It," *Wall Street Journal* (December 21, 1994), p. A-1.
70. Dan Morgan, "While Washington Talked," *Washington Post Weekly* (September 12-18, 1994), p. 31.
71. Erik Eckholm, "While Congress Remains Silent, Health Care Transforms Itself," *New York Times* (December 18, 1994), p. A-1.
72. Elyse Tanouye and Greg Steinmetz, "Managed-Care Feeding Frenzy Probably Hasn't Ended," *Wall Street Journal* (July 13, 1994), p. B-4.
73. Leonard Robins and Charles Backstrom, "The Role of State Health Departments in Formulating Policy: A Survey on the Case of AIDS," *American Journal of Public Health* 84 (June 1994), p. 905.
74. Eric Harrison, "AIDS Is No. 1 Killer of Young Americans," *Los Angeles Times* (December 2, 1994), p. A-8.
75. Kristine Gebbie, "Formulating Public Health Policy: The Case of AIDS," *American Journal of Public Health* 84 (June 1994), p. 888.
76. Institute of Medicine, *The Future of Public Health* (Washington, DC: National Academy Press, 1988).
77. See Robins and Backstrom, "The Role of State Health Departments."
78. John Broder and Robert Jackson, "Clinton Observes World AIDS Day with Low-Key Private Meeting," *Los Angeles Times* (December 2, 1994), p. A-9.
79. Tammy Tengs et al. "Five-Hundred Life-Saving Interventions and Their Cost-Effectiveness," (Cambridge, MA: Harvard University Center for Risk Analysis, 1994), pp. 17-19.
80. Center on Addiction and Substance Abuse, "The Cost of Substance Abuse to America's Health Care System," (New York: author, 1993), pp. 33, 42.
81. Department of Alcohol and Drug Programs, *Evaluating Recovery Services: The California Drug and Alcohol Treatment Assessment, Executive Summary* (Sacramento: author, 1994), pp. 1-5.
82. Arloc Sherman, *Wasting America's Future* (Boston: Beacon Press, 1994), p. 42.
83. Sherman, *Wasting America's Future*, p. 67.
84. Sara Fritz and Alan Miller, "Clinton Plan for Immunization Raises Questions," *Los Angeles Times* (July 17, 1994), p. A-1.
85. Congressional Budget Office, *Reducing the Deficit* (Washington, DC: author, 1994), p. 342.
86. One was Uwe Reinhart.
87. Employee Benefit Research Institute, "Sources of Health Insurance and Characteristics of the Uninsured" (Washington, DC: author, 1994), p. 1.
88. Abigail Trafford and Spencer Rich, "Health Care Reform in Congress?" *Washington Post Health* (September 20, 1994).

89. Udayan Gupta, "United American Healthcare Proves Naysayers Wrong," *Wall Street Journal* (August 22, 1994), p. B-2.
90. "Total Quality Madness," *New Republic* (October 3, 1994), p. 7.
91. Adam Clymer, "Hillary Clinton Says Administration Was Misunderstood on Health Care," *New York Times* (October 3, 1994), p. A-9.
92. Interview with Michael McMullan of the Health Care Financing Administration, September 25, 1994.
93. David Hilzenrath, "In Corporate Hands, Health Care Bureaucracy Blooms," *Washington Post* (September 20, 1994), p. A-1.

chapter 3

Welfare: Poor Policy

> *I went to a federal low-income housing project in Newark, New Jersey, and just going inside and climbing the stairs was more exposure to questions of poverty than most people can stand and not pass out. The stairwell was a cascade of filth, a spillway of human urine and unidentifiable putrefying matter. There was nothing on these steps wholesome enough to call trash. It would have cheered me up to see anything as vibrant as a rat.*
> P. J. O'Rourke[1]

To understand welfare is to appreciate the circumstances of poor, often minority families. Prior to the New Deal, poor families were left to fend for themselves, reliant on relatives or local civic associations for aid. Poverty was made a federal case with the establishment of the Social Security Act in 1935, in which the provisions of the Act focused on the working poor. However, the unemployable were given short shrift. Deficiencies in the Social Security Act led President Johnson to declare a "war on poverty" as part of the Great Society of the 1960s. During the 1970s, the war bogged down, and presidents, regardless of party affiliation, distanced themselves from the poor. By the 1980s, poverty had lost much of its sheen for conservatives. On the eve of Ronald Reagan's inauguration, the president-elect's soon-to-be domestic policy advisor, Martin Anderson, suggested that poverty was all but passé: "The war on poverty has been won, except for perhaps a few mopping-up operations," he lamented. "The combination of strong economic growth and a dramatic increase in government spending on welfare and income transfer programs for more than a decade has virtually wiped out poverty in the United States."[2]

Having viewed a steady decline in poverty in the United States during the 1960s and 1970s, the Reagan administration advocated policies that quickly revived it. By the end of the decade, poverty was once again peaking at 1960 levels. As illustrated by Table 3.1, every poverty-related indicator increased—some quite substantially—during the Reagan and Bush presidencies.

Socially-minded journalists marked the feat by introducing "underclass" into the American vernacular. Exploiting public sentiment toward welfare (already eroding), the Reagan administration fashioned one of the more dubious of social program reforms in the Family Support Act of 1988. Taking the cue, presidential candidate Clinton promised to "out-Reagan" Reagan by limiting receipt of welfare to two years. Not to be outdone, conservative Republicans riding high from the 1994 Congressional elections promised more Draconian reforms of welfare, including terminating benefits to legal aliens and unwed teenagers, repackaging welfare programs as block grants to the states, and cutting benefits 20 percent.

As this scenario suggests, there are few constants in welfare policy. Political parties waver considerably in their welfare reform proposals. Democrats have tended to favor social welfare as an unconditional entitlement—that is, until Bill Clinton came along. Republicans have ordinarily favored cutting welfare expenditures—except for President Nixon, who oversaw the greatest expansion of social programs (Nixon even advocated a guaranteed annual income at one point). Of welfare programs, this much can be said: Poverty programs plague politicians because they are financed from general revenues derived from taxes

TABLE 3.1 Poverty rates

Variable	1977	1992	1993
Unemployment rate	7.1%	7.4%	6.8%
Poverty rate (persons)			
All persons	11.6	14.8	15.1
Non-Hispanic white	8.0	9.6	9.9
Black	31.3	33.4	33.1
Hispanic	22.4	29.6	30.6
Child poverty rate (persons)			
All children	16.2	22.3	22.7
Non-Hispanic white	9.9	13.2	13.6
Black	41.8	46.6	46.1
Hispanic	28.3	40.0	40.9
Poverty rate among families with children where householder works	7.7	n/a	11.3
Elderly poverty rate (persons)	14.1	12.9	12.2
Family type (families)			
Married-couple families	5.3	6.4	6.5
Female-headed families	31.7	35.4	35.6
Persons in poverty	24,720,000	38,014,000	39,265,000
Children in poverty	10,288,000	15,294,000	15,727,000

SOURCE: "Despite Economic Recovery, Poverty and Income Trends Are Disappointing in 1993" (Washington, DC: Center on Budget and Policy Priorities, 1994), p. 5.

paid largely by middle-income taxpayers who do not benefit directly from them. Consequently, when increasing welfare expenditures extends a safety net that only seems to trap more people, an already skeptical public becomes increasingly indignant and questions the value of welfare. On the other hand, because poverty programs tend to vary from state to state (there are more than fifty different AFDC programs and over fifty different Medicaid programs), they represent a windfall for policy analysts whose job it is to make sense of the welfare labyrinth. For all the attention directed at welfare, the beneficiaries of social programs remain almost inconsequential. Despite conservative clamoring that more choices should be extended to the poor and liberal alarm about the urgency of needs of the disadvantaged, neither has gone to the trouble of conducting a large-scale study of the experience and preferences of the poor with regard to social welfare benefits.[3]

"WELFARE"

As we have come to understand it, "welfare" includes an odd assortment of "safety net" programs, eligibility for which is predicated on a "means test," or an applicant's low income and limited assets. Welfare programs can be paired according to their funding characteristics: The costs of AFDC and Medicaid are shared almost equally by federal and state government; on the other hand, the financing of Food Stamps and Supplemental Security Income (SSI) is borne primarily by the federal government.[4] Such financing arrangements of welfare programs are not exercises in the arcane. States benefit fiscally when an adult on AFDC becomes eligible for SSI, reducing their obligation from about half of the AFDC grant to virtually zero for the SSI benefit. For that matter, AFDC beneficiaries also recognize the fiscal advantages of SSI. In 1993, the federal SSI grant for an individual was $434 per month, virtually identical to the average AFDC grant for a family of four.[5] Thus, it is in the interests of state government and the poor to optimize their benefits by transferring from AFDC to SSI. Often, the only barrier to the transfer is a disability determination since SSI is reserved for the poor who are over 65 years of age or disabled. Not so coincidentally, as states have been strapped for revenues and have held AFDC grants below the rate of inflation, federal SSI expenditures have skyrocketed. In 1974, 4 million Americans benefited from SSI at an annual cost of $5.2 billion; by 1993, the number of recipients had increased to 6 million, and costs had ballooned to $24 billion.[6]

This fiscal shell game adds nothing to the programmatic integrity of "welfare," as the public has come to understand the term, but it is minor compared to public perception of welfare fraud. Indeed, welfare fraud is so widely assumed to be taking place by the public that it has been the source of some of the more colorful contributions to contemporary folklore, such as "welfare Cadillac." Liberals, of course, chafe at the allegation that the poor manipulate measly welfare benefits, suggesting the accusation is racist because a disproportionate number of the poor are black or Hispanic. In this instance, the public perception is closer to the truth, liberal indignation notwithstanding. In one of the more credible studies that liberals would sooner forget, Kathryn Edin conducted detailed interviews with 25 Chicago families receiving AFDC in 1988 and another 25 families in 1990. The final sample of families was 46 percent African American, 38 percent Anglo, 10 percent Latino, and 6 percent Asian. Edin concluded that none of the families lived solely by the income provided by AFDC; of the 50 families, only two "came close" to getting by on the welfare grant alone. Yet, all of the families found a way to cover their expenses. How?

> Every single mother supplemented her check in some way, either by doing unreported work, by getting money from friends and relatives, or by persuading someone else to pay a lot of her expenses. Not one of these 50 mothers reported all her extra income to the welfare department, and only four reported any of it.[7]

Because all supplemental income must be reported to the welfare department, all of the families Edin studied technically committed welfare fraud. Yet, the error rate in AFDC payments has been reported by the federal government as between 4.7 and 5.0 percent for the past several years.[8]

That poor mothers would seek income to supplement welfare benefits is understandable considering the impossibly low benefit levels of AFDC. In 1994, the median AFDC state benefit for a family of three was only $366 per month, 38 percent of the 1992 poverty level. Including Food Stamps, the grant amounted to $661 per month, or 69 percent of the poverty level. Given such low benefit levels, any conscionable parent would be driven to supplement AFDC illegally in order to provide necessities for her children. Such incentives were particularly strong for Mississippi AFDC families. In 1994, Mississippi AFDC benefits were the lowest in the nation, $120 per month for a family of three, only 13 percent of the poverty level; with Food Stamps, the family's income equaled $415 per month, or 43 percent of the poverty level.[9]

Returning to public sentiment about social programs, is welfare fraud extensive? Not exactly. It's *rampant,* virtually assured by low benefit levels. A close look at poor families reveals that AFDC is but one component of an erratic income flow for poor mothers. For poor mothers, AFDC is a mixed blessing. On the one hand, AFDC comes in inadequate amounts necessitating illegal income supplements. On the other hand, AFDC checks arrive regularly, unlike most other sources of income for poor families. Under these circumstances, it seems natural that poor mothers view AFDC with ambivalence. At best, AFDC becomes a subadequate baseline for family budgeting.

POVERTY

Despite inherent flaws, welfare programs, of which AFDC is most prominent, have been the primary method that liberals have advocated to alleviate poverty. In order to determine the extent of absolute poverty in the United States, the federal government created a formula for the "poverty line" during the 1960s. Simply put, the poverty line consisted of the cost of minimal nutrition multiplied by a factor of three to account for nonfood expenses (such as rent), then adjusted the figures for family size and inflation. The resultant poverty line established a nationwide level of subsistence income. For a family of three, the poverty line in 1992 was $11,186; 14.5 percent of the population (36.8 million persons) fell below this level.[10]

Poverty, of course, has fluctuated according to the economy and government policy. Generally speaking, the number of people living in poverty dropped as a result of government social programs introduced during the War on Poverty, then rose again during the conservative 1980s. Within this general trend, various subgroups fared differently. There are many fewer elderly poor now than a generation ago, yet, paradoxically, the number of poor children has risen substantially after falling during the 1960s.[11] Similar disparities are evident in minority populations. In 1991, the poverty rate for African Americans stood at 32.7 percent and that of Latinos at 28.7 percent, compared to 11.3 percent of Anglos.[12] Liberals have used such discrepancies to indicate the lack of opportunities afforded minorities in the United States.

With reductions in federal social programs during the 1980s, the number of people living in poverty rose. By the end of the Bush administration, the number of poor families had reached a 27-year high.[13] Liberals, predictably, used a rising poverty rate to flay indifferent Republican administrations. Conservatives countered liberal sniping, arguing that the value of noncash benefits be included in the income of the poor. If Food Stamps, housing assistance, and Medicaid were included with public assistance benefits, a truer picture of the economic circumstances of the poor would emerge, they contended. As it turned out, this revision in the computation of the poverty level reduced it significantly, about 30 percent. For example, in 1980 (on the eve of the Reagan administration), the revised poverty level stood at 8.6 percent; by 1989, it had risen slightly to 8.9 percent.[14] Had the Reagan cuts in welfare programs of the 1980s seriously harmed the poor? Barely, suggested the revised poverty figures.

Including the value of noncash benefits in computing poverty served conservatives well in another respect. An axiom of welfare capitalism holds that welfare should pay less than the lowest prevailing wage in order to reinforce the work ethic. By the 1980s, when added to the typical AFDC grant, the value of in-kind benefits approached the income generated by full-time employment at the minimum wage. For example, in 1991 the average value of the public assistance package available to poor American families was a tax-free $8,569: AFDC accounting for $4,333; Medicaid $2,249; Food Stamps $1,898; and school lunches $89. Assuming a 2,000-hour working year, a full-time minimum wage worker pulled in $8,500 *before taxes*.[15] Eventually, many residents of low-income communities realized that minimum wage work was for chumps. Welfare was problematic, to be sure, but it had certain advantages. Obtaining welfare was a nuisance, but the checks came predictably. Moreover, Medicaid came with AFDC, and health insurance rarely accompanied low-income jobs. Finally, AFDC could be supplemented, as Edin's families in Chicago knew. As welfare exceeded the value of work, conservatives found a powerful lever for reducing welfare benefits. Of course, work would be preferable to welfare if the minimum wage were increased, but this was anathema for the Reaganauts. A more ideologically consistent strategy for them was to reduce welfare. In this they relished; during the 1980s, conservatives took every opportunity to whittle, shave, and gouge welfare programs. Much to the dismay of liberals, the working poor—for the most part—applauded the assault on welfare programs, voting by wide margins for Reagan.

Having been ambushed by conservatives in the attempt to use the poverty level to measure the impact of Reagan social policy, liberals resorted to a relative indicator of economic well-being: income distribution. Since 1947, the federal government has used the concept of economic population quintiles to determine disparity in U.S. income. Changes in after-tax income of American families are depicted in Table 3.2. The figures confirm a striking *upward* redistribution in income from the poor to the rich. During the 1980s, individual income for the poorest fifth of the population dropped by 12 percent, whereas that of the wealthiest fifth increased 31 percent.[16]

Conservatives were prepared for this attack, too. Conceding that income was not distributed fairly—an inevitability in a capitalist economy—conservatives presented data on family income showing that poor families were not faring as badly as liberals had claimed. Consider, for example, family income of the lowest tenth of American families between 1977 and 1990. During this period, income fell from $4,277 to $3,805, a drop of 11 percent.

A closer look at the data, however, disputed the liberal allegation that conservative social and economic policies were primarily responsible for the poor becoming poorer. The largest portion of the income loss experienced by the lowest decile of families occurred from 1977 to 1980, during the stagflation of the Carter administration. During Reagan's first term, these families lost some income, though less than during the period from 1977 to 1980. Then, during Reagan's second term, the income of the poorest tenth of families actually increased, almost making up for the income lost during Reagan's first term. Significantly, the family income increase from 1985 to 1990 was 6.7 percent, which

TABLE 3.2 Shares of after-tax income for all families (in percent)

All families	1977	1980	1985	1988	1989	1990
Highest quintile	44.0	44.9	49.2	49.8	49.9	49.5
Fourth quintile	22.8	22.6	21.9	21.4	21.5	21.8
Middle quintile	16.3	16.2	15.2	15.1	15.1	15.1
Second quintile	11.6	11.4	10.1	9.8	10.1	10.0
Lowest quintile	**5.7**	5.4	4.4	4.3	4.3	4.3

Note—Table reads for **boldface** figure that the lowest 20 percent in income of the population in 1977 received 5.7 percent of total after-tax income. Quintiles are weighted for families.
SOURCE: *Overview of Entitlement Programs*, 1993, p. 1507.

was on a par with other income deciles.[17] Did the 1980s permanently retard the income of poor families? Not as uniformly as liberals had claimed; in fact, toward the end of the decade the poorest families were benefiting comparably to families that were more well-off.

CONSERVATIVE WELFARE REFORM

The conservative counterattack against liberal criticism of the Reagan administration reflected a growing sophistication in their comprehension of welfare policy. Early conservative pronouncements about welfare had a reactionary quality that liberals were quick to exploit. George Gilder, for example, suggested that welfare programs induced dependency on the part of the poor. His prescription? What the poor needed most, suggested Gilder, was *not* more government welfare assistance, but "the spur of their own poverty."[18] Not long thereafter, a book appeared that commanded the attention of liberals and conservatives alike for much of the 1980s. *Losing Ground* by Charles Murray proposed even more severe measures, suggesting that real welfare reform required "scrapping the entire federal welfare and income support structure for working-aged persons, including AFDC, Medicaid, Food Stamps, Unemployment Insurance, Worker's Compensation, subsidized housing, disability and the rest."[19] True welfare reform, Murray contended, would consist of taking down the social safety net altogether. Lawrence Mead offered a more plausible suggestion, making receipt of welfare conditional, according to specific behavioral standards. Most important, Mead suggested that AFDC recipients could be expected to work in exchange for benefits.[20] As a group, Gilder, Murray, and Mead challenged the liberal intellectual elite, took a lot of flak for some of their weaker suggestions, and eventually laid the groundwork for conservative welfare reform. For liberals who often saw the flaws in their work, Gilder, Murray, and Mead had become little more than the "Manny, Moe, and Jack" of American welfare philosophy. But any doubt about the prescience of their work soon faded with passage of the Family Support Act of 1988, at the time the most important welfare reform legislation since the War on Poverty.

At the heart of the Family Support Act (FSA) is the concept of reciprocity, the expectation that a standard of conduct would be a condition for receipt of welfare. The conservative idea of reciprocity meant that AFDC recipients would be expected to work or engage in job training in order to obtain benefits. That social program beneficiaries be required to work as a precondition for benefits was not particularly revolutionary. Work, after all, is a precept of social insurance programs, such as Social Security and Unemployment Compensation. But welfare mothers had not been expected to work since AFDC had been established as a widows and dependents program in 1935.[21] Initially, liberals were willing to allow AFDC mothers to work if it was voluntary and not to the detriment of their children. As the women's movement filtered down to the ranks of the poor, some feminists encouraged AFDC recipients to work in order to become financially independent of welfare, an institution that was seen as a surrogate for the irresponsible male who had left the family destitute. But encouraging AFDC mothers to work was difficult because of the low cash incentives allowed them. Working women on AFDC were able to keep the first $30 and one-third thereafter—this was called the "earned-income disregard"—providing their income did not exceed the amount of the AFDC grant. Because AFDC grants were so low, many mothers worked occasionally, but rarely found the job that paid so well that they became financially self-sufficient.[22] As a result, remarriage—not employment—has been the primary cause of women getting off AFDC. Prior to the 1980s when conservatives promoted the idea of making AFDC mothers work for their benefits, there was some program experience in the relationship between work and welfare—an experience summarized by one welfare analyst as "consistently disheartening."[23]

For their part, conservatives were not particularly consistent in figuring out the work/welfare problem. Rather than encourage AFDC beneficiaries to become *more* involved in the labor market, Reagan administration policy changes introduced through the Omnibus Budget Reconciliation Act of 1981 actually penalized welfare recipients who worked. As a result, 408,000 families were terminated from AFDC and 299,000 families saw their benefits reduced.[24] When studies demonstrated that many of these families would again be eligible for AFDC some time in the future, conservatives began to look at the more structural aspects of the problem, eventually conceding that child day care and health care were often the reason why AFDC families returned to the program.

The FSA, then, incorporated incentives and penalties for AFDC mothers in relation to work. The carrot consisted of the Job Opportunities and Basic Skills (JOBS) program that provided job training and "transitional benefits": the continuation of child care, Medicaid, and transportation for one year after securing a job. The stick was the termination of benefits for a mother who refused to participate in "welfare-to-work" and did not have an exempting excuse, such as a preschool-age child. The Act was budgeted at a Reaganesque $3.34 billion over five years. During this period, states were encouraged to develop innovative programs to wean poor mothers from AFDC and assist them in becoming economically self-sufficient.

Actually quite modest in intention, the FSA soon yielded surprises for liberals and conservatives alike. Liberals had long contended that welfare-to-work was little more than badgering poor women into dead-end jobs, exacerbating their hopelessness. Much to the chagrin of liberals, the majority of AFDC mothers responded to their welfare-to-work requirement with interest, if not enthusiasm. Evidently, the prospect of education, job training, and employment was appealing. Furthermore, JOBS offered the prospect of upward mobility for those AFDC mothers who had taken advantage of the earned-income disregard. Contrary to predictions of the Left, AFDC mothers did not stay home or refuse to participate in welfare-to-work programs.

Conservatives got the real surprise, however. The FSA was the first welfare reform clearly bearing a conservative imprimatur. It was traditional in its expectations: AFDC mothers with older children would have to work or participate in a training program. It was fiscally frugal, budgeted at less than $1 billion per year. It encouraged states to experiment with other ways to make welfare beneficiaries more conventional in their behavior. What was more, unanticipated developments favored the conservative cause. States became increasingly ingenious in placing conditions on receipt of AFDC: Wisconsin required children of AFDC to attend school regularly; New Jersey refused to provide more assistance for additional children born to a parent on AFDC; Maryland required school-age children to be vaccinated against communicable diseases.[25] Having found the front of the wave, conservatives discovered it was breaking in ways they could not have imagined. Even poor, disproportionately minority women were showing a genuine interest in improving their financial circumstances. Nearing the end of the 1980s, conservatives celebrated a rather substantial accomplishment. In less than a decade they had taken what had been perceived to be a dependency-inducing, liberal, social welfare entitlement and converted AFDC to a conditional benefit that rewarded traditional values, most importantly self-sufficiency.

And then the data came in.

WELFARE-TO-WORK

To understand the impact of the FSA—or the lack of it, in this instance—requires an appreciation for program research. Social programs are publicly funded, and because taxpayers prefer prudence in the use of their money, outcome studies are often specified in enabling legislation. This became common during the War on Poverty when experimental programs were launched for the poor. Evaluations of Head Start and the Job Corps, for example, became noteworthy for uncovering ambiguous results when program proponents promised, or at least insinuated, consistently positive outcomes. When research failed to confirm liberal aspirations vis-à-vis social programs, conservatives took them to task during the 1980s for overreaching their grasp.

In a retrospective of the poverty programs, Henry Aaron of the Brookings Institution concluded that any indication of cause and effect relationship between public policy and improvement in social condition tends to occur despite the evidence:

> [N]either the initial acceptance and enthusiasm for aggressive federal efforts to solve social problems nor the present rejection of and reticence about such undertakings are based on reliable information or on scholarly findings or indeed on the actual success or failures of the programs themselves. Both the initial commitment to use national policies to solve social and economic problems and the present distrust of such policies rest largely on preconceptions and faiths whose source lies elsewhere.[26]

What conservatives would have learned about their romance with welfare-to-work programs, had they read Aaron, was that they were flying by the seat of their pants and they were coming in for a landing with their feet up.

Considering the ideological baggage associated with welfare, it is fortunate that the primary studies of welfare-to-work initiatives were conducted by a highly respected organization that is widely regarded as nonpartisan, the Manpower Demonstration Research Corporation (MDRC). The MDRC welfare-to-work studies conducted during the 1980s were, in and of themselves, a remarkable achievement. Rather than shirk at the prospect of studying a new program (JOBS) appended to an unpopular welfare program (AFDC) that varied enormously from state to state, the MDRC saw this as an opportunity to conduct field experiments under varying conditions. Among the earlier findings, MDRC researchers concluded that welfare-to-work produced desirable benefits in communities where there were plentiful jobs as opposed to communities in which the unemployment rate was high. It is interesting that benefits of welfare-to-work programs were greatest when targeted at AFDC recipients who had been most dependent on welfare, as opposed to those who had participated more in the labor market.[27] Such findings were less than unqualified endorsements of welfare-to-work, however. Toward the end of the 1980s, Harvard's David Ellwood summarized the early findings of relevant research: "most work-welfare programs look like decent investments, but no carefully evaluated work-welfare programs have done more than put a tiny dent in the welfare caseloads, even though they have been received with enthusiasm." Ellwood calculated that the increased earnings attributed to an AFDC mother participating in welfare-to-work programs ranged from $250 to $750 *per year,* hardly enough to make someone independent of welfare.[28]

In 1991, MDRC published a summary of welfare-to-work field experiments that had been conducted in 13 communities throughout the United States. Four of these are fairly representative and are summarized in Table 3.3. Two elaborations will aid in interpreting the table. First, the Arkansas WORK Program and the San Diego Saturation Work Initiative Model (SWIM) were mandatory and, as a result, served a broad range of AFDC recipients. By contrast, the New Jersey On-the-Job Training (OJT) Program and the AFDC Homemaker-Home Health Aide Demonstrations were voluntary and, as a result, more selective of participants. Second, benefits of welfare-to-work programs are essentially twofold. A successful program would elevate earnings of participants as well as decrease AFDC program costs. Finally, because welfare-to-work programs entail start-up and maintenance costs, independent of the normal operation of AFDC, these administrative costs should be offset by AFDC program savings attributable to welfare-to-work. In the best of all welfare-to-work worlds, earnings would be up, program expenses would be down, and the cost per participant would be low.

The good news is that welfare-to-work programs increase earnings and lower program costs, but not a lot. Only one of the programs increased earnings more than $1,000 for each year after a participant had graduated. As Ellwood had observed, earnings remain too low to liberate the typical AFDC mother from welfare. While welfare-to-work did lower AFDC program costs, these savings were also modest; none of the programs realized savings of $1,000 for each year after a participant had graduated. The bad news is that the cost per participant is not realized until well after a participant has graduated from the program and

TABLE 3.3 AFDC welfare-to-work programs

Program	Type	Cost per Experimental Participant	Outcome	Experimental-Control Difference
Arkansas WORK Program	Mandatory	$118	Earnings	
			Year 1	$167
			Year 2	223
			Year 3	337
			AFDC payments	
			Year 1	−145
			Year 2	−190
			Year 3	−168
San Diego Saturation Work Initiative Model (SWIM)	Mandatory	$919	Earnings	
			Year 1	352
			Year 2	658
			AFDC payments	
			Year 1	−407
			Year 2	−553
New Jersey On-the-Job Training (OJT) Program	Voluntary	$787	Earnings	
			Year 1	n/a
			Year 2	591
			AFDC payments	
			Year 1	−190
			Year 2	−238
AFDC Homemaker-Home Health Aide Demonstrations	Voluntary	$9,505	Earnings	
			Year 1	2,026
			Year 2	1,347
			Year 3	1,121
			AFDC and Food Stamp Benefits	
			Year 1	−696
			Year 2	−858
			Year 3	−343

Adapted from Judith Gueron and Edward Pauly, *From Welfare to Work* (New York: Russell Sage Foundation, 1991), Table 1.1.

is in the labor market for some time. Only Arkansas's WORK Program recovered its investment per participant in the first year after completion of the program. In most of the programs, welfare-to-work investments were not recouped until a few years later. Thus, from an administrative standpoint the welfare-to-work payoff is not immediate, but long term.

MDRC data did not indicate that welfare-to-work had failed as much as they reflected the incredible inertia that impedes upward mobility of poor families on AFDC. In order to generate earnings sufficient to ensure a welfare-to-work program graduate economic independence from AFDC, a huge investment is necessary—on a par with the AFDC Homemaker-Home Health Aide Demonstration's cost per participant of $9,505, as noted in Table 3.3. The likelihood that the federal government would accept so high an investment to make AFDC families self-sufficient is virtually nonexistent. Most programs cost less than this to launch, of course, and their returns are correspondingly modest. Regardless of outcome variable, the returns on getting AFDC mothers to work were small. For pragmatic conservatives who had opposed bleeding-heart liberals throughout the 1980s, the MDRC results had to be disappointing. Subsequent research by the Government Accounting Office (GAO) was no more encouraging. In late 1994, the GAO noted that the JOBS program had failed to move a majority of AFDC recipients off of the program; between 1991 and 1993, only 11 percent of AFDC beneficiaries had participated in JOBS. Ominously, only 24 percent of pregnant teens on AFDC had enrolled in JOBS.[29] Having implicated AFDC in inducing dependency on government and the rise of the underclass, the conservative prescription for welfare reform was not producing the desired results. Welfare-to-work was a wash.

If the welfare-to-work experience discouraged conservatives from engaging further in welfare reform, it was not for long. Undeterred from their assault on welfare, they regrouped and identified another sinister feature of AFDC: the prevalence of illegitimate births. In late 1993, Charles Murray, whose *Losing Ground* had so influenced the welfare debate of the 1980s, announced in the *Wall Street Journal* "The Coming of the White Underclass." The marked increase in illegitimate births within the African-American community was the source of the black underclass, Murray argued, and the rise of illegitimate births among whites was sufficient to expect that a white underclass would follow. Murray's solution to the anticipated white underclass echoed his prescription for the black underclass: "end all economic support for single mothers." The elimination of AFDC, subsidized housing, Food Stamps, and other welfare programs would place them at the mercy of family and community institutions if they had babies out-of-wedlock. In the face of community disapproval, young women would force marriage on their boyfriends or at least reconsider the consequences of their sexual liaisons, Murray reasoned.[30]

By replacing work with illegitimate births as central to their welfare critique, conservatives introduced a range of new issues into the social policy debate. Some were relatively easy for liberal welfare advocates to handle—for example, do AFDC mothers have babies to increase their benefits? The rate of illegitimate births had actually doubled despite the substantial erosion of the value of AFDC benefits during the past two decades. Others would be tricky for conservatives— for example, would eliminating AFDC force young women to abort pregnancies? Probably so, despite the Hyde amendment prohibiting federal funding of abortions.[31] An altogether different set of questions in the welfare reform debate threw the Clinton administration off balance. Not having anticipated the illegitimate births issue, the administration rushed to endorse aspects of welfare reform for which the evidence was even more pessimistic than the assessments of welfare-to-work programs.

"THE END OF WELFARE AS WE KNOW IT"

Among the welfare-to-work field demonstrations, the Arkansas WORK Program was among the most successful. Although earnings of AFDC recipients increased only modestly, participant costs were recovered soon after graduation from WORK. Even if AFDC mothers were not leaving the program in droves, at least the State of Arkansas was saving money. This, doubtlessly, fueled then-Governor Clinton's enthusiasm for welfare reform as part of the Democratic platform during his campaign for the presidency. Other developments served to highlight welfare reform during the presidential campaign. Preoccupied with foreign affairs, particularly the Persian Gulf War, President Bush had paid scant attention to social policy, hoping that "a thousand points of light" would sufficiently illuminate domestic concerns. The American middle class struggled against stagnating incomes to maintain a standard of living. As more working-class families lost health benefits, a paradox became unavoidable: working stiffs were unable to get health insurance while unemployed welfare recipients received Medicaid. Resentment of welfare increased.

Despite passage of the Family Support Act only a few years before, Democrats suspected that welfare reform remained a viable issue. Writers of the Progressive Policy Institute, the think tank appended to the Democratic Leadership Council which was chaired by then-Governor Clinton, proposed a two-year time limit for receipt of welfare.[32] An aggressive welfare-to-work program would provide training and education for two years, after which an AFDC recipient would have to obtain employment in the private sector or accept a government-created job. Limiting AFDC to two years was a relatively safe bet for campaign rhetoric since a study conducted prior to implementation of the welfare-to-work provisions of the 1988 Family Support Act indicated that half of AFDC recipients were on the program less than two years, anyway.[33] With a more adequate JOBS program in place coupled with the exemption of mothers with disabilities or very young children, the number of AFDC mothers facing the cutoff of benefits after two years would be manageable—at least manageable enough for presidential campaign purposes.[34]

After the election, President Clinton moved quickly to reform AFDC once again. Wary of the influence that would be brought to bear on the two-year time limit by liberal interests (89 liberal advocacy groups had transmitted their objection to time-limited welfare), Clinton created a panel of thirty, all of whom held positions within the new administration. The charge to the Working Group on Welfare Reform was fourfold:

Make Work Pay—families with full-time workers should get adequate income supports so that they would not have to resort to welfare;

Dramatically Improve Child Support Enforcement—government should be more aggressive in extracting child support from absent parents;

Provide Education, Training, and Other Services to Help People Get Off and Stay Off Welfare—redoubling JOBS provisions of the Family Support Act would make self-sufficiency more feasible for AFDC mothers;

Two-Year Time Limit—AFDC would become a two-year transitional program if the first three provisions were in place.[35]

The Working Group on Welfare Reform was immediately bogged down with that agenda. Of the primary objectives, three were relatively incontrovertible. With regard to the working poor, steady increases in the Earned Income Tax Credit (EITC), begun during the Reagan presidency, offered a substantial rebate from the Internal Revenue Service to low-income workers. Much of this objective would be accomplished when the president's economic program would be enacted, since it contained a $28 billion increase in the EITC. Improvements in child support enforcement would be tacked onto Title IVD of the Social Security Act, which had been in place since the amendments of 1975. Reinforcing education, training, and other services would be accomplished by investing more in the JOBS provisions of the FSA. Clearly, the sticking point was the two-year time limit.

To take the edge off liberal criticism that his two-year welfare time limit was too harsh, Clinton as candidate had promised a public-sector job when welfare-to-work graduates could not find one in the private sector. Although this assuaged liberals during the campaign, the postelection implications of a government-created job were enormous. To be consistent with the first principle of welfare reform—Make Work Pay—such a job would have to bring a family above the poverty level. For the number of AFDC families who might require public employment, the costs appeared plausible. Yet, it would be blasphemous to ensure AFDC welfare-to-work graduates an income *above* the poverty line when that earned by workers laboring under the minimum wage fell *far below* it. To be fair, the guarantee of a public-sector job would have to be extended to them, too, and the fiscal implications of that were on the order of $43 to 59 billion, an amount that would have taxpayers screaming.[36] This was far more than what the president was prepared to present to Congress for welfare reform.

Other issues complicated the president's welfare reform panel. If welfare-to-work were pursued more vigorously, there would be about 3 million more AFDC mothers seeking training and employment, imposing an enormous demand for child care. The financial implications of such an expansion of day care could cripple welfare reform, particularly if AFDC children were to be guaranteed professional-quality child care.[37] Panel deliberations on financing welfare reform ranged from a new tax on gambling to drawing on savings attained by eliminating welfare benefits for noncitizens in the United States.[38] The ultimate snag, however, remained the two-year time limit. "What happens if a woman is not disabled and has a three-year-old kid who is not disabled, but she does not show up to work?" complained Congressman Robert Matsui (D. California). "Do we take the child away from her and let her wander the streets?"[39]

While the Working Group on Welfare Reform dithered, states forged ahead with their own versions of welfare reform. More than a dozen states had already received federal waivers to experiment with welfare reform by early 1994. Typical welfare reform waivers are subclassified in the following list.

Common Welfare Reform Waivers
A. Earnings and Assets
   1. Allow workers to keep more of their earnings under the Earned Income Disregard.
   2. Allow beneficiaries to retain a higher value of assets.
B. Child Support Enforcement
   1. Immediately garnish any payments in arrearage.
   2. Aggressively determine paternity in hospitals upon birth of a child.
   3. Require absent parents in arrears to participate in JOBS.
C. Electronic Benefit Transfer
   1. Disperse AFDC and Food Stamps benefits via plastic cards with magnetic strips.
   2. Use "smart cards" as a generic access to benefits of various programs.
D. Supporting Intact Families
   1. Allow both parents to live with a family receiving AFDC.
   2. Eliminate the work requirement or unemployment for wage-earners to stay at home.
   3. Eliminate the 100-hour work limit rule for working parents.
E. Transitional Benefits
   1. Extend Medicaid and child care benefits beyond six months.
   2. Adopt a sliding scale to reduce transitional benefits.
F. Job Creation
   1. Use benefits to augment wages of private sector employment.
   2. Develop microenterprise funds to incubate independent businesses.
G. School Attendance and Completion
   1. Institute bonuses and penalties regarding attendance and graduation.
   2. Provide intensive case management for pregnant teens.
H. Time Limits
   1. Establish strict time limits for receipt of benefits, such as 2 years or 30 months.
   2. Individualize contracts with beneficiaries that include stiff penalties for noncompliance.
I. Alternative Benefit Payment
   1. Encourage working families to replace AFDC with the 100-percent federally financed Earned Income Tax Credit.
   2. Allow families to receive lump-sum benefit payments, up to three times the normal grant, on a one-time basis.[40]

Among these, four states proposed reducing or terminating AFDC after two years.[41] Florida proposed putting in place a two-year time limit for AFDC in two counties, a plan similar to Clinton's campaign promise.[42] Under a conservative governor, Wyoming adopted a welfare reform plan that emphasized several traditional themes. AFDC beneficiaries were required to participate in JOBS or accept community service. Asset limits were increased, and child support enforcement was strengthened. In an innovative departure, unemployed parents with child support arrearages were required to participate in JOBS. Finally, JOBS benefits were expanded to include vocational education, as well as training toward a higher education diploma. The Wyoming welfare reform produced dramatic results.

> In the first six months of the initiative, total caseload dropped by over 7 percent statewide even though the trial was limited to three counties. Clients moved into the work force at an unprecedented rate and the earned income of household heads rose. Child support collections accelerated with an estimated savings to the state of $5–6 million in the first biennium.[43]

With some 40 states seeking or having received waivers for welfare reform demonstrations, the administration was suddenly behind the policy curve in welfare reform. Spying an opening, Congressional Republicans patched together a 150-page welfare reform proposal of their own. Included in House Resolution 3500 were Republican suggestions to convert AFDC to a block grant, to require teen mothers to live with their parents in order to receive AFDC, and to eliminate welfare benefits to aliens; it even proposed random drug tests on Supplemental Security Income recipients, the failure of which would immediately terminate benefits.[44] With the president's promise of a welfare reform proposal already overdue, the proposals of others were attracting media attention.

The stalemate within the Working Group on Welfare Reform was finally broken by a suggestion from Paul Offner, an aide to Senator Daniel Patrick Moynihan. Offner was not a member of the panel, but he effectively used the print media to disseminate what was to be a brilliant example of policy incrementalism. The president's welfare reform group had reached an impasse: In order to avoid a punitive two-year limit to AFDC, welfare-to-work provisions would have to be so extensive that the costs of welfare reform would become impractical. Offner's solution was to target generous JOBS benefits coupled with a two-year time limit to only young mothers who were new to AFDC. "Teen-age mothers would have to live with their families to receive AFDC (they could not move out and get their own apartments), and they would have to stay in school until graduation or until they reached the age of 20," Offner proposed. "After receiving their degrees, or reaching the age of 20, they would be offered work, but not welfare." The cost of selective application of welfare reform, speculated Offner, would be no more than $500 million. This was a manageable amount, he argued, and it was a shrewd investment in public funds since it addressed teenagers who were most likely to become dependent on welfare.[45]

On June 14, 1994, President Clinton announced his welfare reform proposal in a Kansas City bank that had hired former AFDC mothers. The proposal targeted education and training benefits for recipients born after 1971, as Offner had suggested. For these prospective beneficiaries, AFDC would be limited to a single two-year, lifetime benefit. Following training, AFDC recipients would have to find private-sector employment or accept a community service job that paid the minimum wage. Failure to comply would be grounds for terminating benefits. In order to dissuade teens from becoming pregnant, the proposal called for a nationwide campaign to reduce teenage pregnancy. Other features of the president's proposal included more aggressive child support enforcement, a national information clearinghouse to reduce welfare fraud, and limits on welfare benefits for legal immigrants. President Clinton budgeted the plan at $9.3 billion over five years.

The public quickly responded. Judith Gueron, president of MDRC, suggested the president's proposal was "a step toward ending the current welfare system," though she suspected it was inadequately funded.[46] Predictably, Will Marshall, president of the Progressive Policy Institute and an early enthusiast for time-limited welfare, characterized the plan as "radical, yet constructive change." If women's rights groups suspected the proposal was punitive toward women, they reserved comment. Conservatives, on the other hand, were fuming. "A joke, a half fraud," remarked Reagan administration Secretary of Education and conservative lightning-rod William Bennett, "marginal tinkering."[47] "Tinkering," echoed Wisconsin Governor Tommy Thompson, whose state had pioneered some of the features Clinton had pirated for his welfare reform plan.[48] The public, however, was clearly behind Clinton. An April *Los Angeles Times* public opinion poll reported that 90 percent of Americans endorsed a two-year limit to welfare, coupled to a job requirement. Moving tactically, editors of the *New Republic* used their editorial column to remind Clinton of the poll and goad him into proposing "two-years-and-work" welfare reform the very week that Clinton made the announcement.[49]

More seasoned welfare reform observers were less sanguine about the Clinton proposal, however. By reserving the time limit to beneficiaries born after 1971, two-thirds of AFDC recipients would remain virtually unaffected by President Clinton's welfare reform. By the year 2000, between 7 and 14 percent of AFDC recipients would be in job training or would have left the program.[50] Such modest expectations led one policy pundit to brand welfare reform à la Clinton as an extension of the Reagan reforms of the 1988 FSA—"much more incremental change in the welfare system than the sweeping reforms [presidents] Nixon and Carter offered."[51]

THE NEXT WELFARE REFORM AGENDA

By the end of the 103rd Congress, whatever momentum the Clinton administration had built around welfare reform ground to a halt. Earlier, the White House had made a tactical decision to delay welfare reform until after health care reform had been considered. Thus sidetracked, welfare reform was held in abeyance, so long, as it turned out, that it would be presented to the 104th Congress. Any hope that the incoming 104th Congress would be progressive in its approach to welfare reform was dashed when the returns of the 1994 midterm elections came in. For the first time in forty years, Republicans gained control of Congress, granting them control over the means of legislation. The jubilant future Speaker of the House Newt Gingrich announced that welfare reform would be a priority for the new Congress. Having proposed more stringent welfare reform than that offered by Clinton, in his much-publicized "Contract with America," Gingrich provided more details immediately after the election. The primary target of Republican welfare reform would be teen mothers who would be denied AFDC benefits; instead, they would be encouraged to place their children up for adoption. Benefit savings would be diverted to establishing orphanages for children of mothers who were unable to find employment or obtain aid from charitable sources.[52] That federal welfare policy as proposed by Gingrich would encourage the proliferation of orphanages was ironic, to say the least. Possibly affecting 5.3 million children at an annual cost of $36,500 per child, orphanages would be considerably more expensive than the current costs of child welfare.[53] Given the high ratio of professional staff to children in residential child care, Gingrich's proposal might have been more accurately named the Social Worker Full Employment Act.

A dispute between Gingrich and Hillary Rodham Clinton quickly erupted. The First Lady labeled Gingrich's idea as "unbelievable and absurd"; Gingrich suggested that the First Lady view the 1938 movie *Boys Town*. On the defensive, Gingrich explained the implications of liberal welfare programs: "We say to a 13-year-old drug addict who is pregnant, you know, put your baby in a Dumpster, that's OK, but we're not going to give you a boarding school." In an attempt to introduce some rationality to the flap, the director of Boys Town, Father Val Peter, suggested that simplified solutions, such as Gingrich's, were poorly conceived because they failed to contend with the diverse problems experienced by troubled families. "You can't mass produce 7 million Boys Towns and have the problem solved," he said.[54]

The flap over orphanages obscured more serious provisions of the Personal Responsibility Act (PRA) part of the Contract with America. In addition to prohibiting public assistance benefits to legal aliens and pregnant women under age 18, the PRA would limit welfare benefits to five years, giving the states latitude to reduce the time limit to two years. Welfare eligibility would require that paternity be established for all children; by the year 2000, 1 million welfare recipients would have to be working. The primary public assistance programs—AFDC, SSI, and Food Stamps—would be converted from open-ended entitlements to capped, discretionary programs in which case appropriations would not expand with eligibility, but be determined annually by Congress.[55] According to the Center on Budget and Policy Priorities, the PRA would cut welfare programs $59 billion from 1996 to 1999; deny welfare to 29 percent of children for whom paternity has not been established; and terminate 2.5 million families from public assistance of whom 5 million are children.[56]

Yet, in formulating the PRA to eliminate the liberal welfare state, Congressional Republicans may have sown the seeds of their own destruction. Significant federal reductions in welfare would pose almost insurmountable problems for state governors, 30 of whom are currently Republicans. Most problematic would be curtailing SSI and Food Stamps, the costs of which are now almost completely borne by the federal government. The tax implications of states assuming full or even partial responsibility for these programs is inconceivable. As a result, governors would prefer that the federal government devolve welfare to states in block grant form, eliminating federal conditions in the process. If, however, Congressional Republicans insist on cutting the federal contribution to block grants by 20 percent, governors would have to resolve the discrepancy between the needs of the poor and public revenues. Republican governors would be unlikely to seek tax increases and more inclined to reduce welfare benefits. With AFDC benefits already having lost 47 percent of purchasing value between 1970 and 1994,[57] it is difficult to imagine how governors could convince poor mothers that they could manage on 20 percent less. On the other hand, block grant devolution of welfare would conveniently let decision makers in Washington off the hook.[58] The reassignment of welfare to states would absolve Gingrich of the problem of deploying orphanages and Clinton of the question of employment after the two-year time limit expires.

Undone by the 1994 election, the Clinton welfare reform proposal has been eclipsed by the issue of Congressional devolution of welfare to the states. If Gingrich's thinking prevails, the outcome may be more punitive measures than what the Clinton administration would have preferred, at best a stalemate that fails to generate any welfare reform plan. Under these circumstances, more innovative thinking is warranted. A more effective strategy to end poverty—and the welfare programs associated with sustaining it—would feature three initiatives:

1. child support assurance,
2. creation of individual development accounts to encourage asset-building, and
3. deconstruction of the welfare bureaucracy.

Child Support Assurance

A primary reason mothers become dependent on AFDC is the failure of fathers to provide child support to their children. Despite the establishment of child support, only half of mothers caring for their children alone receive the full amount of child support due them, leaving many dependent on welfare. If absent fathers met their fiscal obligations, they would contribute from $24 billion to $30 billion to their children—roughly the annual appropriation for the AFDC program.[59] Since 1975, the federal government has assisted states in extracting child support for families on AFDC. Yet, in 1993, $2.2 billion was expended to collect only $9 billion in outstanding child support.[60] The percentage of AFDC payments retrieved from child support enforcement has increased to 12 percent in 1993 after hovering around 11 percent during the previous two years.[61]

Tough child support enforcement is the ideal solution to the AFDC problem, yet in practicality this is not likely to take place. Optimally, states seem unable to recover more than about one-fourth of AFDC payments through child support.[62] The social and economic circumstances of low-income male workers probably accounts for the dismal results of child support enforcement. Whereas many white-collar professionals can afford to be more conscientious about child support payments, men in marginal jobs will be less able to. The advantages of low-wage work for men in marginal employment are not substantial enough to encourage responsibility in meeting their child support obligations. The social and economic circumstances of poor families once again conspire to subvert the best intentions of policy makers.

Child Support Assurance (CSA) was developed by Irwin Garfinkel as a replacement for much of AFDC. According to Garfinkel, CSA has three facets:

Child support is set as a percentage of an absent parent's income.

Child support payments are automatically withheld from wages.

A minimum benefit is assured a child for whom a support order has been established.[63]

CSA functions much like unemployment insurance. For the same reasons that workers who are laid off are not presumed to be responsible for their joblessness, CSA presents child support as an assured benefit for the children of nonsupporting parents. The first two provisions of CSA, Garfinkel argues, would increase child support payments, offsetting the third, an assured minimum benefit. Thus, placing the assured benefit at $2,000 per child, the cost of CSA would be about $1 billion, a bargain for removing one-fifth of the families on AFDC from welfare.[64]

Currently, two states—Wisconsin and New York—have experimented with the first two features of CSA, but no state has tried to incorporate the assured benefit. "The [as]sured benefit is crucial," contended David Ellwood while he was at Harvard's Kennedy School of Government. "Without it, child support reform will mainly benefit upper and middle class single mothers. Child support would then be yet another device that will separate the poor and the nonpoor. Middle class women will support themselves with a combination of work and child support. Working class women will be left with only welfare."[65] Although Ellwood failed to present a budget for his expanded version of child support, he was willing to set an assured benefit at $4,000 per child, a level that would probably cut in half the number of families on AFDC.[66] As late as February 1994, child support enforcement and assurance was included in the draft of the Working Group on Welfare Reform, although no assured benefit level was indicated.[67] But when President Clinton announced welfare reform in his address four months later, Child Support Assurance was noticeably missing, presumably in response to conservative contentions that its would encourage out-of-wedlock births.

Creation of Individual Development Accounts

Early in 1990 readers of the *Wall Street Journal* were greeted with a front-page welfare story. Grace Capetillo, a Milwaukee welfare mother, had scrimped and saved on daily necessities in order to establish an account for her five-year-old daughter's college expenses. After cross-checking Internal Revenue Service data with welfare rolls, the Milwaukee Department of Social Services (DSS) charged Ms. Capetillo with welfare fraud since her assets exceeded the $1,000 allowed under AFDC. Initially, DSS demanded repayment of $15,545, the amount of payments made to her while her savings made her ineligible for welfare. Convicted, Ms. Capetillo was sentenced to one year's probation and ordered to repay $1,000 to DSS.[68] Readers of the *Journal* quickly registered their outrage in editorial letters railing at a welfare program that stifled the most modest attempt at self-improvement—saving for college.

As policy analyst Michael Sherraden has observed, the entire focus of welfare programs has been on income support. The responsibility of government is to provide temporary support for those in need, goes the argument, and the best way to do that is to give the poor cash that they can spend or in-kind benefits for other necessities. Programs such as AFDC and Food Stamps are surrogates for lost earnings, hence their label, "income maintenance." Sherraden argues that a poverty policy that emphasizes income without addressing asset-building errs fundamentally. Income supports barely allow the poor to survive. A close examination of disadvantaged families that escape poverty reveals that they behave economically very much like middle-income families: the escape from poverty lies in accumulating assets.

A long-range strategy for getting people off welfare would be a program of Individual Development Accounts (IDAs). An IDA is an account in which government matches an individual's contribution; it is tax-exempt if funds are used for (1) finishing college or vocational school, (2) buying a home, (3) starting a business, or (4) supplementing a pension. The amount the government would match would vary with an individual's income. Significantly, IDAs would serve to capture capital in low-income communities where it could be reinvested for purposes of community development. Moreover, IDAs could be inherited, thus helping poor families become more prosperous.[69]

Current asset provisions in welfare policy are little more than incremental increases in the current asset limit so that ownership of a car is permissible. Oregon and Iowa are experimenting with IDAs in modest demonstration programs. Indeed, the timing seems right for more directive strategies for inducing the poor to build assets. Economic development projects encouraging women to become entrepreneurs have been successful under the right conditions.[70] Former welfare recipients have been prominent in a worker-owned, for-profit home health co-op in New York City, Cooperative Home Care Associates.[71] The

Mott Foundation and the Aspen Institute have sponsored a range of microenterprise initiatives to help the poor become economically self-sufficient.[72]

Deconstruction of Welfare Bureaucracies

Virtually all welfare is dispensed through public bureaucracies. In the half-century since welfare departments were established through the Social Security Act, these governmental edifices have consumed larger and larger volumes of resources. For 1992, administration of AFDC and Food Stamps cost government $4.4 billion, 13 percent of benefit expenditures.[73] This would be justifiable, perhaps, if not for the consistently inferior quality of service provided through welfare departments. Service is so poor that welfare bureaucrats have refused to conduct studies of efficiency or client perception of welfare services, a remarkable omission considering the magnitude of public expenditures for social welfare. The fragmentary evidence that exists paints a grim picture. Award-winning sociologist Michael Lipsky studied local welfare offices, concluding that "workers on the front lines of the welfare state find themselves in a corrupted world of service. [They] find that the best way to keep demand within manageable proportions is to deliver a consistently inaccessible or inferior product."[74] The working environment of the welfare bureaucracy is so convoluted that workers often deny benefits to citizens, a process Lipsky labeled "bureaucratic disentitlement."[75] A journalistic account of a Los Angeles welfare office depicted a public institution that defied the notion of public service:

> Welfare offices are so understaffed, the workers so burnt out, that some help applicants cheat just to fill unofficial quotas, avoid confrontation, get them out of their hair. It is a system so flawed that the greedy, the lazy, rip and run with ease. The attitude on both sides of the reinforced windows that separate staff from applicants is: Us against Them. The system becomes so cynical that the desperate—the great majority of applicants, by most estimates—are left under a pall of suspicion, clawing even harder to get the help to which they're entitled.[76]

Rather than provide public service in an expedient and prudent fashion, public welfare departments have become organizational fiefdoms insulating civil servants from accountability to taxpayers and clients in urgent need of service.

While welfare departments endure, other public institutions that evolved during the Progressive Era have been experimenting with structural reform. In health care, health maintenance organizations have flourished. In education, experiments are underway with magnet schools, teacher-managed schools, and vouchers. Transformation of the public sector was prodded along by *Reinventing Government* by David Osborne and Ted Gaebler.[77] But, contrary to the times, welfare has remained virtually exempt from discussions of restructuring.

Several options would make welfare departments more responsive institutions. Many social services could be delivered by vouchers, allowing clients more choice in service providers.[78] Communities could be allowed to charter their own welfare departments, much as schools can be chartered in some localities. The decentralization of welfare would complement the deployment of social services at neighborhood schools, an initiative already underway in several communities. The delivery of financial benefits might be contracted out through commercial banks or credit unions, as Los Angeles County has done through its welfare-to-work contract with a for-profit firm, MAXIMUS.[79] Electronic transfer for payment of benefits and use of plastic "smart cards" could make transactions more efficient while destigmatizing beneficiaries ("smart cards" are plastic cards with electronically readable strips). To date, most localities and states have entertained superficial changes in welfare administration when wholesale restructuring is warranted.

This refusal by welfare professionals to take a hard look at the means of program administration contributes to public perception of a notoriously bloated welfare bureaucracy. Unable to see any substantive reform in the management of welfare programs, the public has chosen to simply pull the plug on funding social programs, as in California's Proposition 13. The consequences of complacency on the part of welfare administrators for program beneficiaries is even more troublesome. At best, clients of welfare programs are socially segregated from the mainstream, having to rely on a second-rate and inferior set of services that no middle-income American would tolerate. Former AFDC recipient, Theresa Funiciello, recognizes this in her scathing critique of welfare in America, *Tyranny of Kindness*.

> When affluent people decide some service they want for themselves isn't up to snuff, they vote with their feet and their pocketbooks. In that sense, markets work quite well for anyone with the power to participate in them. As long as poor people are prohibited from having a choice—a say in deciding which services they need and which providers are most capable of satisfying them—the competitive element, if there is one, is entirely in the hands of Big Brother. Most of the people in every form of this business know this: *there is no accountability in the social service field*. None demanded, none supplied.[80]

At worst, poor Americans are denied—by indifferent welfare workers—the benefits to which they are legally entitled. Welfare professionals' disregard of public concern about welfare administration has given conservatives a rich ideological vein to mine. Indeed, socially minded conservatives have joined with African-American intellectuals to develop the "empowerment movement" precisely as a mechanism to liberate poor minorities from an oppressive welfare bureaucracy.

True welfare reform would integrate these initiatives—Child Support Assurance, Individual Development Accounts, and Welfare Bureaucracy Deconstruction. With what we have learned from the JOBS program, we know this could accelerate the upward mobility of poor families. Because poor families vary in their capacity to exploit the different opportunities inherent in these programs, services should be individualized. Rather than circumscribe benefits for all families, as is the thinking now, a menu of options should be available in order to customize an income-and-assets package that is relevant for each family.

Thomas Corbett of the University of Wisconsin's Institute for Research on Poverty has articulated this menu of options in defining three subgroups of poor families.

1. Working-poor families—about 30 percent of the poor—would be encouraged to rely on Child Support Assurance, Individual Development Accounts, and the Earned Income Tax Credit to supplement earnings and build assets.
2. The 40 percent of nonworking families on AFDC for two to eight years would develop detailed JOBS contracts that would ensure them increased earnings, although economic self-sufficiency might take several years.
3. The remaining 30 percent of families who have been welfare dependent would receive intensive social and psychological services to prepare them for JOBS. Time limits to assistance may be a necessary motivator for this subgroup.

Conceding the difficulty in getting the poor off of welfare, Corbett wisely noted the need for multiple strategies: "no single strategy will do the whole job."[81]

Among the field demonstrations of welfare reform that employ nonpunitive innovations, those of New York and Iowa are notable. Begun in the late 1980s, New York's CAP targets single-parent families on AFDC, encouraging them to work and save. Intensive financial management and social services are provided by a case manager. Although CAP falls short of some of the more ambitious strategies noted above, the results are encouraging. More than eight out of ten CAP families have incomes above the poverty level, and seven out of ten families report increased savings. By emphasizing work and child support, an evaluation of the program noted that "CAP families support themselves primarily with their own earnings and child support provided by the absent parent; a relatively small proportion of their income is supplied by public benefits."[82]

The Iowa Family Investment Program (FIP) represents a more radical departure from conservative versions of welfare reform. Under FIP, participating families work out a Family Investment Agreement (FIA) with a case manager; the FIA specifies steps the family will take toward financial self-sufficiency. In exchange for the family's participation, the state promises to provide a more generous job-training and placement package than that of conventional JOBS programs, including the creation of Individual Development Accounts. A family's failure to uphold the agreement results in transfer to a Limited Benefit Plan; complete noncompliance leads to termination of benefits. Preliminary results of the FIP indicated modest success: the cost per case dropped from $373.75 in

September 1993 to $355.39 in February 1994; the percent of families with employment increased from 18 percent to 26.5 percent during the same period.[83]

How, then, does the Clinton welfare reform plan compare with the more substantive initiatives above or, for that matter, the innovations evolving in New York and Iowa? Having deleted Child Support Assurance and all but neglecting Individual Development Accounts, the president's proposal does little to free poor families from poverty. By reinforcing the JOBS program, AFDC will help families with limited employment experience, but most will still require welfare to supplement their wages. Unless Congressional Republicans reform welfare according to their own callous principles, the Clinton White House has indicated that by the year 2000 AFDC will be a more expensive program and that relatively little will have been saved by the trickle of families who have become economically independent of welfare. The president's plan contains one inherent flaw: to be eligible for education, job training, and transitional benefits, one must be a poor mother on AFDC. Work-welfare benefits, in other words, are predicated on getting on AFDC; they are not offered to the working poor, the low-income Americans who play by the rules. Working-class perceptions that AFDC benefits are superior to work will continue to fuel conservative opposition to welfare.

Given Henry Aaron's admonition on the difficulty of attributing social change to any single social policy, the Clinton administration should also pay close attention to preliminary MDRC data regarding teen pregnancy. Of teen mothers from 10 states who enrolled in the New Chance program—an attempt to dissuade them from becoming pregnant again before attaining self-sufficiency—more than half were pregnant 18 months after entering the program.[84] Problems such as these will reinforce the conservative contention that AFDC contributes to a proliferation of the underclass, and they will continue to propel reactionary schemes such as Gingrich's orphanage proposal.

NOTES

1. P. J. O'Rourke, *Parliament of Whores* (New York: Vintage, 1991), p. 123.
2. Martin Anderson, "Welfare Reform," in Peter Duignan and Alvin Rabushka (eds.), *The United States in the 1980s* (Stanford, CA: Hoover Institution, 1980), p. 145.
3. This is most poignantly stated by Theresa Funiciello in *Tyranny of Kindness: Dismantling the Welfare System to End Poverty in America* (New York: Atlantic Monthly Press, 1993).
4. General relief—sometimes called "general assistance"—is also a welfare program; however, it is financed entirely by local government. Because so few local jurisdictions opt for general relief, it is not included in this discussion.
5. Committee on Ways and Means, *Overview of Entitlement Programs* (Washington, DC: USGPO, 1993), pp. 823, 660.
6. Ways and Means Committee, U.S. House of Representatives, *Overview of Entitlement Programs* (Washington, DC: USGPO, 1994), p. 2009.

7. Kathryn Edin and Christopher Jencks, "Reforming Welfare," in Christopher Jencks, *Rethinking Social Policy* (Cambridge, MA: Harvard University Press, 1992), pp. 206-7.
8. *Overview of Entitlement Programs,* 1994, p. 427.
9. *Overview of Entitlement Programs,* 1994, pp. 366-67.
10. *Overview of Entitlement Programs,* 1994, pp. 1154-55.
11. *Overview of Entitlement Programs,* 1993, p. 1314.
12. *Overview of Entitlement Programs,* 1993, p. 1313.
13. James Risen, "Number of Poor in America Hits a 27-Year High," *Los Angeles Times* (September 4, 1992), p. A-1.
14. *Overview of Entitlement Programs,* 1993, pp. 1317-20.
15. U.S. Bureau of the Census, *Current Populations Reports—Series P-60, No. 182RD,* "Measuring the Effects of Benefits and Taxes on Income and Poverty" (Washington, DC, USGPO, 1992), pp. xxii-xxiii.
16. *Overview of Entitlement Programs,* 1993, p. 1500.
17. Kevin Phillips, *Boiling Point* (New York: Random House, 1993), p. 28.
18. George Gilder, *Wealth and Poverty* (New York: Basic Books, 1981), p. 118.
19. Charles Murray, *Losing Ground* (New York: Basic Books, 1984), pp. 227-28.
20. Lawrence Mead, *Beyond Entitlement* (New York: Free Press, 1986).
21. Elizabeth Shogren, "Unintended Consequences Haunt Welfare Reformers," *Los Angeles Times* (June 20, 1994), p. A-1.
22. Mimi Abramovitz and Frances Fox Piven, "Welfare Reform: One More Way to Make Women 'Shape up'," *San Diego Union-Tribune* (September 3, 1993), p. B-7.
23. Laurence Lynn, Jr., "Ending Welfare Reform as We Know It," *The American Prospect* 15 (Fall 1993), p. 85.
24. David Stoesz and Howard Karger, *Reconstructing the American Welfare State* (Lanham, MD: Rowman and Littlefield, 1992), p. 51.
25. Douglas Besharov, "Statement before the Select Committee on Hunger," U.S. House of Representatives, Washington, DC, May 21, 1992.
26. Henry Aaron, *Politics and the Professors* (Washington, DC: Brookings Institution, 1978), p. 10.
27. Stoesz and Karger, *Reconstructing,* pp. 62, 147.
28. David Ellwood, *Poor Support* (New York: Basic Books, 1988), p. 153.
29. Elizabeth Shogren and Ronald Brownstein, "GAO Says JOBS Plan Not Working," *Los Angeles Times* (December 19, 1994), p. A-24.
30. Charles Murray, "The Coming White Underclass," *Wall Street Journal* (October 29, 1993), p. A-12.
31. Stephanie Mencimer, "Ending Illegitimacy as We Know It," *Washington Post Weekly* (January 17-23, 1994), p. 24.
32. Will Marshall and Martin Schram (eds.), *Mandate for Change* (New York: Berkley Books, 1993).
33. *Overview of Entitlement Programs,* 1993, p. 714.
34. Tom Morganthau, "The Entitlement Trap," *Newsweek* (December 13, 1993).
35. "Charge to the Working Group on Welfare Reform, Family Support and Independence," (Washington, DC: n.d.).
36. Mickey Kaus, *The End of Equality* (New York: Basic Books, 1992), p. 135.
37. Elizabeth Shogren, "Child Care a Key Hurdle to Clinton Welfare Plan," *Los Angeles Times* (March 6, 1994); Paul Offner, "Day Careless," *New Republic* (April 18, 1994).
38. Paul Offner, "Solid Noncitizens," *New Republic* (June 20, 1994).

39. Ronald Brownstein and Elizabeth Shogren, "Welfare Reform Planners in Deadlock," *Los Angeles Times* (March 22, 1994).
40. Julie Strawn, Sheila Dacey, and Linda McCart, *Final Report, The National Governors' Association Survey of State Welfare Reforms* (Washington, DC: National Governors' Association, 1994).
41. Jason DeParle, "States' Eagerness to Experiment on Welfare Jars Administration," *New York Times* (April 14, 1994), p. A-1.
42. Elizabeth Shogren, "2 Florida Counties to Test Clinton-Style Welfare Plan," *Los Angeles Times* (January 28, 1994).
43. Mark Lusk and Joseph Nies, "New Opportunities, New Responsibilities: Welfare Reform in Wyoming," *Journal of Sociology and Social Welfare* xxi, 4 (December 1994), pp. 52-53.
44. House Resolution 3500, 103rd Congress, 1st session.
45. Paul Offner, "Realistic and Affordable Welfare Reform: Target the Teen Mothers," *San Diego Union Tribune* (January 10, 1994), p. B-5; Paul Offner, "Target the Kids," *New Republic* (January 24, 1994).
46. Jason DeParle, "Plan May Not Satisfy Demands for Basic Change," *San Diego Union-Tribune* (June 15, 1994), p. 31.
47. Ronald Brownstein, "Polarization Politics Seen as Key Obstacle to Welfare Proposal," *Los Angeles Times* (June 15, 1994), p. A-14.
48. DeParle, "Plan," p. 31.
49. "Clinton's Secret Weapon," *New Republic* (June 20, 1994).
50. DeParle, "Plan," p. 31; Elizabeth Shogren, "Clinton Unveils Welfare Reform," *Los Angeles Times* (June 15, 1994), p. A-14.
51. Ronald Brownstein, "Clinton's Welfare Reform Shaped by Predecessors' Frustrated Efforts," *Los Angeles Times* (June 14, 1994), p. A-5.
52. "GOP Promises Quick Action on Welfare Bill," *Idaho Statesman* (November 11, 1994), p. 2A.
53. "Secretary Shalala's Challenge," *Washington Post Weekly* (January 9-15, 1995), p. 26.
54. Richard Whitmire, "Boys Town Director Contends Orphanages Won't Solve Problem," *Idaho Statesman* (December 6, 1994), p. 3A.
55. Barbara Vobejda, "Cutting through Welfare on the Way to Personal Responsibility," *Washington Post Weekly* (December 19-25, 1994), p. 8.
56. Dan Bloom et al., *The Personal Responsibility Act: An Analysis* (Washington, DC: Center on Budget and Policy Priorities, 1994), pp. vii-viii.
57. *Overview of Entitlement Programs*, 1994, p. 377.
58. Mickey Kaus, "Devolution Blues," *New Republic* (January 30, 1995), p. 6.
59. Irving Garfinkel, "Bringing Fathers Back In," *The American Prospect* (Spring 1992), p. 76.
60. *Overview of Entitlement Programs*, 1994, p. 455.
61. *Overview of Entitlement Programs*, 1994, p. 457.
62. *Overview of Entitlement Programs*, p. 795.
63. Garfinkel, "Bringing Fathers," p. 75.
64. Garfinkel places the cost at $500 million, assuming a $1,000 assured benefit level.
65. David Ellwood, "Child Support Enforcement and Insurance: A Real Welfare Alternative" (Harvard University: Kennedy School of Government, 1992), p. 9.
66. Ellwood, "Child Support," pp. 8-10.
67. "Welfare Reform Issue Paper" (Washington, DC: Working Group on Welfare Reform, n.d.), p. 36.

68. Robert Rose, "For Welfare Parents, Scrimping Is Legal, But Savings Is Out," *Wall Street Journal* (February 6, 1990), p. 1.
69. Michael Sherraden, "Stakeholding: A New Direction in Social Policy" (Washington, DC: Progressive Policy Institute, 1990); Michael Sherraden, *Assets and the Poor* (Armonk, New Jersey: M.E. Sharpe, 1991).
70. John Else and Salome Raheim, "AFDC Clients as Entrepreneurs," *Public Welfare* (Fall 1992).
71. Jonathan Rowe, "Up from the Bedside: A Co-op for Home Care Workers," *The American Prospect* (Summer 1990), pp. 88–92.
72. See *Small Steps Toward Big Dreams* (Flint, MI: Mott Foundation, n.d.) and *1992 Directory of Microenterprise Programs* (Washington, DC: Aspen Institute, 1992).
73. *Overview of Entitlement Programs,* 1993, pp. 679, 1609.
74. Michael Lipsky, *Street-Level Bureaucracy* (New York: Russell Sage Foundation, 1980), p. xiii.
75. Michael Lipsky, "Bureaucratic Disentitlement," *Social Service Review* 33, 4 (March 1984).
76. Michael Goodman, "Just Another Day in Paradise," *Los Angeles Times Magazine* (December 19, 1993), p. 30.
77. David Osborne and Ted Gaebler, *Reinventing Government* (Reading, MA: Addison Wesley, 1992).
78. David Stoesz, "Social Service Vouchers" (Washington, DC: Progressive Policy Institute, 1992).
79. In an illustration of this, Maximus, a commercial consulting firm, successfully managed Los Angeles County's welfare-to-work program for years. See Jay Mathews, "LA's Free Enterprise Welfare Experiment," *Washington Post National Weekly Edition* (October 30–November 5, 1989), p. 33.
80. Original emphasis, Funiciello, p. 252.
81. Thomas Corbett, "Child Poverty and Welfare Reform," *Focus* (Madison, WI: Institute for Research on Poverty, 1993), p. 9.
82. *Beyond Welfare* (New York State Department of Social Services, Office of Program Planning, Analysis and Development and Division of Income Maintenance, 1991), pp. viii, xi.
83. "Welfare Reform in Iowa" (Des Moines, IA: Department of Human Services, n.d.).
84. Virginia Ellis, "Welfare Mother Plan Fails to Halt Pregnancy Trend," *Los Angeles Times* (June 22, 1994), p. A-3.

chapter 4

Urban Policy: Mainstreaming the Underclass

> *I see a younger, meaner generation out there now—more lost and alienated than we were, and placing even less value on life. We were at least touched by role models; this new bunch is totally estranged from the black mainstream. Crack has taken the drug game to a more lethal level and given young blacks far more economic incentive to opt for the streets.*
>
> *Nathan McCall[1]*

Since its inception during the Progressive Era at the turn of the century, urban policy has been inextricably bound to twin issues of race and class. Early attempts to remedy minority poverty were the predecessors of modern social service agencies, established during the Industrial Era before the turn of the century: the first Charity Organization Society in Buffalo in 1877; the first Settlement House in New York City in 1887 (followed by the most well-known Settlement—Hull House—in Chicago in 1889).[2] Progressives' concern for effective administration was the basis for attempts to rid municipal governance from the corruption associated with the likes of Tammany Hall's Boss Tweed and George Washington Plunkett. "Good government" became a rallying cry for such luminaries as Jacob Riis, Lincoln Steffens, and Upton Sinclair. Together with settlement house workers, the "good government" progressives laid the groundwork for what was to become the New Deal era. It is significant that many of the architects of the American welfare state were tenants of Jane Addams's Hull House, among them Edith and Grace Abbott, Julia Lathrop, Florence Kelley, Frances Perkins, and John Dewey. Harry Hopkins, a lightning rod for many of FDR's initiatives, had resided at New York's Christadora House Settlement.[3] Since the Progressive Era, successful urban policy has exhibited one central feature: the economic and social integration of the minority poor into the mainstream.

Federal urban policy began with the passage of the Housing Act of 1937, which provided assistance to states and cities for purposes of eliminating unsafe and unsanitary housing. After World War II, the Act was amended to focus on slum clearance and urban renewal.[4] The broad authority granted to local government coupled with the lack of advocacy by minorities and the poor resulted in federally funded projects that severely damaged working-class communities,[5] often replacing them with housing projects that resembled vertical concentration camps. In 1954, the Act was again amended, eliminating a requirement that residential housing be a substantial portion of federally supported projects. As a result, African Americans claimed, by an ironic semantic shift, that the "urban renewal" provision of the Act actually meant "Negro removal."

The War on Poverty, declared by President Johnson, ushered in a series of domestic programs intended to improve the plight of minorities and the poor. Because these populations disproportionately inhabited urban areas, programs targeted for them were particularly beneficial for cities. Among them, the Manpower Development and Training Act of 1962 financed education and job training for the poor; the Civil Rights Act of 1964 enhanced the life opportunities for racial minorities; the Food Stamp Act of 1964 improved nutrition of the poor; the Community Mental Health Centers Acts of 1963 and 1965 funded psychosocial services for the poor; the Medicaid and Medicare amendments to the Social Security Act provided access to health care for the poor and elderly; and the Economic Opportunity Act of 1965, which provided an umbrella for several important initiatives, including Head Start, the Job Corps, the Legal Services Corporation, Model Cities, and the Community Action Program.

The Community Action Program (CAP) quickly became the most controversial facet of the War on Poverty. Because local CAPs administered programs independently of municipal government, they were viewed skeptically by city officials. In many cities, militant African Americans had been organizing minority residents around the theme of "black power," so when CAPs were required to have one-third representation of the poor in decision making, organizers saw this as an opportunity to challenge the power structure at city hall. Eruptions around issues of racial and economic injustice soon followed, to which mayors reacted strongly.[6] The instability generated by "citizen participation" in poverty programs was punctuated by urban riots of the mid-1960s, which were attributed to the prevalence of racism and the absence of opportunity for the poor.[7] Turbulence in federal urban policy was addressed in the Housing and Community Development Act of 1974, which reassigned virtually all of the CAP programs to other agencies, dismantling CAPs as they were known, and relegated participation of the poor to an advisory function. Reinforcing the role of metropolitan government, the 1974 Act incorporated a range of programs—including urban redevelopment and beautification, Model Cities, neighborhood improvement, and historic preservation—which were budgeted at $11 billion for 1978 to 1980. By 1981, the Department of Housing and Urban Development (HUD), the primary agency through which urban policy was implemented, subsidized about 3.5 million housing units.[8] Limited though the federal role was in urban affairs, it would prove ineffectual at countering the social and economic dislocations of the 1980s.

AN URBAN DIASPORA

During the 1970s and early 1980s, substantial shifts in demography and capital affected American cities as millions of Americans abandoned older, industrial cities for the "sunbelt." John Kasarda reported that between 1975 and 1985, "the South and West accounted for more than 85 percent of the nation's population growth."[9] The consequence for select cities is depicted in Table 4.1.

Most of the explosive growth of southern and western cities was fed by flight from urban areas of the Northeast and Midwest. Residents left behind in older cities tended to be minorities. Accordingly, between 1975 and 1985, the minority population of northeastern cities increased from 33 to 42 percent.[10]

The flight of whites and capital from older cities had a devastating impact on poorer neighborhoods. In an analysis of racial segregation in American cities, Douglas Massey and Nancy Denton developed the concept of "hypersegregation" to refer to those cities in which African Americans tended to live together in separate enclaves. Using a segregation index, Massey and Denton chronicled the experience of larger American cities in which more than 60 percent of the black population lived in a distinct ghetto. (See Table 4.2.)

In 1970, sixteen cities were hypersegregated; by 1980, the degree of hypersegregation had dropped only 4.4 percent. Between 1980 and 1990, the degree of hypersegregation fell less: 3.2 percent, reflecting further slowing of

TABLE 4.1 Population changes of selected major cities

City	Population (in thousands)		Percentage Change
	1970	1984	
St. Louis	622.2	429.3	−31.0
Detroit	1,511.3	1,089.0	−27.9
Cleveland	751.0	546.5	−27.2
Buffalo	462.8	339.0	−26.8
Pittsburgh	520.2	402.6	−22.6
Los Angeles	2,816.1	3,096.7	+10.0
Dallas	844.2	974.2	+15.4
San Antonio	654.3	842.8	+28.8
San Diego	696.6	960.5	+37.9
Houston	1,232.4	1,705.7	+38.4
Phoenix	581.6	853.3	+46.7

SOURCE: P. Dearborn, "Fiscal Conditions in Large American Cities, 1971–1984," in M. McGeary and L. Lynn (eds.), *Urban Change and Poverty* (Washington, DC: National Academy Press, 1988), p. 256.

TABLE 4.2 Trends in black-white hypersegregation in sixteen metropolitan areas with largest black population, 1970–1990 (hypersegregation in percents)

Metropolitan Area	1970	1980	1990	1970–1980	1980–1990
Atlanta	82.1	78.5	67.8	−3.6	−10.7
Baltimore	81.9	74.7	71.4	−7.2	−3.3
Buffalo	87.0	79.4	81.8	−7.6	2.4
Chicago	91.9	87.8	85.5	−4.1	−2.3
Cleveland	90.8	87.5	85.1	−3.3	−2.4
Dallas–Ft. Worth	86.9	77.1	63.1	−9.8	−14.0
Detroit	88.4	86.7	87.6	−1.7	.9
Gary–Hammond–E. Chicago	91.4	90.6	89.9	−.8	−.7
Indianapolis	81.7	76.2	74.3	−5.5	−1.9
Kansas City	87.4	78.9	72.6	−8.5	−6.3
Los Angeles–Long Beach	91.0	81.1	73.1	−9.9	−8.0
Milwaukee	90.5	83.9	82.6	−6.6	−1.1
New York	81.0	82.0	82.2	1.0	.2
Newark	81.4	81.6	82.5	.2	.9
Philadelphia	79.5	78.8	77.2	−.7	−1.6
St. Louis	84.7	81.3	77.0	−3.4	−4.3
				Average −4.4	Average −3.2

Adapted from Douglas Massey and Nancy Denton, *American Apartheid* (Cambridge, MA: Harvard University Press, 1993), p. 222.

the already minimal mobility of urban blacks. Despite two decades of social programs following the War on Poverty, most blacks continued to live in ghettos.

Yet geographical residency fails to reflect the opportunity losses that accompanied the flight of whites and capital from American cities. John Kasarda examined the plight of poorly skilled, inner-city residents who had problems finding employment when many jobs had migrated to the suburbs. As Table 4.3 shows, the consequences of poor education and joblessness for urban residents varied considerably by race.

During the past three decades, the employment prospects of black high school dropouts has plummeted, exceeding 50 percent in every region of the United States. Yet attaining a high school diploma was no guarantee of a job for young African Americans either; in every region, the percentage of black high school graduates not working more than doubled since the late 1960s. A similar, but less severe, dynamic affected whites. During the past three decades, the percent of working age, white males not in school and not working spiked upward, indicating increasing scarcity for low-skilled jobs. As has been the case for blacks, whites who did not follow jobs as they left the inner city faced significant obstacles in finding work.

As the prospects of poor, inner city, minority families dimmed, references to an American "underclass" surfaced in discussions of urban affairs. Indeed, Massey

TABLE 4.3 Out-of-school males aged 16–64 not working and residing in the central city, by race, education, and region for selected metropolitan areas

REGION Race & Education Level	1968–1970	1980–1982	1990–1992
NORTHEAST			
White			
Less than High School	15%	34%	37%
High School Graduate Only*	7	17	24
Black			
Less than High School	19	44	57
High School Graduate Only	11	27	31
MIDWEST			
White			
Less than High School	12	29	34
High School Graduate Only	5	16	18
Black			
Less than High School	24	52	63
High School Graduate Only	10	30	41
SOUTH			
White			
Less than High School	7	15	18
High School Graduate Only	3	9	19
Black			
Less than High School	13	29	52
High School Graduate Only	1	19	22
WEST			
White			
Less than High School	18	20	26
High School Graduate Only	10	16	19
Black			
Less than High School	26	44	57
High School Graduate Only	13	14	43

*Completed high school, but no higher education completed. Northeast includes Boston, Newark, New York, Philadelphia, and Pittsburgh; Midwest includes Cleveland, Chicago, Detroit, Milwaukee, and St. Louis; South includes Atlanta, Dallas, Houston, Miami, and New Orleans; West includes Denver, Long Beach, Los Angeles, Oakland, Phoenix, San Francisco, and Seattle.
SOURCE: John Kasarda, "Industrial Restructuring and the Consequences of Changing Job Locations," in Reynolds Farley (ed.), *Changes and Challenges: America 1990* (New York: Russell Sage Foundation, 1995), Table 5.15.

and Denton went so far as to suggest a recipe for creating an underclass—virtually, replicate the experiences of blacks in the United States:

> Throughout U.S. history, the wealthy of all groups have sought to put distance between themselves and the poor. As their levels of education, income, and occupational statuses have risen, Jews, Italians, Poles, Mexicans, and Asians have all sought improved housing in better neighborhoods not dominated by their own ethnic group. What distinguishes blacks from everyone else is that this process of normal spatial mobility

occurs within a segregated housing market. As a result of racial segregation, middle-class blacks are less able to achieve a neighborhood commensurate with their socioeconomic status, and poor blacks are forced to live under conditions of unparalleled poverty.[11]

In no small irony, the Eisenhower Foundation marked the twenty-fifth anniversary of the Kerner Commission report with an admonition:

> We conclude that the famous prophesy of the Kerner Commission, of two societies, one black, one white—separate and unequal—is more relevant today than in 1968, and more complex, with the emergence of multiracial disparities and growing income segregation.[12]

Inexcusably, much of the collapse of poor, minority neighborhoods in older American cities escaped the attention of social scientists. During the 1970s, liberal academics who could have brought the social implosion of older American cities to public attention were dissuaded from doing so. The furor following the publication of Daniel Patrick Moynihan's report, *The Negro Family: A Case for National Action* in 1965,[13] made it emphatically clear to social researchers that investigations of the dysfunctional features of African-American families would not go unchallenged. Instead, researchers were encouraged to focus on the strengths of African-American families in order to identify how, under the most adverse of circumstances, so many had persevered. The consequence of this, as William Julius Wilson argued later, was the failure of the academic research community to chronicle the considerable deterioration of African-American institutions in urban areas during the period.[14] Despite a half-century of academic research in urban affairs, university scholars so assiduously avoided studying the problems faced by poor, minority families, that public discussion of the underclass did not begin until journalist Ken Auletta portrayed the plight of the persistently poverty-stricken in his book, *The Underclass,* published in 1982.[15] The reluctance of liberal social scientists to chronicle the deterioration of life in inner city ghettos coincided nicely with an incoming Reagan administration, which held as a primary tenet that social problems were artificial constructs by academics: City life was not all that bad.

THE REAGAN REVOLUTION

With the inauguration of Ronald Reagan, a half-century of "progress" in federal urban policy abruptly came to an end. The federal reversal of aid to cities was the result of a dual strategy: divesting the federal government of its responsibility for social problems while assigning that task to subordinate levels of government (federalism), and delegating as much of the program function as possible to nongovernmental providers (privatization). By the end of the 1980s, federalism and privatization had had a profound impact on the welfare of America's cities and their peoples.

For the record, it is important to recognize that the Reagan legacy in urban policy was not completely remiss. During the early 1980s, much legislative attention was directed at an initiative that promised to lure industry into the nation's most economically depressed communities. Pioneered in Great Britain and imported to the United States by Stuart Butler, a British analyst recruited by the conservative Heritage Foundation, the Urban Enterprise Zone (UEZ) concept was poised as the Republican antithesis to a series of Democratic urban programs. In designating UEZs, government would offer business special considerations, such as tax rebates, reductions in the minimum wage, and the waiving of certain occupational and health protections in order to induce firms to relocate in poor areas. Aggressively promoted by then-Representative Jack Kemp, UEZ legislation attracted the endorsement of such disparate groups as conservative ideologues, Democratic mayors, and civil rights organizations.[16] Yet obstructionism on the part of a Democratic Congress coupled with the glaring incompetence in the administration of HUD, effectively killed any prospect that UEZs would become national policy. The UEZ concept remained the most viable urban policy option for President Bush, though his administration also failed to persuade Congressional Democrats to pass enabling legislation.

Federalism and privatization provided a powerful rationale for the withdrawal of the federal government in urban policy. From 1980 to 1988, federal spending for housing decreased from $27.9 billion to $9.7 billion.[17] As a result, the supply of low-income housing failed to keep pace with the number of poor households. While the number of poor renter households increased by 3.2 million between 1974 and 1985, the number of low-rent units fell by 2.8 million.[18] This, of course, aggravated homelessness during the same period.

Federal grants to cities declined sharply during the Reagan administration. In the years immediately preceding the Reagan Revolution, federal urban aid had increased dramatically. Between 1975 and 1980, federal aid to subordinate levels of government for community development block grants had increased from $38 million to $3.9 *billion*. Toward the end of Reagan's second term, however, federal aid to the cities actually declined to $3.3 billion by 1987. Similarly, the federal contribution for community services block grants decreased from $557 million in 1980 to $354 million in 1986.[19] The House Ways and Means Committee reported that "for HUD's programs alone, appropriations of budget authority declined (in 1989 dollars) from a high of $57 billion in 1978 to a low of $9 billion in 1989."[20]

From the offices of the nation's mayors, the federal retreat from urban affairs must have been horrifying. In 1973, over 70 percent of metropolitan revenue was derived from federal sources; by 1987, the revenue flow was negative, meaning that cities were actually exporting cash *to* the federal government.[21] By 1991, 13 states faced revenue shortfalls exceeding 10 percent of the previous year's budget.[22] In an attempt to reconcile a $3.5 billion budget gap, New York Mayor David Dinkins proposed a "doomsday budget" and layed off 10,000 city workers.²³ The following year the League of California Cities reported that more than 50 percent of cities in that state had had to delay major construction projects, use reserves, or raise taxes and fees to balance their budgets.²⁴

Still, in some respects the Reagan administration paled in its dunning of urban programs compared to that of its successor. The Bush administration budget for 1991 proposed to further reduce federal assistance for low-income housing by 4.2 percent. For the same year, federal allocations for community development block grants dropped to $2.7 billion, and federal support for community services block grants plummeted to only $42 million.²⁵ In terms of urban policy, President Bush's reference to a "kinder and gentler" America proved vacuous. The Bush administration's failure to reverse a decade of federal neglect of cities served to darken an already bleak metropolitan landscape.

THE RISE OF THE UNDERCLASS

As the white population fled industrial urban areas, the economic base of America's cities changed dramatically—blue-collar jobs requiring less education vanished and were replaced by those of the information and service sectors. This penalized particularly the unskilled and poorly educated minority population left behind in industrial cities of the Northeast and Midwest. Kasarda concluded:

> Unfortunately, the northern cities that have lost the greatest numbers of jobs with lower educational requisites during the past three decades, have simultaneously experienced large increases in the number of their minority residents, many of whom are workers whose limited educations preclude their employment in the new urban growth industries.²⁶

Poor urban families were to find little succor from the Reagan administration. Within seven months of assuming office, President Reagan showed his hand on poverty programs by signing the Omnibus Budget Reconciliation Act (OBRA) of 1981. OBRA proceeded on a dual track, cutting public assistance benefits and combining categorical programs into a Social Services Block Grant. The new AFDC eligibility guidelines were particularly punitive since they were directed at poor families who were participating in the labor force. Suddenly, AFDC family heads who were trying to improve their economic lot found that (1) they could deduct only $160 per month per child for child care; (2) the deduction for work expenses was limited to $75 per month; and (3) the earned income disregard (the first $30 per month and one-third of income thereafter) was eliminated after four months.²⁷ As if to strangle the welfare bureaucracy in paperwork, OBRA required the welfare department to redetermine *monthly* the eligibility of those on AFDC who insisted on working. These, among other measures, had an immediate impact on the AFDC rolls: 408,000 families lost eligibility altogether, and another 299,000 had their benefits reduced.²⁸ Significantly, OBRA disentitled working poor families; 5 percent of the total AFDC caseload became ineligible due to OBRA, and "about 35 percent of those who were working were terminated by the legislation."[29]

For most of the families made ineligible for AFDC by the provisions of OBRA, loss of benefits further submerged them in poverty. Monthly income loss ranged from $229 in Dallas to $115 in Boston.[30] Former AFDC beneficiaries in these cities had also lost Medicaid coverage. In Dallas, 59.2 percent of terminated families could not secure alternative health insurance; in Boston, it was 27.5 percent.[31] A study of AFDC families in Georgia found that 79 percent fell *below* the poverty level as a result of OBRA, compared to 70 percent before 1981.[32] An investigation of the quality of life of 129 AFDC families in New Jersey that had lost benefits was Dickensian in its portrayal.

> More than half the families were below the poverty level, 4 out of 10 families did not have enough to eat, 2 out of 10 were spending less than the amount required to provide a minimally adequate diet, almost 3 out of 4 had problems paying rent and utility bills, and most significantly, nearly 8 out of 10 families had to forego or delay medical and/or dental care.[33]

Despite changes in tax policy that benefited low-income workers, particularly increased tax expenditures through the Earned Income Tax Credit, the poor fared badly during the 1980s. The tax rebates given the poor through tax policy failed to compensate for the losses of benefits through welfare programs. "Low-income families, especially the working poor, lost appreciably more by cuts in government services than they gained in tax reduction," admitted conservative analyst Kevin Phillips.[34]

Increasingly reliant on public assistance programs that were not indexed for inflation, poor minorities saw their benefits drop precipitously during the 1980s. Between 1970 and 1994 the value of AFDC benefits declined 47 percent due to inflation. Combining benefits for Food Stamps and AFDC left the 1993 median benefit for an American family of three at $661 per month—31 percent below the poverty level.[35] In 1983, the median worth in assets of nonwhite and Hispanic families was only $6,900, 12.7 percent of that of white families; but by 1989, it had fallen to $4,000, 6.8 percent of that of white families.[36]

The consequences of such deterioration in life opportunity were predictable enough. Many urban neighborhoods began to show characteristics that were qualitatively different—and more troubling—than those of communities that were simply poor. "What distinguishes members of the underclass from those of other economically disadvantaged groups," wrote William Julius Wilson, "is that their marginal economic position or weak attachment to the labor force is uniquely reinforced by the neighborhood or social milieu."[37] By the 1990s, areas of many industrial cities were imploding.[38] The "wilding" of New York teenagers who savagely beat a female jogger was replicated when a gang of Boston youth raped and murdered a young mother.[39] Gang killings in Los Angeles soared 69 percent during the first eight months of 1990.[40] Gang-related murders in the nation's capital reached a three-year high, leading the police department's spokesperson to quip, "at the rate we're going the next generation is going to be extinct."[41]

Observers of urban poverty described a serious deterioration in inner-city communities of the 1980s contrasted to those of the 1960s. "In many of our major cities, we are facing something very like social regression," wrote Daniel Patrick Moynihan.[42] "It is defined by extraordinary levels of self-destructive behavior, interpersonal violence, and social class separation intensive in some groups, extensive in others."[43] Even social institutions usually thought safe from violence succumbed: during the 1993-1994 school year, students of New York City public schools committed 4,011 violent crimes against teachers and staff.[44]

Into the socioeconomic vacuum that had developed in the poorest urban neighborhoods, the sale and consumption of drugs became central to community life, affecting young African Americans disproportionately. As of 1988, 43 percent of those convicted of drug trafficking were African American. In New York, Hispanics and African Americans accounted for 92 percent of arrests for drug offenses in 1989. In 1990, a criminal justice reform organization, the Sentencing Project, reported that one-fourth of all African-American males between the ages of twenty and twenty-nine were incarcerated, on parole, or on probation. Harvard economist Richard Freeman calculated that 35 percent of all African-American males aged 16 to 35 had been arrested in 1989.[45] By the early 1990s, data indicated that the urban minority poor were increasingly segregated into an underclass. Government programs that were essential for integrating the minority poor into the American mainstream had been withdrawn, leaving behind an ever-mounting heap of social debris. Yet, as the life opportunities of urban minorities collapsed during the 1980s, those of suburban whites took an entirely different turn.

PLUMPING THE OVERCLASS

While industrial urban areas withered, postindustrial cities expanded dramatically as a result of massive infusions of capital. Rejuvenating the economy had been a primary concern for the Reagan administration, especially after a blistering campaign assault on the "stagflation" that plagued the Carter presidency. More immediately, the severe depression of the early 1980s made it imperative that the administration move swiftly. In short order, Congress agreed to a sizable tax cut that benefited wealthy individuals and corporations, and it stripped much of the regulatory red tape from the financial industry. The latter action would ultimately lead to the greatest financial debacle in the nation's history—the Savings and Loan (S&L) scandal. Through the deregulation of the S&L industry, supply-side Reaganauts abetted by laissez-faire Democrats created an enormous development program—one that ultimately favored the burgeoning cities of the "sunbelt" at the expense of those of the "rustbowl."

By deregulating the financial industry, the Reagan administration was able to replace a diminished, yet enduring, government urban policy with a de facto corporate policy that outspent federal programs of the previous half-century. The amount of this "corporate urban policy" was roughly the amount taxpayers would fork over during the 1990s to repay depositors for money lost to speculative investments, primarily in real estate—between $300 and $500 billion.[46] Because S&Ls in conservatorship tend to be located in the sunbelt, the S&L bailout represented an unprecedented, intranational transfer of funds. According to financial analyst Edward Hill, 37 states would finance the liquidation of debt incurred in the other 13 states. Of these, several stood to gain substantially: "Texas will receive 43.2 percent of the gross bailout funds, followed by Arkansas (7 percent), Florida (6.8 percent), California (6.7 percent), New Mexico (5.1 percent), Louisiana (4.6 percent), Arizona (4.2 percent)." Correspondingly, the bailout would penalize the "frostbelt" states in the amount of $123 billion.[47] In presenting his analysis, Hill identified the bailout as an "economic development program in the same sense that debt forgiveness" is offered to third-world nations, except in reverse. "The bulk of the transfer will be coming from the Northeast and Midwest, regions that have been trying to renew their economies. The recipients are mainly located in regions that have experienced rapid job growth," noted Hill. "Money capital is being taken from regions that are attempting to renew their infrastructure, or physical capital, and given to regions with the newest physical capital."[48]

Although the S&L scandal has substantial implications for urban policy, it also affects the national culture. If one aspect of the Reagan legacy in urban policy is the rise of the "underclass" due to cutting benefits to the poor, its corollary is the rise of the "overclass" as a result of tax cuts for the wealthy, and fiscal wheeling and dealing. In an exhaustive analysis of the excesses of the Reagan era, Kevin Phillips profiled the American "plutocracy" that emerged during the 1980s, concluding that "corporate executives and investors were the prime 1980s beneficiaries."[49]

The following is Sidney Blumenthal's acerbic portrayal.

> The overclass is the distorted mirror image of a caricature of the underclass. It is not the old establishment of Prescott Bush, George's father; it is, rather, the demimonde of rentiers who, under Reagan, elbowed their way to the top, where they hastily built mahogany-paneled offices to create an aura of settled legitimacy. This overclass piled up vast wealth shuffling junk bonds, paper assets, and real estate. Its monuments are not factories but Atlantic City casinos and boarded-up department stores. The overclass battened under Reagan; under Bush it sought to consolidate its respectability.[50]

Yet, the contradictions posed by an ostentatious overclass could not be so facilely reconciled with a stricken underclass. Consider that the $1 billion in indiscretions of the Silverado S&L—in which the former-President Bush's son, Neil, was implicated—easily exceeded the $691 million proposed by his father in aid for the homeless for 1991. Or, that the amount taxpayers would absolve

Lincoln S&L's Charles H. Keating, Jr., of $2.5 billion, eclipsed what the Bush administration proposed for the Women, Infants, and Children Supplemental Food Program for 1991.[51]

THE INNER CITY BESIEGED

By the early 1990s, many American cities were convulsing from the excesses and inadequacies of the Reagan/Bush era. Opulent, gated communities for the overclass sprang up in the sunbelt, leaving older, rustbowl cities with fewer resources to serve an increasingly troublesome underclass. Federal divestiture of its obligation to aid distressed urban areas left mayors with little recourse but to appeal to state legislatures for aid. When this proved unsatisfactory, the only solution was to cut city services. As poor, minority families struggled to make money through work, work began to prove increasingly futile. The outmigration of unskilled and semiskilled jobs coupled with cutbacks in social welfare programs left families destitute—without a traditional means of support.

For many observers, the results were predictable: a dramatic increase in antisocial, deviant behavior. Having lost their grounding in established community institutions and their orientation to a morally acceptable code of conduct, many of the minority poor sought refuge on the social margin. Incapable of meeting social expectations conventionally and denied supplemental support through public programs, a critical mass grew to the point that its presence began to disrupt daily metropolitan life. It reached the critical point in Los Angeles when a jury acquitted police of charges of beating Rodney King, generating the worst riot in recent memory. Although marginalization of the poor was evident in a variety of ways, in public view, that alienation was manifest in two primary problems: drug-related gang violence and homelessness.

Gang Violence

By 1990, American cities seemed to be vying for the title of murder capital of the nation. The murder rate of Boston was up 45 percent over 1989; Denver, 29 percent; New Orleans, Dallas, and Chicago, over 20 percent; Los Angeles, 16 percent; New York, 11 percent. Yet none eclipsed Washington, DC, which continued to report the greatest number of homicides. Whereas poverty, drugs, and hopelessness were widely reported as responsible for the malignancy ravaging cities, journalists also attributed "a new street ethic that in many cases almost requires young men to commit murder to prove manhood."[52] The National Center for Health Statistics noted that the firearm death rate for adolescents aged 15 to 19 had risen to 23.5 per 100,000, the highest in the nation's history. From 1985 to 1990, the rate of gun deaths for black teenage males tripled, reaching 105.3 deaths per 100,000 people.[53] "We're talking about younger and younger kids committing more and more serious crimes," observed Jeff Modisett, an Indianapolis prosecuting attorney; "Violence is becoming a way of life."[54]

None of this was supposed to happen. Demographers had traced the social consequences of the baby boom, and they predicted that late adolescent deviance would abate as the baby boom aged.[55] Although the S&L and junk bond scandals suggest that a few well-heeled boomers successfully navigated the shoals of justice and emerged as pillars of white-collar crime, their numbers were small. On the contrary, minority youth engaged in drug-related street crime have rocketed crime rates upward. Despite a five-year reduction in cocaine use, in 1991 the number of weekly cocaine users jumped 29 percent. Cocaine-related emergency room admissions increased 30 percent, to 25,370 from April to June of 1991.[56]

During the Reagan/Bush administrations, federal efforts to control drug-related urban violence favored interdiction over treatment. Federal funds for law enforcement increased from $800 million in 1981 to $1.9 billion in 1986; yet funding for prevention, education, and treatment decreased from $404 million in 1981 to $338 million in 1985, a drop of 40 percent when adjusted for inflation.[57] By 1991 the "war on drugs" cost federal, state, and local government $23.7 billion.[58] Despite such massive infusion of funds, by the late 1980s, most experts were admitting that supply interdiction had failed. "We have not yet come to understand the resolute, determined, amoral nature of the major drug traffickers or their enormous power," concluded the late Sidney Cohen, former Director of the Division of Narcotic Addiction and Drug Abuse of the National Institute of Mental Health.

> Perhaps we do not even recognize that, for tens of hundreds of thousands of field workers, collecting coca leaves or opium gum is a matter of survival. At the other end of the pipeline is the swarm of sellers who could not possibly earn a fraction of their current income from legitimate pursuits. If they are arrested, they are out after a short detention. If not, many are waiting to take their place.[59]

If efforts to dampen the import of illicit drugs were proving futile, control of street selling was no less so. A kilogram of cocaine that wholesaled in 1981 for $60,000 was only $10,000 by the late 1980s.[60] The price of crack-cocaine was so low that suppliers were offering free hits to recruit new users, charging regulars as little as $2.[61] Still, conservative lawmakers pushed a hard line, insisting that drug abusers be incarcerated. By the early 1990s, the number of inmates in American prisons topped 1 million. The U.S. incarceration rate was second to Russia, and exceeded that of other developed nations: England and Wales by a factor of 5, Japan by a factor of 14. Drug-related convictions played a central role in the inmate increase; between 1980 and 1992, the number of prisoners convicted of drug infractions increased fivefold.[62] Frustrated with the futility of more prosaic efforts to contain rampant drug abuse, the Bush administration went for the headlines, invading Panama and arresting Manuel Noriega on drug charges.

In the absence of federal success in controlling illegal drugs, states experimented with different tactics. Prominent among them was the idea of "boot camps" for first-time offenders. At such boot camps,

> inmates would receive physical training, military discipline, and drug-abuse treatment, all under the direction of military personnel and with the aim of preparing them for a life that would combine . . . the requirement of regular drug tests and the opportunity for gainful employment.[63]

Resonating with public perceptions that drug thugs got light sentences, boot camps had been developed in 25 states by 1993. Just as rapidly, however, enthusiasm faded. A study of Georgia facilities commissioned by the Justice Department concluded that boot camps failed as deterrents for young offenders. "There is no reason to believe that individuals on the street will be deterred by the threat of serving time in a boot camp prison," concluded researcher Doris MacKenzie.[64] Not long thereafter, Connecticut closed its National Guard boot camp citing "rampant gang activity, assaults on weaker inmates, marijuana use, sexual activity and gambling."[65] New York correctional officials reported mixed results with boot camps; although the state had saved $305 million since instituting the concept, the recidivism rate was no different for boot camp graduates than other inmates. The National Institute of Justice concurred, and after studying eight states, they noted that recidivism of boot camp inmates was similar to those in traditional correctional facilities.[66]

As city coffers emptied, mayors searched for more effective methods of social control. The idea of community policing captured the attention of many. Introduced in Houston by a new police chief during the early 1980s, dispersing police into neighborhood beats was a method for rehabilitating a reputation for brutality that had tarnished Houston's public safety department.[67] Police chief Lee Brown's redeployed officers became neighborhood diplomats in addition to their role as crime fighters. Community policing quickly picked up converts. For 1992, New York City budgeted $90 million for the city's Community Patrol Officers Program, which dispersed officers to 14 high-crime precincts.[68] Police officials serving suburban Baltimore claimed a 16-percent increase in public satisfaction with police services after instituting community policing.[69] After the Los Angeles riots in April 1992, incoming Chief of Police Willie Williams announced plans to introduce community policing in Los Angeles.[70] Meanwhile, other police officials were finding that community policing was not the panacea advocates had promised. As part of his 1991 campaign for mayor of Houston, Bob Lanier promised to get tough on crime. His first act was to terminate "neighborhood-oriented policing," and in three years crime dropped 30 percent.[71]

In light of disappointing state and local efforts to reduce gang predation, public debate about crime became more impassioned. The vicious murder of a California girl, Polly Klaas, by a felon on parole for multiple crimes galvanized state legislators who quickly enacted a "three strikes and you're out" law, mandating life imprisonment for three-time felons. Noting that U.S. prisons already held 925,000 inmates at the time, columnist David Broder suggested that such measures would bankrupt government.[72] California officials projected the need for $10 billion in new prison space during the 1990s in order to implement its law-and-order approach to crime.[73]

Jerome Skolnick noted the irony of locking up young offenders for life. For many gang members, prison was a rite of passage, validating a reputation unavailable by more conventional means. By incarcerating young offenders for ever-longer sentences, the subsequent program had become "the most expensive, taxpayer-supported middle-age and old-age (housing and medical care) entitlement program in the history of the world."[74] Skolnick was referring to the fact that the annual cost of maintaining an inmate in a state prison is about $20,000; at more humane federal correctional facilities, the cost rises to about $30,000.[75]

Homelessness

During the winter of 1982–1983, a homeless advocacy group, the Center for Creative Nonviolence (CCNV), established a mock cemetery on the Ellipse, a small park opposite the White House. Presumably, reasoned Mitch Snyder of CCNV, viewing the false headstones commemorating the homeless who had died of exposure would lead the Reagan administration to more humane treatment of the destitute poor. One headstone noted that in 1976, 671 homeless Americans had died of exposure; by 1977, the number had risen to 898; for 1978, 928. In testimony before Congress, CCNV put the number of homeless at 2.2 million during the early 1980s, a figure they contended would swell as a result of cuts in poverty programs exacted by Reagan.[76] When other guerrilla tactics, such as mock funeral processions, failed to move an intransigent District of Columbia City Council or the Reagan administration, Snyder began a hunger strike—one of many that would permanently impair his vision—eventually forcing the opening of shelters for the homeless. As significantly, Mitch Snyder had become something of a national figure—the spokesman for the homeless.

Lack of leadership from a less than sympathetic Reagan administration compounded by federal cuts in social programs not only drove the number of homeless higher but also made it the *cause célèbre* of the Left. Liberals responded to an increasingly destitute number of homeless persons by establishing shelters when facilities could be located or at least soup kitchens when circumstances permitted. By 1981, there were 30,850 shelter beds in 182 cities; by 1989, the number had risen to 116,730.[77] Complementing the array of programs, a small but dogged group of grass-roots organizers promoted care for these most destitute of Americans. As the numbers of homeless grew, so, it seemed to them, had their composition. Initially consisting predominantly of single men, a growing number of the homeless were families with young children. The plight of homeless families was dramatized in Jonathan Kozol's *Rachel and Her Children,* an account of a homeless family in New York. Citing the purposeful underestimation of the number of homeless on the part of the

Reagan administration, Kozol put the number of homeless at "between 2 and 3 million," agreeing with Snyder that the magnitude of the problem was vastly greater than what was commonly believed.[78]

Eventually, impressionistic depictions of homelessness gave way to more scientific assessments of the population. Typical among them was a study of the Chicago homeless conducted in 1986.[79] Of the homeless studied there, 70 percent were male, 69 percent were black, the average age was 37 years, and the average education was 10.9 years. The study indicated that the homeless were a troubled group: 16 percent had been hospitalized for mental problems, and 20 percent exhibited symptoms of alcoholism. Whereas a majority, 52 percent, were single, 18 percent were single parents. Most, 60 percent, received some form of public assistance. Despite the adversity of homelessness, 32 percent of the homeless worked. Predictably, much of the monthly income of those working, $243.38, was consumed by rent, $137.71 per month, leaving the working homeless dependent on shelters for some period during the month.[80]

The picture that emerges from the Chicago study is one of complexity. About one-third of the homeless have serious problems with substance abuse or mental disorders that impair their judgment. About one-fifth are responsible for young children. About one-third work, but at very low wages. Accordingly, any attempt to remedy homelessness necessitates multiple approaches. Recognition of the diversity of the homeless population represents the maturation of homeless advocates. Clearly, they had come a long way from the early simplification offered by Kozol: *The cause of homelessness is lack of housing.*[81]

As homeless advocates used hyperbole to state the case for more services for the down-and-out, academics were gradually developing a more precise understanding of the magnitude of the problem. During the late 1980s, Martha Burt of the Urban Institute assessed homelessness in 20 American cities and put the number between 500,000 to 600,000. Burt criticized those who estimated that the homeless numbered 2 to 3 million, a figure that represented one percent of the U.S. population. According to calculations based on the use of shelter beds, Burt figured the rate of homelessness at about 0.2 percent of the population. Still, according to her calculations, the number of homeless has risen markedly during the 1980s, roughly tripling between 1981 and 1989.[82]

The 1990 census gave demographers an unprecedented opportunity to obtain more definitive data. Toward that end, the Census Bureau deployed 15,000 census interviewers on one March 1990 evening to literally count each homeless individual. But this strategy was not without problems: Suspecting the one-night count would suppress a more accurate—and much higher—census, CCNV's Mitch Snyder urged the homeless not to cooperate. Subsequently, many agreed that the Census Bureau's tabulation of 228,821 homeless was much too low.[83]

In a later review of research on homelessness, Christopher Jencks suspected that Burt's figures were a little high. Jencks guessed the number of homeless in March 1980 at 125,000, increasing to 216,000 by January 1984. For 1987 to 1988, the period when many city surveys were conducted, Jencks figured the number of homeless peaked at 402,000. By March 1990, he approximated the number of homeless had dropped to 324,000, primarily due to a low unemployment rate.[84] During the anti-welfare 1980s, Jencks indicates the number of homeless increased two and a half times. That, he noted, is a substantial increase, yet it was far below the 3 million number pulled out of the air by Snyder. Without saying as much, Jencks suggested that homeless advocates had misled the public, overestimating the number of homeless by a factor of ten. Assuming Burt's figures were more accurate, the deception was somewhat less: The number of homeless had only been overestimated by a factor of five.

Accuracy in counting the homeless was rather academic given the intransigence of the Reagan and Bush administrations. Between 1987 and 1991, when the number of homeless was peaking, only $2.3 billion was actually spent out of $3.4 billion authorized under the Stewart B. McKinney Act. For 1992, the Bush administration proposed spending only $776 million of the $1.13 billion authorized for the homeless. "This amount sounds substantial," observed homelessness researcher Joel Blau, "but by the time these funds had been distributed throughout the whole country, they had thinned out into a vital, though insufficient, resource."[85]

In the winter of 1993, one incident symbolized the urgency of making cities habitable. Three days after Thanksgiving, a 43-year-old homeless woman lay down on a bench to sleep in Washington, DC. Yetta Adams had children, but they were grown; she had been homeless for a decade, a condition that aggravated her chronic depression and diabetes. She was well known to workers of the shelters she had frequented, but for her last night, she chose not to seek help from a shelter, nor did she use the $300 in her possession to rent a room. As the temperature sank into the low 30s, Adams lost what tenuous hold she had on life. When her body was found the following morning, police reported that she had died in front of the office of Henry Cisneros, Secretary of the Department of Housing and Urban Development.[86]

Cisneros immediately recognized the irony of Adams's death—since being appointed by Bill Clinton, homelessness had been his top priority at HUD.[87] Cisneros attended Adams's funeral, then redoubled his efforts to revitalize American cities. He did not have much to work with. The administration announced a $2 billion cut in HUD's budget for housing assistance, almost halving the $4.2 billion available for public housing.[88] Meanwhile, the White House urged Congress to increase funding for the homeless, hoping to double appropriations to $1.7 billion by 1995. The objective was a comprehensive approach to homelessness featuring three basic components: emergency shelter, rehabilitative services, and permanent affordable housing.

On May 18, 1994, Cisneros announced the first of a set of demonstration grants to implement the service model: $20 million to the District of Columbia.[89] Three days later, Cisneros notified Los Angeles that it would receive a second $20 million grant.[90] Given White House disinterest in homelessness during the 1980s, homeless advocates eagerly anticipated the new funding, at the same time recognizing that it would not go far. Fred Karnas, director of a 40-city network of agencies serving the homeless, spoke for many: "It's doomed to disappoint," he said.[91]

That the Clinton administration would increase funding for the homeless by gouging appropriations for public housing did not set well with Vince Lane, Chairman of the Chicago Housing Authority. In 1988, Lane left his partnership in Urban Services and Development, a private development firm, to rehabilitate Chicago's notoriously crime-ridden public housing projects. On a salary of $1 a year, he quickly established a reputation for being innovative and impatient with housing reform, winning plaudits from liberals and conservatives alike.[92] Lane's popularity with public housing tenants soared when he began "sweeps" of entire high-rises—sealing off the building with police, ejecting nontenants, immediately painting and repairing apartments, then implementing a security system whereby only valid tenants could gain access to the building.[93]

Lane's long-range strategy for revitalizing public housing is grounded in "income mixing," limiting the number of poor families to a building so that more affluent, working families establish community norms. Lake Parc Place is an example of Lane's strategy. In the late 1980s, the building was typical of Chicago's public housing gulags. The halls reeked of urine; lights were smashed; members of the El Rukn gang patrolled the building. Closing the building, Lane diverted $14 million in HUD funds to enhance the security and landscaping, then put $60,000 into rehabilitating each apartment unit. Reopened, tenants to Lake Parc Place were carefully screened, and half of all units were reserved for middle-income working families. By the early 1990s, Lake Parc Place was proving a successful experiment for tenants, if an expensive one for the Chicago Housing Authority.[94]

But Lane's most recent campaign was to raise the ire of civil libertarians. Seeking to evict gangs from Robert Taylor Homes, a 28-block line of public housing high-rises, Lane authorized warrantless searches for weapons in units. Within one week, 15 shootings and 5 deaths had provoked Lane to place Fourth Amendment rights second to tenant safety. Tenants reported that gang members were using high-powered rifles to pick off rival thugs from the upper stories of high-rises.[95] During the summer of 1993, several children had fallen out of windows, but Housing Authority crews sent to install window guards were driven off by gang gunfire. Before the sweeps began, Lane consulted with 19 tenant councils, securing approval from 18 of them. The American Civil Liberties Union (ACLU) charged that the sweeps violated Fourth Amendment protections against "unreasonable" search and seizure, and obtained an injunction against further such action by the Housing Authority.[96] Whereas attorneys sought a compromise, such as incorporating permission for a weapons search in a tenant lease, Lane wondered how he could secure the remaining $300 million to rehabilitate Cabrini-Green, a 70-acre vertical ghetto of 91 buildings housing 7,000 poor families.[97]

THE CLINTON URBAN POLICY

President Clinton's strategy for dealing with increasing social and economic segregation of the urban poor appeared in *A Vision of Change for America*, released for his joint address to Congress in February 1993. In order to bolster a flagging economy, the president proposed a $16.3 billion stimulus package. Included in it were several urban aid programs: $1 billion for a youth summer employment program; $15 million for a National Service Program; $2.5 billion for an urban Community Development Block Grant; accelerating allocation of the $2.5 billion HOME housing program; and $423 million to support urban housing.[98] Banking on a Democratic Congress, Clinton anticipated that the economic stimulus package would be the first of a series of domestic policy initiatives marking his presidency. But this proved not to be the case. Unable to hold the allegiance of Senate Democrats or to claim Senate Republican defections, the stimulus package foundered before a filibuster led by Bob Dole.

A much-chastened Clinton tried again through his 1994 budget proposal. Laboring beneath the 1993 budget reconciliation act, which required that any increase in discretionary allocations be made up for by cuts in other programs or tax increases, the administration elected to straddle a very narrow budget fence, balancing specific program expansion with select program rescissions, a tax increase on the wealthy providing a small buffer. The result bore an uncanny resemblance to the budgets submitted by the Bush administration that often pulled funding from one social program to establish another—a fiscal shell game. (See Table 4.4.)

In the Clinton proposal, the only significant departure in urban aid was the introduction of an $800 million Project-Based Community Development Grants program.

TABLE 4.4 Proposed changes in select federal programs in urban aid

Program	Proposed FY 1995	Major Increases (in millions of dollars)	
		Increase	Increase
Housing Certificates and Vouchers	$2,743	$1,380	101.3%
Homeless Grants	1,120	275	32.5%
Summer Youth Employment	1,056	144	15.8%
Adult Training Grants	1,130	115	11.4%

Program	Proposed FY 1995	Major Decreases (in millions of dollars)	
		Decrease	Decrease
Emergency Food Assistance Program	$40	–$83	–67.5%
Elderly & Disabled Housing	553	–$1,056	–65.6%
Public & Indian Housing Construction	413	–349	–45.8%
HOME Housing Grants	$1,000	–309	–23.6%

Adapted from Paul Leonard and Robert Greenstein, *Life Under the Spending Caps* (Washington, DC: Center on Budget and Policy Priorities, 1994), p. 16.

A construct of fiscal frugality, the Clinton 1994 budget proposal diverted funding from existing urban programs to enhance others. In the shuffle, some programs took major hits. "Total fiscal year 1995 appropriations for housing programs serving low-income households would fall $856 million below fiscal year 1994 levels, after adjusting for inflation," reported the liberal Center on Budget and Policy Priorities.[99] Job training for the homeless was reduced from $13 million to $5 million, a reduction of 60.4 percent; funding for Severely Distressed Public Housing was cut from $799 million to $500 million, a reduction of 37.4 percent.[100] The Clinton 1995 budget would not be received enthusiastically by mayors having to contend with rising tides of homelessness and gang violence.

These reductions in discretionary appropriations were tactical concessions to conservative Democrats and Republicans who placed deficit reduction as a priority in budget policy. Clearly, the importance of deficit reduction had been highlighted by Ross Perot's presidential campaign, a grass-roots revolt that threatened to reignite if Congress failed to cut the deficit substantially. Constrained by the 1993 budget reconciliation agreement and influenced by the deficit reduction "hawks," who fell beneath Perot's shadow, Clinton's proposed 1994 budget passed each house of Congress by breathtakingly slim margins.

In substance, the Clinton vision of urban policy bore little resemblance to the ambitions voiced during the campaign. In part, this was due to circumstance: A deficit-reduction agreement negotiated during the Bush administration effectively placed the funding of entitlements above discretionary programs. Since most federal urban assistance programs were discretionary programs, they were at a disadvantage going into the budget process. On the other hand, the administration's leadership was anything but deft. In its first months, the White House staff displayed little political savvy. What limited political capital remained from an election won by a 43-percent plurality was squandered on a poorly timed economic stimulus package. Unfortunately for big-city mayors, many of the provisions of the stimulus package, so sorely needed to repair a neglected urban infrastructure, were characterized by Republicans as wasteful "tax-and-spend" programs that had tarred liberal Democrats. For Congressional deficit hawks, Clinton's attempts to redefine urban social programs as "investments" were nothing more than a smokescreen for a long-suspected liberal tendency toward domestic policy. By the time the White House regained its composure for the 1994 budget battle, many of the urban program measures of the stimulus package had been deleted.

The result of this misadventure in urban affairs was a budget grounded in monetary policy. Having cut federal social program obligations in order to reduce the budget deficit, the administration counted on private investors to keep interest rates low, thereby extending the economic recovery. Eventually, an expanding economy would benefit the nation: enhancing job opportunities, expanding production, and increasing tax revenues. To be sure, this was trickle-down economics, admittedly not the outcome Clinton had expected for his administration. On the heels of NAFTA, the administration's 1995 budget proposal looked anything but the product of a Democrat, even a conservative Democrat. In a moment of despair, Clinton admitted his budget resembled more that of a conservative Republican than a "new Democrat."[101]

To his credit, Clinton was at least candid in his intentions. He admitted that the concession for revitalizing a naggingly slow economic recovery was placating Wall Street, and that necessitated cuts in federal social programs. By contrast, Reagan had embarked on deregulating banking and commerce, leading to massive misappropriations of capital, the consequences of which both Reagan and Bush administrations were loath to admit. Conveniently oblivious to the sacking of the nation's S&Ls, the Republican presidents of the 1980s knew full well that publicly funded insurance would cover losses to depositors. In effect, taxpayers underwrote in the hundreds of billions of dollars the capricious investments fancied by Reagan-era financiers. Thus cornered by the consequences of the excessive 1980s, Clinton did what he had to—he stole from Peter to pay Paul. In so doing, the execution was not pleasant, nor was it masterful; but, in contrast to his predecessors, it was at least forthright.

THE NEXT URBAN POLICY AGENDA

Despite the constraints imposed by budget deficits, a feckless Congress, and a skeptical public, the Clinton administration's urban policy revealed tentative steps toward a mainstreaming strategy to counter social and economic segregation. The National Service Corps, limited to only 20,000 volunteers in its first year, was a heartening boost to a dormant civic ethic in American culture and offered at least minimal assistance to poor communities.[102] The allocation of $382 million for a nationwide system of community development banks to be modeled after Chicago's Shorebank provided badly needed capital and technical assistance to economically ravaged neighborhoods in older cities.[103] Unemployed workers in need of job retraining were doubtlessly encouraged by Clinton's announcement of a $13 billion employment training and counseling proposal that could enhance their upward mobility.[104] If such proposals showed a glimmer of new thinking, they also betrayed a fault: With minimal funding extended over five-year periods, they were unlikely to create the momentum necessary to reverse the decay characteristic of many urban neighborhoods. If the record of the Clinton White House would disappoint big-city mayors, the 1994 midterm elections in which Republicans gained control of Congress would throw them into a panic. No sooner had the ballots been counted than the incoming Speaker of the House—Newt Gingrich—promised that Clinton urban aid programs would be reviewed and all "pork" excised. Thus, if the Clinton administration offered tardy attempts to mainstream the urban poor, a conservative 104th Congress threatened to reverse even these small gains, further diminishing the prospect of urban reclamation.

In the absence of a coordinated initiative to salvage destitute neighborhoods, a politics of desperation has begun to pervade American cities. When federal and state government abrogated their responsibility to provide essential services to the minority poor during the 1980s, they became ripe for exploitation. Petty operators manipulated the deprivation of the urban poor for personal gain. Often drawing resources from philanthropy and government, poverty pimps easily profited from the poor, and in the process built personal empires. Hustlers, such as Al Sharpton,[105] exploited organizations that allegedly helped the downtrodden, but which were little more than "postmodern Tammany Halls"—organized manifestations of social opportunism and political cynicism. The complement of such predation consisted of the spontaneous acts of poor people driven by their despair with literally nothing to lose. For them, abandoned buildings and unsupervised goods became symbols of social justice denied. In Milwaukee, a Black Panther Militia threatened civil disorder, its uniformed members marching through poor neighborhoods;[106] in New York, the city's department of Housing Preservation and Development was confronted with illegal groups of squatters who took over condemned buildings, organized by a group calling itself Inner City Press/Community on the Move.[107] Acting like modern-day Robin Hoods, such groups have taken "guerilla welfare" to the streets, challenging the very governmental agencies that were supposed to help the poor. In both instances, the civic glue that had held inner cities together had crumbled.

In light of this erosion of civic values, the few demonstration projects that have accelerated the *upward* mobility of the underclass have been welcome. Indeed, together with the tentative steps of the Clinton administration, such initiatives, as listed below, could signal the beginning of an urban renaissance, provided such tentative beginnings are not quashed by Republicans during the 104th Congress.

Disperse Public Housing

The most prominent program designed to disperse public housing is the *Gautreaux* project in Chicago. Named after Dorothy Gautreaux, whose 1966 class action suit against the Chicago Housing Authority (CHA) on the grounds that it maintained segregation in housing patterns, the program will eventually provide housing vouchers to 7,100 minority families.[108] The *Gautreaux* ruling required the CHA to help families resettle outside the public housing projects that it maintained; by the early 1990s, over 4,500 families had been dispersed throughout metropolitan Chicago. Sadly, the 15-year delay in implementing the suit was of little use to Gautreaux, who died before its provisions were to take effect.

Because housing vouchers allowed CHA tenants to obtain housing on the private market without restrictions as to where they lived, researchers saw that the *Gautreaux* decision set up a de facto field experiment through which it would be possible to track the experience of low-income families. Would minority families who elected to move to integrated, suburban neighborhoods fare better than those who left the projects for predominantly black, inner city areas? Tracking families that were relocated through the *Gautreaux* ruling, researchers found that poor African-American families that moved to the suburbs prospered more than those that stayed in the city. "The suburban move greatly improved adult employment, and many adults were employed for the first time in their lives," concluded the researchers.

The suburban move also improved youths' education. Compared with city movers, the children who moved to the suburbs were more likely to be (1) in school, (2) in college-track classes, (3) in four-year colleges, (4) employed, and (5) employed in jobs with benefits and better pay. The suburban move led also to a considerable amount of social integration, friendships, and interaction with white neighbors in the suburbs.[109]

That the results of the *Gautreaux* experiment have been so uniformly positive has led John Bolger, a law professor at the University of North Carolina, to propose a National Fair Share Act, a 10-year, $5 billion program to disperse public housing tenants throughout the nation's metropolitan areas.[110]

Establish Youth Enterprise Zones

In order to combat drug-related gang violence in San Diego, Arthur Ellis began the Youth Economic Enterprise Zone (YEZ) program in 1990. Noting that minority youth had few socially acceptable alternatives outside of school, Ellis organized YEZ as a way to encourage gang-prone adolescents to establish their own businesses. "Part business school, part business incubator,"[111] YEZ introduces youth to the world of business through eight weeks of classroom work followed by six months of real work in small businesses. Among the early YEZ businesses were a magazine, and ventures in catering and apparel design.[112] Within a year, Ellis had captured the attention of the U.S. Department of Education, which provided $80,000 in funding for training the first cohorts of YEZ small business operators. During the second year of operation, YEZ expanded from its first storefront in one of San Diego's poorer neighborhoods to two additional disadvantaged communities. By the third year, the City of Phoenix adopted YEZ as a model for gang prevention. Ultimately, Ellis dreams of a youth-owned-and-operated shopping plaza where disadvantaged youngsters can trap the capital that is now leaving poorer neighborhoods. A YEZ strategy would complement other initiatives that focus on youth.

Through "Choice," an intensive program designed to steer at-risk youth away from gangs, advocates shepherd adolescents on a daily basis for three to six months, making certain they attend school, engage in constructive activities, and stay out of trouble. Choice reports that 73 percent of the youth it serves stay clear of trouble six months after they graduate from the program.[113] One of the more impressive ventures in revitalizing a predominantly poor, minority neighborhood, Boston's Dudley Street, relied on youth to assume major responsibilities. Beginning with a Youth Committee that was represented on the board of the Dudley Street Neighborhood Initiative (DSNI), Dudley Street kids undertook a range of activities to reverse negative stereotypes of minority youth and then developed a Young Architects and Planners group that reclaimed a drug-infested neighborhood park.[114] Programs such as Choice and DSNI represent the "empowerment" of poor minority communities, a capacity too often underappreciated. Hugh Price, the new president of the Urban League, echoes that refrain by his call to African Americans to "tithe with our time and, more importantly, our money" to help urban youth.[115]

Forge Urban Compacts

Innovative as they are, initiatives such as *Gautreaux* and YEZ are unlikely to reverse the rapid deterioration of cities in the absence of a strategy that addresses structural deficits. The varying capacity of American cities to maintain a productive economy—while ensuring essential services but without being overwhelmed by the minority poor—has been explored by David Rusk, former mayor of Albuquerque. Rusk differentiates between cities that enforce hypersegregation of the minority poor and "elastic" cities that expand economic and social resources. Traditional prescriptions for urban problems—the "Big Buck" strategy of liberals and the "Big Bootstrap" strategy of conservatives—both assume a degree of social and economic segregation that is as fatal for urban prosperity as it is for the life opportunities of the minority poor. Rusk lists essentials for metropolitan government:

1. "fair share" housing policies (supported by planning and zoning policies) that will encourage low- and moderate-income housing in all jurisdictions;
2. fair employment and fair housing policies to ensure full access by minorities to the job and housing markets;
3. housing assistance policies to disperse low-income families to small-unit, scattered-site housing projects and to rent-subsidized private rental housing throughout a diversified metro housing market; and
4. tax-sharing arrangements that will offset tax-base disparities between the central city and its suburbs.[116]

Given the federated nature of American government, how can multiple and often antagonistic levels of government be made to work in tandem to address transjurisdictional problems? An optimal strategy would be to design a template for urban assistance, an "urban compact." An urban compact would be a framework explicating specific program objectives; funding would be contingent on an organization's agreement to join the compact. As such, an urban compact would state the deficits of a metropolitan area and the steps taken to rectify them.[117] Accordingly, urban compact performance would determine the extent to which funding sources provide aid to specific metropolitan areas. In this sense, the urban compact would be a cross between a city's bond rating and an environmental impact statement. As an intergovernmental and intersectoral initiative, the overall design of the urban compact should be the product of a panel representing major public and private institutions, such as HUD, state and city government, major philanthropic foundations, the National Urban League, and the National Civic League, complemented by representatives of poor neighborhoods.

A prototype for an urban compact was forged early in 1994 when leaders of government, with help from a number of philanthropists, announced an $86.7 million package for low-income housing in 23 cities. Leveraging this urban investment was the National Community Development Initiative (NCDI), a coalition of corporations, government, and foundations organized by Peter Goldmark, Jr., president of the Rockefeller Foundation.[118] NCDI wisely drew from the experience of two nonprofit organizations with extensive experience in generating low-income housing: the Local Initiative Support Corporation and the Enterprise Foundation. Eventually, Goldmark projects, the initial investment will generate $660 million from other sources.[119] A bonus as large as NCDI's could prove instrumental in inducing cities to undertake the structural reforms required of an urban compact.

The key to reclaiming American cities is to mainstream the underclass. Through hypersegregation, a largely minority population has been consigned to a netherworld, a fate utterly inconsistent with the American ethos. Socially and economically isolated from the mainstream, the underclass evinces shocking levels of violence and predation. Immune from traditional controls on deviance, such as sanctions by community leaders and eviction from neighborhood institutions, young conscripts in the cadres of the underclass—gangs—have accepted early incarceration and premature death as facts of life. In so doing, they have gone far beyond flaunting social conventions; indeed, they have made a parody of the most extreme measures of social control.

In this context, much of the Clinton crime bill is flawed. The proposal contains provisions—adding 100,000 police to the nation's streets, locking up third-time felons for life, spending $10.5 billion on new prisons, and creating 50 new death-penalty crimes—that may resonate with voters, but would mean little to the petty "gangsta's" in our inner cities. The problem with the crime bill is not that it is punitive, but that it is irrelevant to much of what happens daily in underclass neighborhoods. On the other hand, the proposal's crime prevention provisions almost certainly have value—not because they would prevent crime, but that they would, in a very modest way, contribute to mainstreaming the underclass. Although the Clinton crime bill narrowly avoided Congressional sabotage,[120] the Republican Congressional victory of 1994 raised the doubts about its viability. No sooner had Republicans gained control of Congress than they announced they would revisit the crime bill and remove all the funding for prevention programs. Even more threatening, Republicans suggested radical surgery, dismantling entire federal agencies, such as HUD. The Clinton administration scrambled to position itself in front of the wave of events and proposed a three-part overhaul of the agency: consolidating 60 housing programs into three by 1998 (including a voucher program to replace public housing); devolving urban aid to states in the form of block grants; and transforming the Federal Housing Administration into a government-owned corporation. Thus restructured, the Clinton administration promised $800 million in savings over five years.[121]

This denouemont in urban policy borders on the tragic—given the circumstances in American cities. To be sure, some metropolitan areas appear to thrive, despite crumbling infrastructure, unprecedented levels of violence, and depletion of resources. But many cities teeter at a precipice with little hope of reclamation. David Rusk has ranked the most troubled cities in the nation according to three factors: population loss, percent minority population, and city-to-suburb income ratio. For want of a better classification system, Table 4.5 provides a plausible list of metropolitan areas most in need of assistance.

The American failure in urban policy, of which the Clinton record is but a small part, is one of will. Clearly, we have the resources to create solutions, as

TABLE 4.5 Cities in trouble

City	Population Loss by 1990	Minority Population	City-to-Suburb Income Ratio
1. East St. Louis, Illinois	50%	98%	39%
2. Camden, New Jersey	30	86	39
3. North Chicago, Illinois	26	47	39
4. Newark, New Jersey	38	82	42
5. Benton Harbor, Michigan	33	92	43
6. Trenton, New Jersey	31	59	50
7. Detroit, Michigan	44	77	53
8. Hartford, Connecticut	21	66	53
9. Cleveland, Ohio	45	50	54
10. Gary, Indiana	25	85	59
11. East Chicago, Illinois	41	81	60
12. Atlantic City, New Jersey	43	69	61
13. New Haven, Connecticut	21	47	62
14. Youngstown, Ohio	44	35	64
15. Philadelphia, Pennsylvania	23	45	64
16. Dayton, Ohio	31	36	64
17. Baltimore, Maryland	23	60	64
18. Saginaw, Michigan	29	40	66
19. Chicago, Illinois	23	60	66
20. St. Louis, Missouri	54	50	67
21. Buffalo, New York	43	37	69
22. Flint, Michigan	29	52	69
23. Birmingham, Alabama	22	64	69
24. Holyoke, Massachusetts	26	35	69

SOURCE: David Rusk in Lori Montgomery, "Expert Prophecies Doom for Many U.S. Cities," *Albuquerque Journal* (December 25, 1994), p. B-5.

the S&L bailout demonstrates. Similarly, we have more than a decade of field demonstrations funded by prominent foundations, conducted in cities throughout the nation and evaluated by reputable agencies. And we have undertaken more momentous challenges in the past. Metaphorically, breaking down the wall of hypersegregation is not unlike tearing down the Berlin Wall. Indeed, if we can free a people imprisoned by decades of propaganda to say nothing of a nuclear-armed police state, why are we unable to liberate our fellow citizens who have been shackled by race and poverty? The challenges posed by the economic and racial isolation of the minority poor by market forces and public programs are similar to travesties confronting ethically oriented Americans in earlier periods: for example, the abolitionist crusade against slavery, or the progressive purges of municipal corruption. In each of these instances, moral suasion triumphed over civic evil. An underclass in America is a comparable construct—abrasive to the social fabric, inconsistent with our national character.

During the past three decades, we have effectively written off an entire generation of children bound by race and poverty. Our inaction has made Swedish philosopher Gunnar Myrdal's an American "dilemma"[122] an American tragedy. Even more dismaying, this has been unnecessary; by nature, the forces of markets and policy are human constructs. That we should debate the best way to ameliorate the conditions that confine the minority poor is perhaps inevitable considering our democratic polity; that we should delay alleviating the circumstances that so obviously oppress destitute children in our cities is untenable for any civil society, regardless of its political economy. If the purpose of public policy is to provide some general direction to the national endeavor, it is difficult to imagine a more urgent priority than the lot of poor children struggling to grow up in American cities.

NOTES

1. Nathan McCall, *Makes Me Wanna Holler* (New York: Random House, 1994), p. 403.
2. June Axinn and Herman Levin, *Social Welfare* (New York: Harper & Row, 1982).
3. Howard Karger and David Stoesz, *American Social Welfare Policy* (White Plains, NY: Longman, 1990), p. 339.
4. Karger and Stoesz, *American Social Welfare Policy,* p. 243.
5. Herbert Gans, *The Urban Villagers* (New York: Free Press, 1962).
6. Daniel Patrick Moynihan, *Maximum Feasible Misunderstanding* (New York: Free Press, 1969).
7. National Advisory Commission on Civil Disorders, *Report of the National Advisory Commission on Civil Disorders* (New York: Dutton, 1968).
8. Karger and Stoesz, *American Social Welfare Policy,* pp. 244, 245.
9. John Kasarda, "Jobs, Migration, and Emerging Urban Mismatches," in M. McGeary and L. Lynn (eds.), *Urban Change and Poverty* (Washington, DC: National Academy Press, 1988), p. 154.
10. Kasarda, "Jobs," p. 156.

11. Douglas Massey and Nancy Denton, *American Apartheid: Segregation and the Making of the Underclass* (Cambridge: Harvard University Press, 1993), p. 145.
12. Ronald Ostrow, "New Report Echoes 'Two Societies' Warning of 1968 Kerner Commission," *Los Angeles Times* (February 28, 1993), p. A-23.
13. Daniel Patrick Moynihan, "The Negro Family: The Case for National Action," (Washington, DC: U.S. Department of Labor, 1965).
14. William Julius Wilson, *The Truly Disadvantaged* (Chicago: University of Chicago Press, 1987).
15. Ken Auletta, *The Underclass* (New York: Vintage, 1982).
16. David Stoesz, "The Case for Community Enterprise Zones," *Urban and Social Change Review* (Summer 1985), pp. 20–23.
17. P. Leonard, C. Dolbeare, and E. Lazere, *A Place to Call Home* (Washington, DC: Center on Budget and Policy Priorities, 1989), p. 32.
18. Robert Greenstein and Paul Leonard, *Bush Administration Budget* (Washington, DC: Center on Budget and Policy Priorities, 1990), p. 21.
19. *Statistical Abstract of the United States, 108th ed.* (Washington, DC: USGPO, 1988), pp. 260, 337.
20. Committee on Ways and Means, *Overview of Entitlement Programs* (Washington, DC: USGPO, 1990), p. 1311.
21. Michael Spechter, "The New Domestic Tug-of-War," *Washington Post Weekly* (April 8-14, 1991), p. 6.
22. David Rosenbaum, "States and Cities with Deficit Woes May Slow Rebound," *New York Times* (May 31, 1991), p. A-1.
23. Barry Bearak, "Mayor Presents a 'Doomsday' Budget for N.Y.," *Los Angeles Times* (May 11, 1991), p. A-2; David Treadwell, "New York City Lays Off 10,000 Workers," *Los Angeles Times* (June 29, 1991).
24. Bill Billiter, "Most Cities Facing a Threadbare 1992," *Los Angeles Times* (January 9, 1992), p. A-3.
25. Greenstein and Leonard, *Bush Administration Budget,* Table 1.
26. Kasarda, "Jobs," p. 178.
27. David Stoesz and Howard Karger, *Reconstructing the American Welfare State* (Lanham, MD: Rowman and Littlefield, 1992), p. 51.
28. Committee on Ways and Means, *Overview of Entitlement Programs* (Washington, DC: USGPO, 1985), p. 376.
29. Robert Mofitt and Douglas Wolf, "The Effect of the 1981 Omnibus Budget Reconciliation Act on Welfare Recipients and Work Incentives," *Social Service Review* 61 (1987), pp. 247–48.
30. *Overview of Entitlement Programs,* 1985, p. 377.
31. *Overview of Entitlement Programs,* 1985, p. 377.
32. John Wodarski et al., "Reagan's AFDC Policy Changes," *Social Work* 31 (1986), pp. 273, 275.
33. Isabel Wolock et al., "Forced Exit from Welfare," *Journal of Social Service Research* (Winter 1985–Spring 1986), pp. 71, 94.
34. Kevin Phillips, *The Politics of Rich and Poor* (New York: Random House, 1990), p. 87.
35. Committee on Ways and Means, *Overview of Entitlement Programs* (Washington, DC: USGPO, 1994), p. 367, 377.
36. Lawrence Mishel and David Frankel, *The State of Working America* (Washington, DC: Economic Policy Institute, 1991).

37. William Julius Wilson, "Public Policy Research and *The Truly Disadvantaged,*" in Christopher Jencks and Paul Peterson (eds.), *The Urban Underclass* (Washington, DC: Brookings Institution, 1991), pp. 460, 474.
38. Christopher Jencks, "Deadly Neighborhoods," *New Republic* (June 13, 1988); Juan Williams, "Hard Times, Harder Hearts," *Washington Post* (October 2, 1988).
39. "Eight Boston Teenagers Charged in Savage Slaying of Young Mother," *Los Angeles Times* (November 21, 1990), p. A-4.
40. Louis Sahagun, "Gang Killings Increase 69%, Violent Crime Up 20% in L.A. County Areas," *Los Angeles Times* (August 21, 1990), p. B-8.
41. Gabriel Escobar, "Slayings in Washington Hit New High, 436, for 3rd Year," *Los Angeles Times* (November 24, 1990), p. A-26.
42. Daniel Patrick Moynihan, *Came the Revolution* (San Diego: Harcourt, Brace, Jovanovich, 1988), p. 291.
43. Moynihan, *Came the Revolution,* p. 291.
44. Joe Sexton, "Young Criminals' Prey: Usually Young," *New York Times* (December 1, 1944), p. A12.
45. Jonathan Marshall, "Targeting the Drugs, Wounding the Cities," *Washington Post Weekly* (May 25-31, 1992), p. 23.
46. William Greider, "The Great S&L Clearance," *The American Prospect* 1 (Summer 1990), p. 11.
47. For this calculation, a ratio used by Hill was employed. Hill's penalty for the frostbelt states was placed at $51.6 billion, but this was based on an earlier, low assessment of bailout costs.
48. Edward Hill, "The S&L Bailout," *Challenge* 33 (1990), p. 44.
49. Kevin Phillips, *The Politics of Rich and Poor* (New York: Random House, 1990), p. 166.
50. Sidney Blumenthal, "Chapped Lips," *New Republic* 33 (July 30 and August 6, 1990), p. 20.
51. Details on Neil Bush's activities can be found in K. Day "Going after Neil Bush," *Washington Post Weekly* (July 23-29, 1990); those on Charles Keating, in J. R. Adams *The Big Fix: Inside the S&L Scandal* (New York: Wiley, 1990). Budget figures are from Robert Greenstein and Paul Leonard, *The Bush Administration Budget* (Washington, DC: Center on Budget and Policy Priorities, 1990).
52. Guy Gugliotta and Michael Isikoff, "The Plague of Our Cities," *Washington Post Weekly* (October 28-November 4, 1990), p. 6.
53. Barbara Vobejda, "Faster than a Speeding Bullet," *Washington Post Weekly* (March 29-April 4, 1993), p. 37.
54. Barbara Kantrowitz, "Wild in the Streets," *Newsweek* (August 2, 1993), p. 42.
55. James Q. Wilson and John DiIulio, Jr., "Crackdown," *The New Republic* (July 10, 1989).
56. Michael Isikoff, "What Was Down Came Back Up," *Washington Post Weekly* (December 30, 1991-January 5, 1992), p. 33.
57. Mathea Falco, *The Making of a Drug-Free America* (New York: Times Books, 1992), pp. 26-27.
58. "U.S. War on Drugs Cost $23.7 Billion in '91," *San Diego Union Tribune* (December 2, 1993), p. A-11.
59. Sidney Cohen, "The Drug-Free America Act of 1986," *Drug Abuse and Alcoholism Newsletter* (San Diego: Vista Hill Foundation, 1987), pp. 1-3.
60. Falco, *The Making of a Drug-Free America,* p. 29.

61. Barry Bearak, "A Room for Heroin and HIV," *Los Angeles Times* (September 27, 1992), p. A-18.
62. Steven Holmes, "Ranks of Inmates Reach One Million in a 2-Decade Rise," *New York Times* (November 28, 1994), pp. A-1, A-9.
63. Wilson and DiIulio, "Crackdown," p. 23.
64. Rhonda Cook, "Georgia's Prison Boot Camps Don't Work, Study Says," *San Diego Union Tribune* (May 8, 1994), p. A-32.
65. "Connecticut Suspends Gang-Riddled Youth Boot Camp," *San Diego Union Tribune* (June 12, 1994), p. A-6.
66. Marianne Yen, "A Shock that Seldom Jolts," *Washington Post Weekly* (November 28–December 4, 1995), p. 10.
67. Dean Murphy, "When Cops Go Back on the Beat," *Los Angeles Times* (August 27, 1991), p. A-1.
68. Bill Turque, "A New Line Against Crime," *Newsweek* (August 27, 1990).
69. Sam Fulwood, III, "Pulling the Plug on Violence with Problem-Solving Policing," *Los Angeles Times* (December 11, 1991), p. A-5.
70. Jim Newton, "A Gamble to Reform the LAPD," *Los Angeles Times* (April 17, 1994), p. A-1.
71. Richard Serrano, "Hiring More Police in Houston Pays Off as Overall Crime Rate in City Plummets," *Los Angeles Times* (May 30, 1994), p. A-15.
72. David Broder, "Programs, Not Prisons," *Washington Post Weekly* (November 19-25, 1990); David Broder, "'3 strikes' May Send Us to Debtors Prison," *San Diego Union Tribune* (April 18, 1994), p. B-5.
73. Sharon LaFraniere, "Running Hard, But Losing Ground," *Washington Post Weekly* (May 6-12, 1991), p. 31.
74. David Broder, "When Tough Isn't Smart," *Washington Post Weekly* (March 28–April 3, 1994), p. 4.
75. Charles Colson, "Let's Get Soft on Criminals," *Washington Post Weekly* (July 25-31, 1994), p. 24.
76. Mary Ellen Hombs and Mitch Snyder, *Homelessness in America* (Washington, DC: Center for Creative Non-Violence, 1983), pp. xvi, 15. Christopher Jencks documents that Snyder later admitted that the figure was baseless, though he continued to insist that Reagan administration figures on homelessness were conveniently low. See Christopher Jencks, *The Homeless* (Cambridge, MA: Harvard University Press, 1994), pp. 1-3.
77. Guy Gugliotta, "The Ways that Homelessness Counts," *Washington Post Weekly* (May 23-29, 1994), p. 38.
78. Jonathan Kozol, *Rachel and Her Children* (New York: Crown, 1988), p. 10.
79. Jencks has aggregated several studies conducted during this period, the findings of which are similar to the Chicago study. Studies cited by Jencks reported more males, fewer Blacks, more mental hospitalizations, and more substance abuse. Considering the methodological problems of this nature of research, these differences are probably not important. What is significant about studies cited by Jencks is the 41 percent of the homeless having spent time in jail or prison. This might suggest that the homeless are more criminally inclined, hence their imprisonment. But it could also mean that they are often arrested for misdemeanors and sent to jail. The former implies deviance; the latter being a victim of circumstance. See Jencks, *The Homeless*, p. 22.
80. Michael Sosin, "Homeless in Chicago," *Public Welfare* (Winter 1989), pp. 25-27.

81. Kozol, *Rachel and Her Children,* p. 11; emphasis in the original.
82. Martha Burt, *Over the Edge* (New York: Russell Sage Foundation, 1992), pp. 3-4, 211.
83. Gugliotta, "The Ways that Homelessness Counts," p. 38.
84. Jencks, *The Homeless,* pp. 16-17.
85. Joel Blau, *The Visible Poor* (New York: Oxford University Press, 1992), p. 112.
86. Henry Cisneros, "A Death on the Nation's Doorstep," *Washington Post Weekly* (December 13-19, 1993), p. 23.
87. Marcelo Rodriguez, "Henry Cisneros and the Politics of Ambivalence," *Los Angeles Times Magazine* (February 27, 1994).
88. Elizabeth Shogren, "White House Reportedly Plans Public Housing Funds Cuts," *Los Angeles Times* (January 8, 1994), p. A-4.
89. Elizabeth Shogren, "U.S. Vows Major Cut in Homeless," *Los Angeles Times* (May 18, 1994), p. A-1.
90. Ted Rohrlich, "Clinton Plan for Homeless Could Be L.A. Windfall," *Los Angeles Times* (May 21, 1994), p. B-3.
91. Shogren, "U.S. Vows Major Cut in Homeless," p. A-11.
92. Andrew Cooper, "Enabling the Underclass: Vince Lane's Campaign to Restore Rights and Responsibilities in Chicago's Public Housing" (Washington, DC: Progressive Policy Institute, 1990).
93. "High Noon at the Housing Project," *Ebony* (August 1989).
94. Stephen Braun, "New Life for Notorious High-Rises?" *Los Angeles Times* (June 2, 1994), p. A-1.
95. David Savage, "Clinton Calls for Steps to Rid Projects of Guns," *Los Angeles Times* (April 17, 1994), p. A-16.
96. John Leo, "Gun Sweeps in the Projects Hardly 'Unreasonable' Search," *Albuquerque Journal* (April 25, 1994), p. A-7.
97. Braun, "New Life," p. A-12.
98. Bill Clinton, *A Vision of Change for America* (Washington, DC: USGPO, 1993), pp. 30-35.
99. Greenstein and Leonard, *Bush Administration Budget,* p. 20.
100. Greenstein and Leonard, *Bush Administration Budget,* p. 20.
101. Bob Woodward, *The Agenda* (New York: Simon and Schuster, 1994), p. 165.
102. Paul Richter, "Clinton Unveils Plan for College Aid, Service," *Los Angeles Times* (March 2, 1993), p. A-1.
103. Judy Pasternak, "Chicago's Shorebank Earns Interest as Model for Rebirth, *Los Angeles Times* (February 22, 1994), p. A-1; Paul Richter, "Clinton Announces Credit Plan for Poor," *Los Angeles Times* (July 16, 1994), p. A-17.
104. David Lauter, "Job Retraining Backed but Clinton Plan Has Obstacles," *Los Angeles Times* (March 30, 1994), p. A-22.
105. Jim Sleeper, "The Clash," *The New Republic* (September 19 and 26, 1994).
106. David Maraniss, "Trouble Brewing in Milwaukee," *Washington Post Weekly* (July 30-August 5, 1990), p. 9.
107. Barry Bearak, "A Turf War for Urban Squatters," *Los Angeles Times* (February 27, 1994), p. A-1.
108. Douglas Massey and Nancy Denton, *American Apartheid: Segregation and the Making of the Underclass* (Cambridge: Harvard University Press, 1993), pp. 190-91.
109. James Rosenbaum et al., "Can the Kerner Commission's Housing Strategy Improve Employment, Education, and Social Integration for Low-Income Blacks?" *North Carolina Law Review* 71, 5 (June 1993), p. 1553.

110. John Bolger, "Toward Ending Residential Segregation: A Fair Share Proposal for the Next Reconstruction," *North Carolina Law Review* 71, 5 (June 1993).
111. Ronald Powell, "On Some Rising Young Entrepreneurial Stars," *San Diego Union-Tribune* (May 15, 1993).
112. L. Erik Bratt, "Teens Will Fend for Selves—On the Job," *San Diego Union* (February 18, 1993).
113. Joe Klein, "Shepherds of the Inner City," *Newsweek* (April 18, 1994), p. 28.
114. Peter Medoff and Holly Sklar, *Streets of Hope* (Boston: South End Press, 1994), chapter 8.
115. E.J. Dionne, Jr., "Hugh Price's Radical Alternative to Farrakhan," *Washington Post Weekly* (August 1-7, 1994), p. 28.
116. David Rusk, *Cities Without Suburbs* (Washington, DC: Woodrow Wilson Center Press, 1993), p. 123.
117. As described here, "urban compacts" expand Rusk's notion of conditions for receipt of federal assistance to cities.
118. "From Devastation to Urban Rebirth," *Los Angeles Times* (April 3, 1994).
119. Paul Houston, "$87-Million Aid Earmarked for 23 Cities," *Los Angeles Times* (March 22, 1994), p. A-23.
120. William Eaton, "Long-Stalled Crime Bill to Get Jump-Start," *Los Angeles Times* (July 26, 1994), p. A-14; Michael Ross, "Vote on Crime Bill Is Blocked; Major Setback for Clinton," *Los Angeles Times* (August 12, 1994), p. A-1.
121. Elizabeth Shogren, "Drastic Pruning Reportedly Planned to Save HUD Itself," *Los Angeles Times* (December 15, 1994), p. A-42; Marlene Cimons, "Administration Sees a 'Reinvented' HUD," *Los Angeles Times* (December 20, 1994), p. A-32.
122. Gunnar Myrdal, *An American Dilemma: The Negro Problem and Modern Democracy* (New York: Harper, 1944).

chapter 5

Education: Slouching toward the Twenty-First Century

> *How many potential Colin Powells, Condoleezi Rices, Sally Rides, Barbara McClintocks, Wilma Mankillers, Daniel Inouyes, and Cesar Chavezes is our nation going to waste before it wakes up and recognizes that its ability to compete and lead in the next century is inextricably intertwined with its poor and nonwhite children as with its white and privileged ones, with its girls as well as its boys?*
>
> Marian Wright Edelman[1]

Education policy in the United States is an anomaly. On the one hand, among the basic provisions associated with an advanced welfare state—health care, employment, housing, income—education is the only commodity offered Americans solely as a right of citizenship. On the other hand, even though the right to education is ensured by government, it is an obligation on the part of local and state authorities, making education highly decentralized. In the United States, there are 50 different state boards overseeing education and 15,000 local school boards.[2] On account of its atomistic nature, coordinating public education for the purposes of attaining any given goal nationally has about the same plausibility as herding cats.

To compound matters, public education is subject to shifts in public sentiment. Sometimes these are relatively uncontested, as in the movement to upgrade student performance in math and science after the launching of Sputnik. At other times, these lead to violent conflict, as in the attempt to integrate schools by busing students after the *Brown* and *Swann* decisions. Most recently, widely shared concerns that American students were inferior to those in other industrialized nations led to the "excellence movement," an initially conservative attempt to reform education by reinstilling traditional values.[3] This movement has provoked a sometimes volatile debate around issues such as chartering independent schools, providing vouchers so that parents can claim a tax deduction for private school tuition, and allowing parents a choice as to which schools their children can attend.[4]

Liberal response to the "excellence movement" has been mixed. Secular humanists have suspected that conservative concern about academic reform is nothing less than a smokescreen for a traditionalist social agenda, including objectives such as prayer in the classroom. How coincidental, liberals may wonder, that parents can choose among schools just as teachers can choose among sources of creation. The transformation of education from a public utility to a market commodity has been vigorously rejected by traditional liberals.[5] In *Savage Inequalities,* a poignant review of the condition of schools in poor, minority communities, Jonathan Kozol argues that debates about restructuring and choice serve to distract Americans from the very urgent need to reverse the resegregation of our schools.[6]

From this polemic, a consensus is gradually emerging: American education, today, is underperforming in contrast to other nations, and dangerously so. Underlying this assessment is a recognition that education in the United States is encumbered by institutional residues of the past. A nine-month academic year, as a conspicuous example, hails from an agricultural culture in which children were needed to help in the harvest. Less obviously, a focus on basic skills, learned by rote, was more meaningful in the Industrial era when work was a mindless repetition of routine tasks on an assembly line. An information-driven postindustrial economy, by contrast, places a premium on the manipulation of systems of symbols, a degree of literacy far beyond the "three R's." Before becoming Secretary of Labor, Robert Reich underscored the importance of educating "symbolic analysts" in order for the nation to be competitive in the twenty-first century.

> American children as a whole are far behind their counterparts in Canada, Japan, Sweden, and Britain in mathematical proficiency, science, and geography. Some American children receive almost no education, and many more get a poor one. But some children—no more than 15 to 20 percent—are being perfectly prepared for a lifetime of symbolic-analytic work.[7]

By the early 1990s, tentative—but substantive—steps were being taken to accelerate reform in American education. Through *America 2000,* then-President Bush proposed the funding of $1 million for each of 535 new American schools under the cultivation of the New American Schools Development Corporation, a public-private collaboration.[8] The RJR Nabisco Foundation designated almost $30 million to 42 Next Century Schools.[9] In the face of public support of school reform, the major teachers' unions, the National Educational Association (NEA) and the American Federal of Teachers (AFT), became more amenable to experimentation in education, reversing two decades of ambivalence. Governors of several southern states—ordinarily intransigent about reform of *any* sort—overhauled state public education. Among these "education governors" was the governor of Arkansas, Bill Clinton. As president, Clinton would designate another "education governor"—Richard Riley of South Carolina—as Secretary of Education. The early 1990s were propitious for educational reform, propitious indeed.

A HISTORY OF AMERICAN EDUCATION

Free public education in the United States is widely attributed to the "common school" concept advocated by leaders such as Horace Mann. Since the 1830s, many communities levied taxes to prepare youngsters for their future role as citizens by providing a basic education.[10] In 1874, a Michigan Supreme Court decision validated the use of taxes for public high schools, extending the right to an education to adolescents.[11] In so doing, what had been an elite institution reserved for relatively few well-off families became accessible to the masses.

The prospect of a first-rate public education through high school was soon compromised by two developments: the immigration of millions of poorly educated Europeans and an emerging technology of testing that was embraced by American educators. The turn of the century found the nation experiencing its greatest influx of immigrants. From 1900 to 1910, almost 8.8 million foreigners came to America, the largest number—1.3 million—arriving in 1907. By 1910, 15 percent of the U.S. population was foreign-born.[12] Not long thereafter, Lewis Terman adapted the intelligence test first presented in 1908 by French psychologists Alfred Binet and Theodore Simon. Terman's use of what became known as the Stanford-Binet Intelligence Scale had an enormous influence on public education when his test results indicated that 80 percent of immigrants were feeble-minded! Citing genetic deficits, such as race, for immigrants' poor performance, Terman suggested that they be "segregated in special classes."[13]

The use of tests in education dovetailed with Progressive enthusiasm for application of the scientific method in many social circumstances. With public schools filling with foreigners, American educators quickly embraced the rational ordering of the learning process insinuated by instruments such as the Stanford-Binet. In 1918, this orientation to public education was reified in *The Cardinal Principles of Secondary Education,* a report by the National Commission on the Reorganization of Secondary Education, a panel created by the National Education Association. *The Cardinal Principles* rejected an academic orientation to education that emphasized intellectual development in favor of a utilitarian approach that provided the basic preparation for citizenship. The Commission followed conventional educators of the day in thinking that "immigrant students surging into the schools were incapable of mastering academic subject matter."[14] In this manner, *The Cardinal Principles* provided a scientific rationale for offering students of public schools a second-class education. Public educators' response to the Commission's report was gradual, but no less consequential. Just after the turn of the century, academic subjects occupied two-thirds of the high school curriculum, with one-third being nonacademic courses; by 1930, the ratio was reversed, with two-thirds of high school courses involving "commercial, general, or trade subjects."[15]

The leveling of American education was not endorsed by all Progressives, to be sure. John Dewey argued that critical thinking was essential for a viable democracy and advocated a strong academic curriculum toward that end.[16] Dewey's admonitions notwithstanding, public education became sodden as training in home economics, shop, civics, and driver education replaced education in literature, science, and the fine arts. An obvious problem of the utilitarian paradigm in public education, however, was assessing student performance. Whereas standards had existed for evaluating a student's facility to comprehend Greek tragedy, use proofs in geometry, or appreciate baroque architecture, how did one evaluate a student's ability to tighten a lug nut, vote, or bake a cupcake? Educators' solution to the problem was "social promotion," the advancing of students within public education based on age and attendance, regardless—and sometimes in spite of—poor academic performance.[17]

The era of World War II reinforced utilitarian public education. The armed services functioned optimally, of course, with personnel who were well versed in basic skills. An education in the liberal arts was at best frivolous, a distraction from successful prosecution of the war, or at worst an impediment as when conscripts cited Thoreau as a basis for their pacifist resistance to the draft. Escaping virtually unscathed from the war after having obliterated its major industrial competitors, the United States blithely continued its inferior educational practices, quite ignorant of their ultimate consequences. All the world needed, it seemed, was a little American know-how, a touch of Yankee panache.

American complacency in education came abruptly to an end in the 1950s. Local school districts were jolted out of lethargy in 1954 when the Supreme Court ruled in *Brown* that separate but equal education for African Americans violated the equal protection provisions of the 14th Amendment. But *Brown* was limited to the five school districts that were part of the litigation.[18] Ultimate reversal of *Plessy* would entail hundreds of challenges to local school districts before *de jure* segregation would be abandoned. Despite obstructionism that stalled desegregation for years, the *Brown* decision put local school districts on notice that thought, if not action, was suddenly necessary to salvage public education.[19] In 1957, the Soviet Union launched Sputnik in a dramatic display of technological prowess. Immediately, public officials were put on the spot having to explain how America's communist enemy could exhibit such obvious superiority in space, to say nothing of the security implications for the nation. In the same year, Congress passed the National Defense Education Act, pumping millions of dollars into math, science, and foreign language programs in the nation's educational institutions.[20]

During the mid-1960s, as part of his War on Poverty, President Johnson signed into law two acts elevating the federal role in education policy: the

Elementary and Secondary Education Act (ESEA), which targeted federal aid for poor schools; and the Equal Opportunity Act, which established Head Start. ESEA was the most prominent federal educational program, initially funneling $1.5 billion to schools with disproportionate numbers of poor children for educational training, research, and instructional materials.[21] While receiving far less appropriation—less than $200 million—Head Start captured the nation's attention when it was introduced during the Summer of 1965. Under the administrative direction of Sargent Shriver and the academic leadership of Dr. Edward Zigler, Head Start was designed to provide cultural enrichment to preschool children from poor families.[22] For 1966, Head Start served 733,000 poor, mostly minority children, an annual enrollment that was still not exceeded by 1990.[23]

Any residual optimism from the 1960s about public education quickly evaporated during the 1970s. Certainly, a few skeptics had predicted trouble in American schools. James Coleman, for example, had begun what was to become a series of studies, the results of which challenged liberal conventional wisdom in education. The first "Coleman report" on compensatory education, of which ESEA and Head Start were prototypes, was released in 1966 and suggested that the gains from special programs to aid poor, minority children were apt to be subverted by family characteristics and environmental features of the neighborhood. The second report completed under Coleman's direction appeared in 1975 and concluded that desegregation had prompted whites to flee cities for the suburbs, effectively resegregating schools. The third report to which Coleman contributed was released in 1981 and concluded that private, parochial schools were superior to public schools.[24] Although Coleman took a good deal of flak from disillusioned liberals, in retrospect much of his research reflected various dynamics in the rapid deterioration of American education.

Educational journalist Thomas Toch put it bluntly: "The 1970s left public education in a shambles." A conspiracy of events contributed to the disassembling of the nation's schools. A massive exodus of whites from cities to suburbs left urban school districts devoid of more capable students and the tax base represented by their families. A tax revolt—California's Proposition 13 and Massachusetts' Proposition 2½—capped property taxes, thereby limiting revenues for public schools. As teachers felt the compression of increasing numbers of poorer students but less revenues to serve them, they engaged in job actions, undertaking more than 1,000 strikes between 1975 and 1980. Further straining urban schools, additional requirements were introduced to educate the handicapped through the 1973 Rehabilitation Act and the 1975 Education of All Handicapped Children Act.[25]

As local school districts struggled to reconcile increasingly disparate variables in a more convoluted education equation, they were to find little relief from the federal government. Upon his inauguration as president in 1981, Ronald Reagan indicated that, rather than redouble federal assistance to troubled schools, one of his administration's top priorities would be to eliminate the federal Department of Education.

"A RISING TIDE OF MEDIOCRITY"

Reagan's reversal of the federal education policy represented the culmination of conservative frustration with a liberal-inspired "equity movement" that had opened education to underserved groups, while at the same time diluting the curriculum. "Within the equity movement the traditional measures of scholastic success (high school graduation and college admission) came to be seen not as rewards to be earned through achievement," Thomas Toch wrote in summarizing the conservative case, "but as compensation that all students were entitled to, regardless of their performance."[26] A leading conservative critic was Chester Finn, Jr., whose resume boasted Republican (the Nixon White House) and Democratic (Senator Daniel Patrick Moynihan's office) appointments. In the early 1980s, Finn claimed that a "liberal consensus" was responsible for the deterioration of the skills of American students. The liberal consensus, however, was not some amorphous collection of well-intended values, Finn argued, but specific actions taken by some of the most powerful and influential institutions in American culture. Among them were the elite universities with schools of education (Harvard, Columbia, Stanford); the nation's top philanthropists (Ford and Carnegie); the major teachers' unions (the NEA and AFT); prominent policy institutes (Brookings and Aspen); and minority advocacy groups, all aided and abetted by various members of Congress.[27]

The conservative critique of liberal education focused on competence, broadly understood. Not only were American students poorly schooled in the arts, sciences, and humanities, but educators were also finding gaping holes in basic skills: reading, writing, and math. For the better part of the century, the liberal design in American education had sacrificed academic performance for a utilitarian focus—which was bad enough, as conservatives viewed education, but now even basic skills were deteriorating. Having lost the academic-versus-utilitarian debate decades before, conservatives viewed the latter half of the century with skepticism. If liberals controlled the nation's educational apparatus, as Finn contended, perhaps the best strategy for conservatives would be to decommission federal educational policy altogether.

But the prospect of losing what little leverage the federal government represented in reforming the nation's schools was unacceptable to Reagan's incoming Secretary of Education, Terrel Bell. Rather than close down the Education Department, Bell assiduously worked to highlight the evident crisis in American education. Within a year of the Reagan inauguration, Bell had established the National Commission on Excellence in Education, a blue-ribbon panel that solicited public testimony from a wide range of organizations in all regions of the United States. In 1983, the Commission's report, *A Nation at Risk*, was released, attracting unprecedented public attention. "Our Nation is at risk," the report warned. "Our once unchallenged preeminence in commerce, industry, science, and technological innovation is being overtaken by competitors throughout the world." American workers were not only unprepared for an increasingly competitive world, but their performance was below that of an earlier generation:

> [T]he *average graduate* of our schools and colleges today is not as well-educated as the average graduate of 25 or 35 years ago, when a much smaller proportion of our population completed high school and college. The negative impact of this fact likewise cannot be overstated.

Then, in phrases that reverberated throughout American education, the report portrayed the crisis in stark metaphor:

> [T]he educational foundations of our society are presently being eroded by a rising tide of mediocrity that threatens our very future as a Nation and a people. . . . If an unfriendly foreign power had attempted to impose on America the mediocre educational performance that exists today, we might well have viewed it as an act of war.[28]

A Nation at Risk sparked a rigorous self-examination of American schools on the part of dozens of commissions. Their conclusions were not pretty. In 1991, the National Commission on Children concluded:

> Assessments of 20 school systems around the world rank American eighth graders 10th in arithmetic, 12th in algebra, and 16th in geometry. Even America's top students fare poorly in international comparisons: among the top 1 percent of high school seniors, American students ranked last. Achievement in science is no better. Among 10-year-olds in 15 countries, Americans rank eighth. Among 14-year-olds in 17 countries, Americans tie with children in Singapore and Thailand for 14th place. Among advanced science students in 12 nations, Americans are 11th in chemistry, 9th in physics, and last in biology.[29]

If American high school graduates were not performing favorably compared to those from other countries, the nation's college graduates were becoming something of an embarrassment. The Wingspread Group on Higher Education, another panel of leaders in American education, reported that "56.3 percent of American-born, four-year college graduates are unable *consistently* to perform simple tasks, such as calculating the change from $3 after buying a 60 cent bowl of soup and a $1.95 sandwich." In wry understatement, the report observed that "tasks such as these should not be insuperable for people with 16 years of education."[30] The Educational Testing Service (ETS) reported findings from a study of four-year college graduates indicating that only 35 percent could do such things as write a letter to explain a billing problem, and that only 42 percent were capable of writing an argument contrasting two views from newspaper articles. Noting that college does enhance literacy, the ETS observed that graduates of two- and four-year institutions of higher education demonstrate "levels of literacy [ranging] from a lot less than impressive to mediocre to near alarming, depending on who is making judgment."[31] Yet while the academic performance of American students slid compared to their peers in other developed nations, this did not seem particularly disturbing to them. In ironic counterpoint to their lack of academic knowledge—and as affirmation of the social promotion doctrine—American students ranked themselves first in self-esteem.[32]

A DECADE OF EXPERIMENTATION

By confirming the inadequacy of public education, *A Nation at Risk* fanned the flames of a grass-roots rebellion already evident in many communities. Starved for cash and dejected at the loss of abler students, education officials in older cities grasped for reforms that might reverse the condition of urban schools. The urgency and extent of disrepair among many of the nation's metropolitan school districts was as acute as it was extensive. The problem was not confined to individual schools; rather, entire districts were affected. Nor were deficits limited to elementary or secondary levels; instead, faults ran up and down the educational continuum, fracturing kindergartens as well as community colleges. Jonathan Kozol described the implications of pervasive deterioration in public education for children in Chicago's schools. "For children who begin their school career at Anderson Elementary School, for instance, the high school dropout rate is 76 percent. For those who begin at McKinley School, the high school drop out rate is 86 percent." From these figures, Kozol extrapolated that "nearly half the kindergarten children in Chicago's public schools will exit school as marginal illiterates." The implications for higher education? "At the city's community colleges, which receive most of their students from Chicago's public schools, the noncompletion rate is 97 percent. Of 35,000 students working toward degrees in the community colleges that serve Chicago, only 1,000 annually complete the program and receive degrees."[33]

Amid the tumult that typified urban schools, a handful of committed educators searched for solutions largely within existing parameters. Among them, Marva Collins stood out. She was a Chicago teacher known for her innovation and nurture; in 1975, exasperated with conventional public education, Collins joined an alternative school, Daniel Hale Williams Westside Preparatory School, in one of the city's poorest black neighborhoods. Her students excelled due to a method that combined schooling in the classics with individual caring.[34] In 1968, psychiatrist James Comer brought an interdisciplinary approach that included parental participation to two troubled Boston schools. Comer's School Development Program (SDP) emphasized individual attention for troubled students, integrated mental health services with the curriculum, and brought parents into governance of local schools. Improvement in students' skills attracted national attention, and "Comer schools" emerged in several communities.[35] During the late 1970s, Los Angeles teacher Jaime "Kimo" Escalante began preparing his

Garfield High School students for the Advanced Placement (AP) test in calculus. His initiative seemed Quixotic at best. Ninety percent of Garfield students were Latino, 80 percent were poor; and in 1975, Garfield High almost lost its accreditation. Nonetheless, 18 of Escalante's students took the calculus AP test in 1982, and although 14 had to retake the test because ETS suspected copying on the first exam, all of the students passed. In one decade, Escalante had elevated an unchallenging math program in a typical barrio high school to one that produced more calculus AP students than all but three public schools in the nation, an accomplishment later recounted in the film, *Stand and Deliver*.[36]

Despite the isolated successes of innovators like Collins, Comer, and Escalante, many educators and parents began to perceive the problems of urban education in more fundamental terms—rather than reform schools, they called for "restructuring." An early restructuring experiment occurred in District 4 in East Harlem, one of the poorest neighborhoods in New York City. In 1974, District 4 began to designate alternative schools, each with a specific curriculum; students then elected which school they wished to attend. Under the direction of Seymour Fliegel, the number of alternative schools increased from three in 1974 to 26 in 1982. Proponents of District 4's experiment with "school choice" argued that the empowerment of students and parents yielded improved performance. When the experiment began, District 4 ranked lowest in the 32 school districts in student skills; only 15 percent of students were reading at grade level. By 1982, District 4 ranked fifteenth of 32 districts, and 60 percent of students were reading at or above grade level.[37] In 1974, fewer than twenty District 4 students were admitted to New York City's select high schools; by the early 1990s, the number exceeded 300.[38] Such improvements among a student population that was two-thirds African American, one-third Latino, and uniformly poor, led to its distinction as a model of school choice.[39]

A more radical experiment in restructuring evolved in Milwaukee in 1987. Public schools there were beset with problems typical of a city where 28 percent of minority family heads were unemployed; 60 percent of children lived below the poverty line; the teen pregnancy rate was double the nation's average; the high school dropout rate was 40 percent; and the student turnover rate was up to 70 percent in certain schools. Earlier recommendations by two commissions designated to reform public education had been ignored for the most part.[40] To improve public education for Milwaukee's poor, minority kids, State Representative Annette "Polly" Williams proposed that poor children receive a voucher for attendance at the school of their choosing. In advancing the idea, Williams was hardly the typical anti–public education conservative—she was African American, the single parent of four children, a member of Milwaukee's Black Panther Militia, and twice chair of Jesse Jackson's presidential campaign in Wisconsin.[41] As enacted, Milwaukee's school choice program offered poor children $2,500 vouchers to attend a nonsectarian private school. In its first year of operation, only 600 of 60,000 eligible poor children opted to participate, and seven of 21 private schools indicated their willingness to accept the voucher students.[42] An unsuccessful legal challenge to the program was overruled by the

Wisconsin Supreme Court, and one of the private schools that accepted many choice students folded, creating confusion. Still, enrollment increased from 562 in 1991 to 632 the following year. A thorough assessment of the Milwaukee school choice program has yet to be completed, yet impressionistic evidence indicates that parents are pleased. Ernest Boyer, president of the Carnegie Foundation for the Advancement of Teaching, made this observation:

> Those participating in the Milwaukee experiment appear to be happy with the way it is working. A majority of students say they feel safe. Few have reported drug or alcohol problems in their new schools. More than 80 percent of the participants believe they are getting a good education. Eighty-four percent of parents graded the private schools "A" or "B"; only 32 percent felt that way about the public schools.[43]

Infrastructural collapse of urban school districts led some school officials to wonder if corporate management would make public schools more efficient, while at the same time enhancing teacher productivity and raising student test scores. In 1986, Educational Alternatives, Inc. (EAI), was founded in Minnesota as an educational management firm. EAI adapted a children's science fiction term, "Tesseract," as its teaching method, emphasizing "more technology, more staff in the classroom, and more [teacher] training."[44] Beginning with contracts to manage one school each in Arizona and Minnesota, EAI attracted the attention of Wall Street when it secured the support of Baltimore's first African-American mayor and negotiated a five-year, $133 million contract to manage nine schools. Early results of EAI's performance in Baltimore were mixed: teachers' organizations complained of more work, parents appreciated a marked upgrading in building maintenance, and student performance remained comparable to that of city schools. Nevertheless, by mid-1994, EAI was among the largest of educational management firms, reporting annual revenues of $32 million, and they were negotiating agreements to manage schools in Hartford and San Diego.[45]

Among the most dynamic of educational firms is Sylvan, a company reporting annual earnings of $40 million. Begun fifteen years ago, Sylvan was a marginal firm until 1991 when two young Baltimore entrepreneurs acquired it. Since then, Sylvan has developed a reputation tutoring poor kids with severe learning deficits within some of the nation's poorest schools. Through subcontracts using Title I funds, Sylvan has demonstrated significant improvements in reading and math skills of students who had been written off by their schools. Sylvan's track record has led to future negotiations with an additional 10 to 15 school districts.[46]

More than anyone else, Christopher Whittle has taken the corporate ethos and applied it to public education. In 1986, Whittle invested capital from his revitalization of the fading *Esquire* magazine and began Channel One, an attempt to introduce commercial advertising in public schools in exchange for "free" in-depth news on contemporary events. Although few schools initially accepted Channel One, Whittle persisted, designating $55 million in order to upgrade public education. By the early 1990s, Whittle was speculating on the cost of deploying a nationwide system of for-profit schools using the latest in teaching methods and technology, called the "Edison Project." Reasoning that the per capita expenditure in public education could yield profits if done under corporate management, Whittle attracted a handful of prominent educators to form the core team of the Edison Project. Prominent members of the core team included Chester Finn, an education professor and Bush-appointee to the Education Department; John Chubb, a policy analyst from the Brookings Institution; and Benno Schmidt, outgoing president of Yale University. The objectives of the Edison Project were lofty: 1,000 Whittle schools educating 2 million children by 2010.[47]

Unable to raise the capital necessary for a full-fledged corporate assault on public education, Whittle's Edison Project lowered its sights, opting for the deployment of 10 to 40 primary schools, beginning with management of existing public schools, if necessary.[48] By 1993, Whittle's aspirations were materializing: Channel One generated $100 million in annual revenue, and the Edison Project had formulated six school designs that maximized teaching innovations and media technology within reach of the economic parameters of public education. The Edison Project approximated Whittle school tuition at $6,000 annually, somewhat more than the $5,600 spent for public education.[49] Still, the Edison Project anticipated that many parents would pay the increase to escape an inferior public education. Moreover, if families were offered vouchers, parents would only have to pay the difference, substantially lowering the amount they would have to pay. For 1995, Whittle's group negotiated a contract with Wichita, Kansas, school authorities to manage three schools, in the process agreeing to invest between $1.5 and $3 million in each school for research and development.[50] But investor enthusiasm for the Edison Project faltered. Whittle's tendency to oversell programs was caught by auditors, and executives of the Edison Project were suddenly distancing themselves from its founder. By early 1995, educational analysts wondered if the Edison project would survive, with Whittle, or without him.[51]

THE SCHOOL CHOICE DEBATE

In quite different ways, the structural changes introduced by District 4, Milwaukee's vouchers, EAI, Sylvan, and the Edison Project reflected a challenge to public education. The standard critique, usually—but not exclusively—associated with conservatives, contended that public education was a monopoly, insulated from change. Public schools, accused one group of corporate reformers,

> are moribund institutions because they are organizations hopelessly out of sinc with the realities of modern economic, social, and political life. They are a bureaucratic monopoly which cannot last. If schools stay as they are, they will be abandoned across the board, just as they have been in our great cities.[52]

If subjected to competition, the logic went, public education would be effective in several ways: educators would be more responsive to students' families; schools would be more cost-effective; the curriculum would be updated continually. The key to educational reform, then, was breaking up the publicly held education monopoly.

Much of the educational reform debate of the 1980s focused on different ways to deregulate the public education monopoly. Many reformers argued that competition could be injected into public education by allowing parents to choose which schools their children would attend. But the school "choice" option was not simple. If parents were allowed to select their child's school, should they be allowed to choose from all schools, private and public? Should parochial schools be included? Within the choice debate, traditionalist conservatives argued that parochial schools should be included, while traditionalist liberals objected to this as an indirect subsidy by the state of religious schools. The Milwaukee voucher program reflects this concern by allowing parents to choose among private schools but not giving the option of using the vouchers for parochial schools. On the other hand, education reformers John Chubb and Terry Moe have outlined a choice model that includes aid to parochial schools.[53] In this manner, the choice argument has moved more to the center. Options offered parents are: They might choose among private schools, but sectarian schools were excluded (a concession to conservatives); or parents could choose only among public schools (a concession to liberals).

Choice proponents understood that competition in public education was meaningless unless there were funding consequences. Thus, vouchers had a value that schools could secure upon enrollment of a student. As schools performed better, their enrollments would increase, generating additional revenues that could be used for program enhancement; diminishing enrollment in inferior schools would put educators on notice that improving the school was needed to continue operations. But what should be the value of a voucher? If a voucher were to cover the full cost of tuition at a private school, the costs of a full-blown choice program would be astronomical—$22 billion.[54] If vouchers are valued at less than full tuition, however, the specter of dual educational systems looms, since well-off parents will subsidize their vouchers in order to place their children in better schools, leaving poorer parents to choose among inferior schools. Solutions to this problem include prohibiting the supplementation of vouchers or equalizing vouchers. Rather than allowing parents to use vouchers directly, Chubb and Moe have suggested a de facto voucher arrangement whereby school districts maintain accounts of all enrolled students, billing various parties for educational services rendered. Through such an "equalization approach," wealthier districts could be billed more than poorer districts, effectively transferring funds to disadvantaged communities.[55]

As this brief discussion indicates, the variations possible in school choice arrangements multiply rapidly. During the 1980s, the proliferation of choice schemes seemed to parallel an increasingly vociferous ideological debate about school restructuring: conservatives promoting education as a market; liberals insisting on it as a public utility. Two more modest reform models have emerged that tend to refocus the debate away from ideological polemic and back on the education of students. In "magnet schools," the curriculum is built around specific themes—sciences, performing arts, humanities, for example—and students are screened for admission. In addition to a more customized curriculum, magnet schools tend to feature smaller classes that allow more individual attention. As a result, magnet schools often attract more motivated students from outside a traditional school district, thus improving the caliber of the student body. The District 4 experiment has adopted the magnet school strategy. By the early 1990s, the magnet school concept was enjoying immense popularity; nationwide, magnet schools were estimated to number 10,000.[56]

A more recent candidate for education reform is the "charter school" concept, first introduced in Minnesota. As advocated by Ted Kolderie, a chartered school was one authorized by the state to function parallel to the public school system. The proliferation of independent charter schools, Kolderie argued, would divest government of its education monopoly, at the same time offering students' families choice of schools children would attend.[57] By prohibiting certain practices in charter schools, problems associated with school choice can be eliminated. Charter schools "may not have a religious character, or charge tuition; cannot pick and choose their students, or discriminate. . . . [parents] are free to remove their children if they are not satisfied."[58] By allowing educators, parents, or other interested parties the option to establish a public school independent of a local school board, advocates of charter schools avoided two of the most contentious issues associated with the school choice movement: tuition and private education. By 1991, school reform legislation led to several schools being chartered in Minnesota and California.[59] Three years later, eight states had authorized charter schools.[60]

AMERICA 2000

Inferior student performance, extensive state and local experimentation, and a volatile restructuring debate exerted force on the federal government to take action in educational reform. In 1991, George Bush, otherwise reluctant to take the lead in domestic policy, revealed a national plan for school reform: *America 2000*. Among the plan's major features were the development of national standards of student performance, upgrading teacher preparation, and evaluating local schools through "report cards." *America 2000* called for the creation of a New American Schools Development Corporation that would redesign public education. In order to garner legislative support, the proposal designated one $1 million model school in each Congressional district, more than 535 in total. Notably, the plan endorsed school choice, both for public and private schools. Rather than force federal expectations on state and local government, however, *America 2000* asked states and localities to conform their schools to the national plan, after which they would be designated *America 2000* communities.

States and cities responded quickly to *America 2000*. Within a year, some 32 states and hundreds of communities had subscribed to the plan. More than $50 million had been raised by the New American Schools Development Corporation to design model schools.[61] As a template for educational renewal, *America 2000* received wide praise, even if some of its features, such as school choice, were problematic. As social policy, however, the proposal was inadequate to reverse public perception that the Bush presidency was short on domestic initiative. When President Bush failed to win a second term, the future of *America 2000* suddenly became very much in doubt.

Contravening the tradition of incoming presidents, Bill Clinton embraced the intent, if not certain aspects, of *America 2000*. Revised as *Goals 2000: The Educate America Act*, the Clinton education reform package endorsed national performance standards for students, then articulated specific objectives that American schools should achieve by the end of the millennium:

- all American children would "start school ready to learn";
- the high school graduation rate would be at least 90 percent;
- after completing grades 4, 8, and 12, all students will be proficient to varying degrees in English, math, science, civics, foreign language, economics, arts, history, and geography;
- the continuing education of teachers would incorporate new knowledge of curriculum as well as student diversity;
- American students would be "first in the world in mathematics and science";
- every American would be literate as well as have the skills to participate fully as global citizens;
- every school would be free of drugs and alcohol, unauthorized firearms, and violence; and
- every school would involve parents in the education of children.

To prod the nation along, *Goals 2000* designated a National Education Goals Panel, a National Education Standards and Improvement Council, and three research and development centers: a National Institute on Educational Governance, Finance, Policy-Making, and Management; a National Institute on Early Childhood Development and Education; and a National Institute on Post-Secondary Education, Libraries, and Lifelong Learning.[62] In signing *Goals 2000*, President Clinton remarked that it would provide $700 million for education for 1995.[63]

Whereas *Goals 2000* elaborated the federal education bureaucracy to a considerable extent, it also encouraged the wide range of experimentation underway in many states. School choice, however, was deftly circumscribed in the plan—"nothing in this Act shall be construed to authorize the use of funds . . . to directly or indirectly benefit any school other than a public school"— effectively limiting it to public schools.[64] Oddly, few educators seemed willing to judge the realism of *Goals 2000*—American children being first in the world in science and math, 100 percent adult literacy, schools free of substance abuse and violence—even though the date of the president's announcement invited as much: the eve of April fool's day. That Americans would attain such lofty objectives in less than a decade had all the prospects of Dan Quayle spelling a three-syllable word correctly.

WHITHER HIGHER EDUCATION?

American colleges and universities were virtually omitted from the *Educate America Act,* conveniently excused from playing a prominent role in educational reform. Of course, much of the research and development of *Goals 2000* would be contracted out to university professors, larding educational research institutes in the nation's premier colleges and universities. But of any direct obligation in education reform, American institutions of higher education were excused, receiving little more than oblique reference. In the Community Partnership Program, for example, universities are lumped with "schools, businesses, and communities" in an appeal to "improve the quality of learning and teaching in the most impoverished urban and rural communities of the United States."[65]

During the 1980s the role of institutions of higher education in American culture was brought to public attention, but only sporadically. Arguably, the most prominent of the critiques of higher learning in America was Allan Bloom's *The Closing of the American Mind.*[66] Citing the divisive and leveling consequences of a democratically-driven curriculum in which race, gender, ethnicity, and a host of other liberal fetishes were primary, Bloom argued that American colleges and universities had forsaken their classical heritage. Instead of a rigorous education in traditional values that served as the foundation of Western culture, American students were dished up gobs and slices from the educational buffet of whatever seemed of momentary interest. Little was substantive; all was relative. The result was mediocrity.

The year following the publication of Bloom's critique of the college curriculum, Charles Sykes weighed in with an indictment of the American professorate. In scathing caricature, Sykes portrayed professors as erudite navel-gazers, more interested in esoteric research and publishing for purposes of securing a position in the academic pecking order than educating students in any real sense. Hiding in research labs and using graduate assistants to front for them in the classroom, professors exploited higher education for its physical comforts and lack of intellectual rigor, virtually unaccountable to students, parents, and taxpayers footing their expenses.[67]

Soon conservatives put the critique of higher education to ideological service. Most of what was wrong with American colleges and universities, they argued, was attributable to a rampant infestation of uncontested liberalism. Dinesh D'Souza accused radical African Americans, Latinos, feminists, and homosexuals of elevating their agendas over the virtues of higher education, in the process trashing truth.[68] Roger Kimball warned that feminists and other ideologically driven groups were deliberately subverting higher values of Western culture through a full, take-no-hostages, assault on the humanities.[69] Russell Jacoby rebutted, arguing that the basic problem with American higher education was pervasive commercialism and a complementary utilitarian curriculum that dimmed the ability of American students to think at all, let alone embrace leftish dogma. As for radical professors, Jacoby suggested they were more concerned about academic protocol—attending committee meetings, making tenure, and the like—than using the university to launch the next revolution.[70]

All this might be dismissed as intellectual mudslinging had American universities not displayed more fundamental flaws. In the Spring of 1991, auditors accused Stanford University of misappropriation of federal funds that Stanford had obtained for "indirect" costs associated with research contracts. When government contracts out research projects, grant applicants are allowed to include in their budgets "indirect" costs: the administrative overhead and other incidental expenses of mounting and completing a research project. The amount of indirect cost varies in relation to the project as well as the institutional applicant, but indirect costs typically exceed 50 percent, meaning they are a substantial revenue source for universities. The assumption was that indirect cost revenues were expended to support research projects, and government rarely audited them for that reason. By the early 1990s, universities collected $2.5 billion from the federal government for indirect costs, out of $9.2 billion in research contracts.[71]

That was until the Stanford case. By the time federal accountants were finished, Stanford's President Donald Kennedy stood accused of using funds for purposes some distance from research support: a $4,000 wedding reception at his home, a 72-foot yacht, an antique commode, and improvements on his bed, including its enlargement and $7,000 for sheets.[72] Kennedy's resignation presaged the sudden retraction of charges on the part of major-league universities for indirect cost billings to the federal government: Stanford withdrew $500,000; MIT $731,000; California Institute of Technology $500,000; Harvard Medical School $500,000; Cornell $310,000; Washington University $550,000.[73] In a separate fiscal dispute, Stanford agreed to reimburse the Office of Naval Research $3.4 million for improper billings.[74]

The credibility of the nation's elite institutions of higher education was further diminished in May 1991 when 23 private colleges and universities agreed to a U.S. Justice Department consent decree that prohibited tuition price fixing. Since 1956, the Overlap Group, a small group of prestigious schools, has met annually to review students who had been admitted to more than one institution in order to designate common financial aid packages for them. In so doing, the Justice Department alleged, the Overlap Group acted as a cartel that subverted any competition among member institutions for more desirable students.[75] Among institutions alleged to have violated antitrust law were several that had been found to be misusing federal research funds—Cornell, Harvard, MIT, and Stanford—institutions for which typical tuition and fees approximated $15,000 annually.[76]

The image of higher education that emerges from the dithering about "political correctness," the scandal over indirect research charges, and the collusion around setting tuition is one of academicians and administrators more concerned about battening their positions than taking seriously the crisis in American education. During the 1980s, leaders of the nation's colleges and universities scaled ever higher in elaborating their institutional edifices, evidently ignorant of—or conveniently disregarding—the collapse of public education. Rather than assume a social responsibility for which the nation's premier institutions of higher education were ideally suited, educators amused themselves with the petty puzzles of the academy. The performance of American college students may have stagnated, and the percent of black male high school graduates attending college may have dropped five points from 1990 and 1992 to 30 percent,[77] but tuition was going up, and neither students nor parents were doing much more than balking about the rising cost of a college degree. By intellectual standards, the management of higher education was light lifting, so why complicate matters unnecessarily—even if the schools in the adjoining neighborhood did resemble the third world? Given the unpredictable nature of involvement in community affairs, the captains of the nation's flagship universities opted for the proven, the successful, and the insular. Far better to commiserate in the Chancellor's Office than walk into the neighborhood next door. Their credo: don't just do something, sit there.

THE NEXT AGENDA IN EDUCATION POLICY

The formulation of a national educational reform plan must acknowledge the decentralization of American schools as well as the roles played by various levels of government. The former reinforces the pluralism of American society; the latter recognizes that the federal government will not be dominant in educational policy. The federal government accounts for no more than 6 percent of K-12 educational expenditures.[78] On the other hand, coupling this with federal funding for preschool programs and student loans for higher education places the federal government in a strong position to negotiate partnerships with state and local government as well as private schools for the purpose of forging a national educational plan.

A national educational plan should have a dual focus: drawing state and local schools and private educational institutions together so that they work in consort, and bringing together various services to accelerate the development of poor children. With respect to drawing together public and private schools, the *Goals 2000: Educate America Act* is a fine beginning, but its appeal to the various entities involved in education to voluntarily adopt a national plan must be reinforced. As is the practice in many funding arrangements, the availability of federal funds should be contingent on state and local government and private schools signing on to a national educational reform plan. *Goals 2000* errs in highlighting objectives that are for the most part unachievable given the state of American education; far better to pull together relevant parties and hammer out a realistic plan that harnesses the tremendous potential of our educational institutions and guides the nation through the next century.

Any national educational reform initiative should emphasize investments in young Americans. The virtues of early education are obvious: Preschool youngsters prepared for learning are not only apt to be more successful but they are also less likely to become a drain on society, as shown in Figure 5.1.

Using these foci as a rationale, four specific initiatives should be undertaken to reform American education: School-Based Human Services, Preferred School Choice, Apprentice Warranties, and Universities in the Public Interest.

School-Based Human Services

Anecdotal evidence and empirical research confirm bleak prospects for preschoolers from poor communities. Of six areas of readiness for school, kindergarten teachers indicated that "serious problems" existed with five: 21 percent of students had serious problems with "moral awareness," 31 percent with "social confidence," 38 percent with "general knowledge," 43 percent with "emotional maturity," and 51 percent with "language richness."[79] Problems such as these are more often encountered by poor children. Preschool deficits are but one facet

FIGURE 5.1 Benefits of early education (by age 19)

SOURCE: Ernest Boyer, *Ready to Learn* (Princeton, NJ: Carnegie Foundation for the Advancement of Teaching, 1991), p. 55.

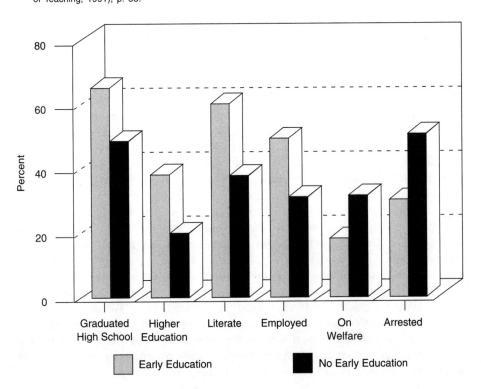

of an environment that is hazardous for a good start in school. "Impoverished parents are often unable to provide their children with the building blocks of early development—adequate nutrition, decent medical care, a safe and secure environment—and at age five, poor children are often less alert, less curious, and less effective at interacting with their peers than are more privileged youngsters," observed author Sylvia Hewlett. "As they start school, poor children are already way behind."[80]

The absence of readiness for school is troubling enough for an individual youngster, but when multiplied as in a classroom, the result is combustible. James Comer's log of his first days at a poor elementary school is perhaps typical:

> The first day was shocking. The second day was even worse. There was constant disarray. It flared into wild disorder many times. There was no quietness, very little listening. There was fighting; there was thumbsucking; there was crying; there were continual cries of "teacher!" There were wails of "I want to go home." "Do we go outside now?" There was no sense of structure, or organization to the schedule of the day.... Every transition, every change during the day, was a disaster. They screamed and yelled and pushed as they lined up at the door downstairs. They rushed down the halls, yelling more. The lavatory with its high ceiling, its echoing walls, its many toilets with doors seemed to incite the children to new heights of excitement and wildness.[81]

More effective sabotage of early education is difficult to imagine.

The most significant program for poor preschool children has been Head Start. Although Head Start is supposed to serve all eligible minority children by 1994, this is improbable. In 1988, only 25 percent of eligible children were enrolled;[82] by 1991, that had increased to only 28 percent.[83] Plans by the Clinton administration to expand Head Start dramatically have been hampered by reports that the program suffers from poor management, that children are not getting required immunizations, and that families have not received adequate assessments.[84] Independent of these difficulties, some child development experts have questioned whether Head Start is an adequate response to the deficits that poor children bring to school.[85]

Recent research indicates that more intensive intervention with poor children beginning early in life produces significant improvements in their educational experience. When "extremely high-risk" children are placed in an educational program by 6 months of age, University of Alabama psychologist Craig Ramey noted that evidence of mental retardation was reduced as much as 80 percent. Moreover, the intelligence quotient (IQ) of these students was 15 to 20 points higher than their peers by age three; by ages 12 and 15, students were pulling away from their classmates in school performance.[86] In another project associated with Ramey, the Carolina Abecedarian Project, educational day care from infancy to age 5 yielded significant improvements in IQ that remained at age 12.[87]

In light of this evidence, it is encouraging that several states have initiated parent-as-educator programs, particularly since formal programs, such as Head Start, typically do not serve children younger than three. Programs in Maryland, Minnesota, Missouri, and Oregon serve children as early as infancy. Typically, parents are given an orientation to their role as early educator; a manual and workbooks are provided; and a peer monitor makes home visits to assist with any problems. Preliminary assessments have been positive, leading the Carnegie Foundation for Advancement in Teaching to advocate for the parent-as-educator to become a national program.[88]

Alone, early learning initiatives and parent-as-educator programs are unlikely to counter the negative environmental circumstances of poor children. At-risk children tend to come from poor families, and the most troubled of these children and families require intensive intervention from several agencies. The American tradition has been to separate these agencies and provide services according to the category that a family fits—hence, we have "categorical" programs. Recently, some cities have experimented with provision of social services at neighborhood schools.[89] The rationale behind redeploying social services at schools grows out of the recognition that services needed by poor parents are often fragmented and located some distance from a family's residence. By relocating social services at a school, parents can obtain services more easily and at one time. Furthermore, by using common eligibility forms, human service workers can cut down on the red tape for which social services are notorious. Locating social services in neighborhood schools is a relatively new development, but it has been accomplished successfully in San Diego.

A more effective provision of human services for troubled families would be to reassign existing programs—Head Start, early education, parent-as-teacher programs, and social services—to neighborhood schools. In order to simplify administration, existing categorical programs should be collapsed and assigned as a block grant to a local "children's authority." Operating parallel to a school system, the children's authority would be responsible for oversight of all services to children and their families within its jurisdiction.[90]

Preferred School Choice

Choice in American education has been prevalent for those who can afford it and in those instances when government has extended that option to the poor. Wealthy families enjoy choice, of course, by electing to send their children to elite private schools. Middle-income families commonly enroll their children in parochial schools. Families without the resources or opportunities to place children outside of the public school system often exercise choice by relocating so that children can attend a public school of their preference. Thus, school choice has been an option for wealthy and middle-income families for some time. If more affluent families prefer to avoid public education, they can; they vote with their wallets.

Government programs contribute to choice, as well. The most celebrated example is the GI Bill. Veterans of World War II were offered a choice of which institution they wished to attend, and the federal government underwrote their tuition and fees. Public, private, and sectarian institutions of higher education participated in the GI Bill. Significantly, African Americans used their GI Bill benefits more than other groups.[91] In higher education, government student aid programs also contribute to school choice by subsidizing colleges and universities that students choose to attend. As in the case of the GI Bill, public, private, and sectarian institutions participate. A Congressional Budget Office review of student aid programs indicated that in 1986 46 percent of undergraduates obtained assistance in higher education, totaling $27.2 billion, of which $18.1 billion was from the federal government. Most aid is prioritized for poorer students; student aid averaged $7,600 for students from the poorest families attending the most expensive institutions.[92]

It is only in elementary and secondary education that the role of government in school choice has been questioned. An early experiment in school choice involved the Alum Rock, California, public schools. Ironically, this school choice program was developed and promoted by the Office of Economic Opportunity (OEO), an agency otherwise noted for its liberal initiatives to empower the poor. For five years beginning in 1972, certain parents were given the option of which school their child(ren) would attend, and this group's experience was compared to a control group of families following traditional enrollment practices in public schools. Although initial reports of the Alum Rock experiment were positive, established educational interests challenged OEO's conclusions as well as its suggestion that California undertake a statewide voucher plan that would include private, though not parochial, schools.[93]

During the 1980s, the virtues of school choice were most often associated with conservatives who used it as an example of privatization, an opportunity to inject competition into public education in order to break up a publicly held monopoly. Paradoxically, conservative rhetoric on school choice was complemented by experimentation in public education underway in several urban school systems. As discussed earlier, school choice programs in East Harlem's District 4 and the proliferation of magnet schools in many cities reflected the willingness of urban educators to reform public education so that schools were more responsive to poor, minority communities. Thus, it is no small paradox that during the 1980s conservative ideologues exploited the school choice field experiments begun by urban educators. Equally so, many liberal intellectuals mistook school choice as a Freidmanesque economic mutation and rejected it outright. For paleoliberals, school choice was a weapon of the far right aimed at the vulnerable underbelly of liberal designs in social policy. As a result, the oddest of political liaisons evolved during the Reagan and Bush presidencies: Wealthy WASP conservatives consorted with poor minority educators to reform public education. At the margin of the debate, ideologically correct liberals remained intransigent, even if some from their camp began to defect to school choice. How far behind the curve the liberal Left had fallen became evident when the U.S. Commission on Children released its report in 1991. Comprised of some of the most esteemed leaders in children's policy—Senator Jay Rockefeller, Marian Wright Edelman, Mary Futrell, and Sid Johnson—the National Commission on Children was clear in its pronouncement on school choice:

> The National Commission on Children encourages states to explore school choice policies as part of an overall plan to restructure and improve public schools. School choice should only be implemented where accountability measures are specified and where the special needs of educationally disadvantaged students are addressed.[94]

Given the quite substantial impediments to education faced by poor children, any school choice plan should offer special assistance to them. The Milwaukee school choice program does this by making the $2,600 school voucher available only to poor families. A more refined approach has been advocated by John Chubb and Terry Moe, who have proposed a "scholarship plan" through which scholarships for poorer students with special needs would be supplemented. Chubb and Moe suggest that federal funds now expended to special needs children "should take the form of add-ons to student scholarships. At-risk students would then be empowered with bigger scholarships than the others, making them attractive clients to all schools—and stimulating the emergence of new specialty schools."[95] As the Milwaukee experiment and the "scholarship" approach of Chubb and Moe indicate, there are methods for evening out the playing field for poor children in a school choice plan. Such strategies illustrate "preferred school choice" because they provide additional aid to poorer children in order to bring them up to par with their well-off classmates. In so doing, preferred school choice ensures poor children the same educational opportunity enjoyed by kids who come from more prosperous families.

Apprentice Warranties

Given the utilitarian ethic that pervaded education through much of the twentieth century, the failure of public schools to prepare students for the labor market is ironic. Federal support for vocational education begins with the 1918 Smith-Hughes Act, preceding the Social Security Act by more than a decade.[96] During the War on Poverty, career-oriented educators proposed that secondary education focus on preparation for real jobs, leading to federal support of career education in 1972. During the 1970s, some 38 career education field experiments were supported by federal funds. Although evaluation of these federally supported career education demonstrations indicated that most federal career education projects enhanced job opportunities for youth, the Reagan administration terminated them in 1981.[97]

By the end of the 1980s, evidence indicated that the nation's approach to public education was out of sync with changes in the labor market. The transition from an industrial mode of production to one that was technologically intensive placed a premium on skills far beyond those taught in conventional K–12 education. As a result, the emerging service economy tended to split into either well-paying, high-tech positions that required substantial investments in upgrading workers' skills, or into low-skilled, minimum-wage "McJobs." More competitive nations such as Germany pumped as much as 3 percent of gross income into job training, but the United States marked less than 1 percent for that purpose.[98] Accordingly, American productivity has dropped from an average annual growth rate of 3 percent between 1937 and 1973 to less than 1 percent since 1973.[99] The U.S. economy was less and less competitive as the postindustrial era expanded.

The consequences of the service economy for new entrants into the labor market were equally significant. For those able to find work, a poor education segregated young workers in dead-end, minimum-wage, no-benefit jobs. Most poorly educated youth were simply unemployable. In 1990, less than half—46.7 percent—of recent high school dropouts were employed.[100] Minority youth found themselves less able to earn the income necessary to assume family responsibilities, as shown in Figure 5.2.

Between 1975 and 1989, salaries of employed high school graduates under 25 years of age lost 40 percent of their value due to inflation.[101] In light of the eroding value of secondary education, many youth questioned why they should stay in school. The high school dropout rate soared, exceeding 50 percent in many cities. Even high schools specializing in trades in order to increase a graduates' labor market value fell victim to student apathy; for example, in 1993 the dropout rate at Manual Arts High School in South Central Los Angeles was 73 percent.[102]

The Clinton administration's response to deteriorating career prospects for youth is the School-to-Work Opportunities Act signed into law in 1994. The Act is a collaborative effort between business and government to improve the performance and job prospects of high school students. Participating students would attend school part time and work part time as apprentices in specific industries. Upon completion of the program, a graduate would have earned "a high school diploma, a skill certificate, and either a first job on a career track, college admission or further training."[103] For 1995, the Act was budgeted at $300 million, although lawmakers' concerns about the budget deficit may reduce that funding level substantially.[104]

As an initiative to elevate the productivity of American workers and make the U.S. economy more competitive, the School-to-Work Act deserves high praise. However, as an effort to upgrade the performance of minority students at risk of dropping out, the Act falls short. With minority teenagers dropping out of high schools that now feature a diluted curriculum, what is to keep them from dropping out when faced with a *more rigorous* education? Ensuring apprentice program graduates good jobs and continued retraining are incentives that would quickly register with students. In effect, such assurances would warrant the credentials granted program graduates. An apprentice warranty would guarantee a good job after completing the School-to-Work program and ensure continued

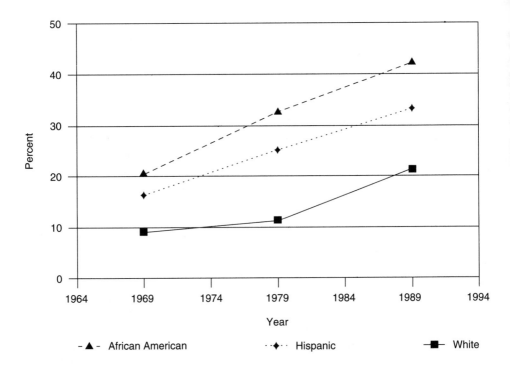

FIGURE 5.2 Proportion of male high school graduates whose income is less than poverty level for a family of four*

*Males, ages 25–54, with 12 years of education whose own earnings are less than poverty level for a family of four. Family income may be higher.

SOURCE: Sheldon Danziger, "The Poor," in David Hornbeck and Lester Salamon, *Human Capital and America's Future* (Baltimore: Johns Hopkins Press, 1991), p. 148, and unpublished data for 1989; *Learning a Living* (Washington, DC: Department of Labor, 1992), p. 7.

upgrading of skills through unlimited retraining. The impediments faced by minority youth in poor communities justifies targeting funding for them. Because of the adversity often encountered by individual minority youth who elect mainstream rewards, the Apprentice Warranty initiative should be designed for a cohort of School-to-Work students. A group of ten School-to-Work apprentices who go through the program together are more likely to complete it, and they are more likely to make a positive impression on classmates.[105]

Universities in the Public Interest

The relationship of higher education to the social order of which it is a part has not been frequently addressed. An unstated American maxim has held that colleges and universities are institutions above—and therefore removed from—the conventional wisdom of the lay public. This ivory-tower depiction of higher education has been reinforced by the dynamics of the postindustrial era. In a knowledge-intensive society, those organizations that generate and transmit information are increasingly valued. A society becomes data-driven to the extent it requires not only new information but also new ways to arrange and exploit *systems* of information in order to be economically competitive. This has enormous implications for higher education as a societal endeavor. The historical tendency for higher education to be indecipherable to the public, attributable to a highly specialized academic curriculum, is compounded by the refinements and dictates of knowledge in the information age. Thus, when administrators and professors wind their raison d'être with the esoteric rhetoric typical of the academy, the result is often an obfuscating obscurantism that baffles the public and stymies reasoned oversight. Lost altogether is the obligation that colleges and universities have to the greater social order; at the institutional level, higher education has violated its social contract with the very agencies that sustain it: government, business, and students.

Operating from such a narrow vision of public purpose, colleges and universities used the most superficial of indicators to claim social relevance.[106] For example, a university's affirmative action program might induce more minority students to enroll in professional schools in medicine, education, and social work, but the community near where these students lived remained untouched, resembling the slum of a developing nation. Anecdotal as well as empirical evidence suggests that the tether between the university and mainstream culture has begun to fray. Richard Hersh, president of Hobart and William Smith Colleges, has lamented a "culture of neglect" that typifies university students:

> We have failed to teach an ethic of concern and to model a culture of responsibility. We have created a culture characterized by dysfunctional families, mass schooling that demands only minimal effort and media idols subliminally teaching disrespect for authority and wisdom. It is as if there were a conspiracy of parents and educators to deliberately ruin our children. College students reared in the culture of neglect externalize any notion of obligation and responsibility.[107]

A 1994 survey of college freshmen conducted by UCLA's Higher Education Research Institute found that only 16 percent "frequently discussed politics" and that only 31.9 percent thought keeping up with politics was important, both all-time lows in the history of the 29-year survey.[108] To the survey's director, Alexander Astin, the results indicated that college freshmen "don't see themselves as being part of the democratic process; [they] don't even understand how democracy works."[109]

To be sure, some units within colleges and universities have intended to serve the public. Professional schools in medicine, nursing, social work, and other disciplines provide public service while training students. A smaller number of institutions have centers or institutes that specialize in areas of public policy, such as health, education, and welfare. For the most part, however, the mission of professional schools has been to educate students; the assumption being that their graduates will then serve the public. Public policy institutes state their purpose as educating the public and decision makers about issues of public concern—the assumption being that citizens and lawmakers consume an institute's reports. But these activities are basically self-serving. Training professionals benefits administrators and professors; generating reports is the grist of technicians with high credentials. In neither case is an institution of higher education expected to tackle an important social problem. Former Harvard president Derek Bok stated:

> Whether you are looking at entire schools, like schools of education, or schools of public administration or social work ... you are struck by what an inverse correlation there is between what society needs from these institutions and what we are taking most seriously. If you take some of the basic problems facing our society ... and then make a list of all the things that a university could contribute ... and ask yourself how do all these things rank in the list of priorities as the modern university, one is struck by how low they rank.[110]

Rarely do American universities stray beyond what is institutionally safe and wander into areas of compelling social relevance—even when opportunities are just next door. Fortunately, some do. Among administrators in higher education, this is what marked John Silber as a maverick. As president of Boston University (BU), Silber committed the university to revitalizing a defunct school system in Chelsea, Massachusetts, a poor, mostly minority suburb of Boston.[111] Since assuming management of Chelsea schools, BU reports that the number of Chelsea graduates going on to vocational education or college has increased from 52.6 to 72.3 percent; although Scholastic Assessment Test (SAT) scores initially dropped because of increasing numbers of students taking the test, from 1992 to 1994 the average score has increased from 620 to 644.[112] Although the results of BU's attempt to reform education in Chelsea may be ambiguous and disputed, Silber serves as a prototype for how higher education can serve the public interest. Consequently, there have been revived commitments, such as when the incoming president of Cornell University, Hunter Rawlings III, stated his intent to commit the resources of that university to addressing social problems.[113]

As part of an exemplary career interweaving academic with community pursuits, Harvard psychiatrist Robert Coles has encouraged students to engage the most troubled residents in poor neighborhoods.

> Our colleges and universities could be of great help to students engaged in community service if they tried more consistently and diligently to help students connect their experiences in such work with their academic courses. Students need more opportunity for moral and social reflection on the problems that they have seen at first hand, and such

intellectual work would surely strengthen both their academic lives and their lives as volunteers.[114]

That institutions of higher education can be held to a standard of public purpose is based in their receipt of public funds. Virtually every college and university in the United States benefits from federal student grants and loans, and most enjoy governmental support from indirect costs billed to the government through contracts. As a condition of receipt of public dollars, institutions of higher education can be expected to serve the public interest. Institutions developing projects that clearly demonstrate public service may be designated "Universities in the Public Interest," a status that would given them an advantage in seeking governmental grants and contracts. A public interest audit conducted by the federal Office of Technology Assessment would determine the merit of projects and identify those worthy of national replication.

Much of public education in America is provided through bureaucracies that evolved during the Industrial Era. Educators devised a utilitarian curriculum to train masses of workers consistent with the economic and civic needs of the period. In this way, public education served the working and middle classes reasonably well. With elevated social and economic expectations, the wealthy avoided public education by paying tuition to private schools. For those residing in the lower registers of the socioeconomic hierarchy, basic education could be obtained in public elementary schools; secondary education was unnecessary so long as youth had lower expectations and strong backs. Having destroyed prospective competitors during World War II, the United States could afford a casual approach to public education.

The Industrial Era mold of public education is no longer tenable, however. A knowledge-starved service economy situated within an increasingly competitive global economy has antiquated the industrial model of public education. The United States can no more afford to produce a cadre of minimally prepared workers than it can afford to relegate thousands of poor, minority kids to a marginal existence within the underclass. To be productive on a par with other postindustrial economies, the United States must upgrade the performance of mainstream students *and* it must elevate the skills of poor, minority youngsters as well. That the nation can no longer afford the indifference that has characterized educational policy regarding the minority poor is no longer an argument contended on moral grounds. Postindustrial capitalism dictates that nations that maintain Industrial Era educational practices and neglect the minority poor do so at their own risk—the penalty being loss of competitive position internationally.

The reform of public education indicated by these dynamics is addressed in part by the *Goals 2000: The Educate America Act*. However, much more needs to be done to integrate at-risk children into the mainstream. School-based human services, preferred educational choice, apprentice warranties, and universities in the public interest are initiatives that can focus resources on the families and communities of minority children. Collectively, they can enable and empower our most vulnerable youth to accept confidently the challenges of the next century.

NOTES

1. Marian Wright Edelman, *The State of America's Children* (Washington, DC: Children's Defense Fund, 1991), p. 19.
2. Louann Bierlein, *Controversial Issues in Educational Policy* (Newbury Park, CA: SAGE, 1993), p. 152.
3. Thomas Toch, *In the Name of Excellence* (New York: Oxford University Press, 1991).
4. Louis Gerstner et al., *Reinventing Education* (New York: Dutton, 1994).
5. Jeffrey Henig, *Rethinking School Choice* (Princeton, NJ: Princeton University Press, 1994).
6. Jonathan Kozol, *Savage Inequalities* (New York: HarperPerennial, 1991).
7. Robert Reich, *The Work of Nations* (New York: Knopf, 1991), p. 227.
8. Bierlein, *Controversial Issues,* p. 147.
9. Gerstner, *Reinventing Education,* p. x.
10. Bierlein, *Controversial Issues,* p. 6.
11. Toch, *In the Name of Excellence,* p. 42.
12. Russell Jacoby, *Dogmatic Wisdom* (New York: Doubleday, 1994), p. 151.
13. Quoted in Toch, *In the Name of Excellence,* pp. 43-44.
14. Bierlein, *Controversial Issues,* p. 7.
15. Toch, *In the Name of Excellence,* p. 48-49.
16. Bierlein, *Controversial Issues,* pp. 7-8.
17. Toch, *In the Name of Excellence,* p. 49.
18. Bierlein, *Controversial Issues,* p. 136.
19. Taylor Branch, *Parting the Waters* (New York: Simon and Schuster, 1988).
20. Bierlein, *Controversial Issues,* p. 9.
21. Bierlein, *Controversial Issues,* p. 9; Thomas Dye, *Understanding Public Policy* (Englewood Cliffs, NJ: Prentice Hall, 1992), p. 171.
22. Lisbeth Schorr, *Within Our Reach* (New York: Doubleday, 1988), pp. 184-92.
23. Committee on Ways and Means, U.S. House of Representatives, *Overview of Entitlement Programs* (Washington, DC: USGPO, 1993), p. 1690.
24. Diane Ravitch, "The Coleman Reports and American Education," in Aage Sorensen and Seymour Spilerman, *Social Theory and Social Policy* (Westport, CT: Praeger, 1993), pp. 129-41.
25. Toch, *In the Name of Excellence,* pp. 4-6.
26. Toch, *In the Name of Excellence,* p. 58.
27. Toch, *In the Name of Excellence,* p. 57.
28. National Commission on Excellence in Education, *A Nation at Risk* (Washington, DC: USGPO, 1983), pp. 5, 11.
29. National Commission on Children, *Beyond Rhetoric* (Washington, DC: USGPO, 1991), p. 179.
30. The Wingspread Group on Higher Education, *An American Imperative: Higher Expectations for Higher Education* (Racine, WI: The Johnson Foundation, 1993), p. 15.
31. Cassandra Burrell, "Study Finds Variation in College Grads' Skills," *Idaho Statesman* (December 10, 1994), p. A-8.
32. Jacoby, *Dogmatic Wisdom,* p. 89.
33. Kozol, *Savage Inequalities,* pp. 58, 59.
34. Marva Collins and Civia Tamarkin, *Marva Collins' Way* (Los Angeles: J.P. Archer, 1982).

35. James Comer, *School Power* (New York: Free Press, 1980).
36. Jay Mathews, *Escalante* (New York: Henry Holt, 1988).
37. Ted Kolderie, Robert Lerman, and Charles Moskos, "Educating America," in Will Marshall and Martin Schram (eds.), *Mandate for Change* (New York: Berkley Books, 1993), p. 133.
38. Ernest Boyer, *School Choice* (Princeton, NJ: Carnegie Foundation, 1992), p. 43.
39. Henig, *Rethinking School Choice*, pp. 111-12. The improvement of students in District 4 has not gone unchallenged. See Billy Tashman, "Hyping District 4," *The New Republic* (December 7, 1992), pp. 12-13.
40. Boyer, *School Choice*, pp. 64-65.
41. Henig, *Rethinking School Choice*, p. 113.
42. Paul Taylor, "The Bearer Is Entitled to Private Schooling," *Washington Post Weekly* (June 3-9, 1991), p. 34.
43. Boyer, *School Choice*, pp. 68-69.
44. William Trombley, "For-Profit Public Schools Test Is Off to a Mixed Start," *Los Angeles Times* (December 22, 1992), pp. A-1, A-36.
45. Gary Putka and Steve Stecklow, "Do For-Profit Schools Work?" *Wall Street Journal* (June 8, 1994), pp. A-1, A-6.
46. LynNell Hancock, "A Sylvan Invasion," *Newsweek* (December 19, 1994), pp. 51, 53.
47. Charles Trueheart, "Chris Whittle's New Thought of School," *Washington Post* (July 21, 1992).
48. Peter Passell, "Public Schools for Profit, Phase 2: The Sales Pitch," *New York Times* (January 19, 1994), p. B-8.
49. Jean Merl, "One Giant Leap for Education," *Los Angeles Times* (March 8, 1993).
50. Steve Stecklow, "Wichita Schools Agree to For-Profit Edison Project," *Wall Street Journal* (May 12, 1994), p. B-7.
51. Peter Applebome, "A Venture on the Brink: Is Education Profitable?" *New York Times* (October 30, 1994), p. 16.
52. Gerstner et al., *Revinventing Education*, p. 2.
53. John Chubb and Terry Moe, "Choice *Is* a Panacea," *Brookings Review* (Summer 1990).
54. Bierlein, *Controversial Issues*, p. 111.
55. Chubb and Moe, "Choice," p. 8.
56. Toch, *In the Name of Excellence*, p. 255.
57. Ted Kolderie, *Beyond Choice to New Public Schools* (Washington, DC: Progressive Policy Institute, 1990).
58. Kolderie et al., "Educating America," p. 133.
59. Bierlein, *Controversial Issues*, p. 96.
60. Tom Mirga, "Rebels with a Cause," *The New Democrat* (April-May 1994).
61. Bierlein, *Controversial Issues*, pp. 146-48.
62. Public Law 103-227, 103rd Congress, Title I.
63. Elizabeth Shogren, "Clinton Signs Education Law that Sets U.S. Standards," *Los Angeles Times* (April 1, 1994), p. A-2.
64. Public Law 103-227, sec. 1020.
65. Public Law 103-227, 108 STAT. 255.
66. Allan Bloom, *The Closing of the American Mind* (New York: Simon and Schuster, 1987).
67. Charles Sykes, *ProfScam* (Washington, DC: Regnery Gateway, 1988).
68. Dinesh D'Souza, *Illiberal Education* (New York: Free Press, 1991).

69. Roger Kimball, *Tenured Radicals* (New York: Harper & Row, 1990).
70. Russell Jacoby, *Dogmatic Wisdom* (New York: Doubleday, 1994).
71. Brian Hecht, "Schools for Scandal," *New Republic* (August 19 and 26, 1991), p. 15.
72. Hecht, "Schools," p. 14.
73. Kenneth Cooper, "The Ivory Tower Isn't Looking So Pristine Lately," *Washington Post Weekly* (May 13-19, 1991), p. 31.
74. Coleen Cordes, "Settlement for Stanford," *Chronicle of Higher Education* (October 26, 1994), p. A-31.
75. Scott Jaschik, "Ivy League Agrees to End Collaboration on Financial Aid," *Chronicle of Higher Education* (May 29, 1991), p. A-1.
76. "Tuition and Fees of American Colleges and Universities," *Chronicle of Higher Education* (October 23, 1991), pp. A-31-36.
77. Retha Hill, "Giving Up and Getting Out," *Washington Post Weekly* (March 28-April 3, 1994), p. 31.
78. Bierlein, *Controversial Issues*, p. 19.
79. Ernest Boyer, *Ready to Learn* (Princeton, NJ: Carnegie Foundation for the Advancement of Teaching, 1991), p. 37.
80. Sylvia Ann Hewlett, *When the Bough Breaks: The Costs of Neglecting Our Children* (New York: Harper Perennial, 1991), pp. 70-71.
81. Comer, *School Power*, pp. 78-79.
82. Edelman, *The State of America's Children*, p. 76.
83. *Overview of Entitlement Programs*, 1993, p. 1690.
84. May Jordan, "A New Start for Head Start," *Washington Post Weekly* (April 5-11, 1993), p. 33.
85. Douglas Besharov, "Fresh Start," *New Republic* (June 14, 1993).
86. Rochelle Sharpe, "To Boost IQs, Aid Is Needed in First 3 Years," *Wall Street Journal* (April 12, 1994), p. B-5.
87. Bruce Brower, "Growing Up Poor," *Science News*, Vol. 146 (July 9, 1994), p. 25.
88. Boyer, *Ready to Learn*, pp. 43-45.
89. The federal departments of Education and Health and Human Services have begun collaborative work in this direction. See *Together We Can: A Guide for Crafting a Profamily System of Education and Human Services* (Washington, DC: Department of Education, 1993).
90. For details on the "children's authority," see Lela Costin, Howard Karger, and David Stoesz, *Child Abuse Politics* (New York: Oxford University Press, forthcoming).
91. D. O'Neill, "Voucher Funding of Training Programs: Evidence from the GI Bill," *Journal of Human Resources* (Fall 1977).
92. Congressional Budget Office, *Student Aid and the Cost of Postsecondary Education* (Washington, DC: author, 1991), pp. xiv, xvii.
93. Henig, *Rethinking School Choice*, pp. 119-20.
94. Original emphasis, National Commission on Children, *Beyond Rhetoric* (Washington, DC: author, 1991), p. 207.
95. Chubb and Moe, "Choice," pp. 9-10.
96. Bierlein, *Controversial Issues*, p. 7.
97. Kenneth Hoyt, "Collaboration: The Key to Success in Private Sector/Education System Relationships," *Youth Policy* (October 1993), p. 12.
98. "Transition from School to Employment," *Youth Policy* (October 1993), p. 5.
99. *Learning a Living*, Part 1 (Washington, DC: Department of Labor, 1992), p. 4.
100. "Scope of the Problem: Supply," *Youth Policy* (October 1993), p. 9.

101. Thomas Rosenstiel, "Senate Sends Clinton Apprenticeship Bill," *Los Angeles Times* (April 22, 1994), p. A-25.
102. Lynn Franey, "Failure Stalks the Halls in L.A.," *San Diego Union Tribune* (December 12, 1993), p. A-33.
103. "Overview of School-to-Work Initiative," *Youth Policy* (October 1993), p. 26.
104. Rosenstiel, "Senate Sends Clinton Apprenticeship Bill," p. A-25.
105. For a description of the adversity faced by mainstream-oriented students, see Ron Suskind, "In Rough City School, Top Students Struggle to Learn—and Escape," *Wall Street Journal* (May 26, 1994). The circumstances that make success so difficult for minority youth are captured in Katherine Boo, "Alonzo's Battle," *Washington Post Weekly* (October 18-24, 1993), p. 6; Nathan McCall, "'If You Can Dream,'" *Washington Post Weekly* (February 21-27, 1994); and Barbara Vobejda, "No Exit," *Washington Post Weekly* (March 15-21, 1993).
106. As an illustration of a limited interpretation of social relevance of higher education, see John Hope Franklin, *The Inclusive University* (Washington, DC: Joint Center for Political and Economic Studies, 1993).
107. Richard Hersh, "The Culture of Neglect," *Newsweek* (September 26, 1994), pp. 11-12.
108. Ruben Navarrette, Jr., "Why So Many Young People Keep Politics at Arm's Length," *Los Angeles Times* (January 15, 1995), p. M-6.
109. Amy Wallace, "Survey Finds Political Apathy Among Freshmen," *Los Angeles Times* (January 9, 1995), p. A-14.
110. John Goldman, "Universities Rated 'F' for Inability to Help Solve Society's Problems," *Los Angeles Times* (August 7, 1990), p. A-5.
111. Mark Starr, "Not a 'Miracle' Cure," *Newsweek* (September 17, 1990).
112. Julie Nicklin, "When a University Takes Over the Public Schools," *Chronicle of Higher Education* (October 26, 1994), p. A-22.
113. William Honan, "New President Sees Cornell Helping to Solve Society's Problems," *New York Times* (December 11, 1994), p. 23.
114. Robert Coles, "Putting Head and Heart on the Line," *Chronicle of Higher Education* (October 26, 1994), p. A-64.

chapter 6

Immigration: The Closing of the American Dream

>   La gallina de arriba siempre caga en la de abajo.
>   *(The chicken on top always defecates on the one below.)*
>   *New Mexican dicho*[1]

Immigration is arguably the most volatile of social issues. As a source of public debate, it often lies dormant, until political and economic forces ignite a latent xenophobia, and government officials are charged with reinforcing our borders against an influx of aliens and expelling those here illegally.[2] Occasionally, such purges become ugly, giving rise to nativist hate groups, such as the Ku Klux Klan.[3] California's 1994 Proposition 187, "Save Our State" (cleverly—"SOS"), the ballot initiative that would deny 14th Amendment protections to U.S. residents is a more recent incarnation of immigrant bashing.[4] In either event, the result is a parody of the human condition—former immigrants redoubling their efforts to drive out new arrivals. Longitudinally, this is more than a little perplexing. The anthropological evidence demonstrates that the Americas are populated completely by immigrants, beginning with natives traversing the Bering Strait not that long ago. In a literal sense, we are *all* immigrants.

The other side of the immigration coin is a romanticization of those who have fled to America. Here, the culprits are typically religious intolerance, political persecution, and famine and poverty. The Statue of Liberty and the hallowed words of Emma Lazarus ("Give me your tired, your poor, your huddled masses yearning to breathe free . . .") serve as a potent symbol of America as no less than a savior of millions of innocents victimized by circumstance. The metaphor "Immigrants as pilgrims to a promised land" has been elaborated in variations of the Horatio Alger myth. The immigrant heritage of Americans who have achieved heroic proportion is an essential feature of their, and therewith the nation's, biography: the "founding fathers," Andrew Carnegie, Thomas Edison, Carl Sandburg, Georgia O'Keeffe, Cesar Chavez, and Arnold Schwarzenegger, to name a few. Indeed, it is impossible to conceive of events quintessentially American—the Constitution, the hamburger, Levis, the bomb, "West Side Story"— without acknowledging the contribution of immigrants.

Paradoxically, debate of the nation's immigrant heritage often proceeds without appreciation of historical precedent and in the virtual absence of social and economic data. Even today, few accounts of immigration include the fate of Native Americans at the hands of alien Europeans, or the disenfranchisement of Latinos of the Southwest after the 1848 Treaty of Guadalupe Hidalgo. Indeed, the involuntary immigration of African Americans is often omitted altogether[5]— as if the importation of human cargo still remains a question for customs. Implausibly, despite the inundation of data generated by an informationally insatiable culture, until quite recently first-rate studies of immigrants were virtually nonexistent. Without good research, the immigration debate tends to degenerate into caricature, oscillating between the vilification or celebration of immigrants.[6] Rarely has any phenomenon experienced so intimately by so many been so poorly understood.

THE EUROPEAN MIGRANT WAVES

Historical convention holds that the U.S. population was predominantly Anglo-Protestant well into the nation's first century. Of the signatures to the Declaration of Independence, 95 percent were of English Protestant men. During the first half-century of the United States, it is unlikely that immigration exceeded 250,000.[7] But by the mid-nineteenth century, this changed dramatically. Political instability and economic stagnation in Europe contrasted with expanding opportunity in the New World, and Europeans emigrated to the United States, Canada, Brazil, and Argentina in droves.[8] Facilitating the journey, shipping companies collaborated with European governments to ease the passage. The Cunard Line constructed dormitories that accommodated 2,000 people, provided Kosher food for Jews, and employed a multilingual staff. The Hamburg-Amerika Line went a step further, constructing "an immigrant village for transients with its own railway station, churches, and a synagogue." Immigrants were disinfected, examined by health personnel, and provided with inexpensive food and board.[9]

Promises of inexpensive land enticed immigrants, and their travel was encouraged by shipping companies who stood to benefit from their travel. For its part, the United States was indiscriminate in accepting new arrivals; only a few states had enacted immigration regulations. In 1891, Congress established the Bureau of Immigration to oversee the arrival of foreigners, and authorized the construction of a new immigration processing facility on Ellis Island that was completed in 1901.[10] During this period, immigration regulations were so lax that passengers arriving first- or second-class were automatically admitted, "exempt from any inspection or careful scrutiny."[11]

The first wave of immigrants was largely from northern and western Europe. From 1880 to 1889, 5.2 million immigrants had come to the United States, and 68.5 percent of those had emigrated from the United Kingdom, Ireland, Scandinavia, and the German Empire. Three decades later, these nations counted for only 14.9 percent of immigrants. From 1910 to 1919, 6.3 million foreigners had immigrated, and 55 percent had come from Poland, Russia, and Italy, nations that represented only 9.4 percent of immigrants three decades earlier.[12] This shift in region of origin was significant. Earlier immigrants were more likely to come from English-speaking nations, and they were better educated and skilled. By contrast, immigrants from southern and eastern Europe were non-English speakers, and their education and job skills were inferior.

Whatever the differences among immigrants' nationalities, their impact was unavoidable. Between 1880 and 1919, 23.5 million foreigners had come to the United States. By the turn of the century, 14.2 percent of Americans were foreign-born.[13]

Immigrant families easily accounted for more than half the population of American cities: 69 percent in Boston, 86 percent in Milwaukee, 78 percent in San Francisco.[14] Prior to the enactment of government social programs, immigrants had little to expect in the form of assistance, save for the sporadic and condescending aid extended by the newly established Charity Organization Societies. Consequently, immigrants marshaled what resources they had in their ethnic enclaves and established self-help, mutual assistance organizations.[15]

Despite the social insularity of community enclaves and the economic emphasis on self-sufficiency, immigrants were often met with hostility by American-born natives. The "alien menace" posed by immigrants grated against provincial perceptions of the young nation held by citizens. Anti-Catholicism and anti-Semitism often fueled the vitriolic rhetoric of nativist groups. In 1887, the American Protective Association was founded by Henry Bowers in Clinton, Iowa, to expose Vatican influences allegedly imported by Catholic immigrants. In 1894, the Immigration Restriction League was established by aristocratic Bostonians to limit immigration through the institution of literacy tests. In 1905, the Asiatic Exclusion League was organized in San Francisco to pressure the Board of Education to restrict Japanese students to schools attended by Chinese students. Such groups presaged the revival of the Ku Klux Klan, which used the immigrant issue to rebuild a membership that had flagged after the Civil War.[16]

Xenophobia was not restricted to the ill-educated, however. Many intellectuals of the period took their cues from Social Darwinism, celebrating the superiority of race and the ultimate beneficence of deprivation. Social Darwinism thoroughly permeated the immigration issue after the turn of the century. Yale University sociologist Graham Sumner argued that millionaires were the product of natural selection; conversely the poor had to bear the consequences of their inferiority. Sumner held that prosperity depended on a ratio of men to land, and that overpopulation reflected the exhaustion of antiquated institutions. Clearly, this typified the Old World that was generating immigrants, and it was only natural, Sumner thought, that they would come to the New World:

> If you have abundance of land and few men to share it, the men will all be equal. Each landholder will be his own tenant and his own laborer. Social classes disappear. Wages are high. The mass of men, apart from laziness, folly, and vice, are well off.[17]

Other academics noted that, consistent with Social Darwinist tenets, immigrant groups fared differently. Writing of the later decades of European immigration in which southern and eastern Europeans predominated, professor Ellwood Cubberley contended that

> these southern and eastern Europeans are of a very different type from the north Europeans who preceded them. Illiterate, docile, lacking in self-reliance and initiative, and not possessing the Anglo-Teutonic conceptions of law, order, and government, their coming has served to dilute tremendously our national stock, and corrupt our civic life.

Cubberley's solution to the evils accompanying immigration was to break up ethnic conclaves in order to resocialize foreign children into the American mainstream.[18]

University of Wisconsin sociologist Edward Alsworth Ross was similarly concerned about the racial dilution that invariably attended immigration.

> Observe immigrants not as they come travel-worn up to the gang-plank, nor as they issue toil-begrimed from pit's mouth or mill gate, but in their gatherings, washed, combed and in their Sunday best. You are struck by the fact that from ten to twenty percent are hirsute, low-browed, big-faced persons of obviously low mentality. . . . These oxlike men are descendents of those who always stayed behind.[19]

As noted earlier, Stanford psychologist Lewis Terman used the newly developed IQ test to demonstrate that 80 percent of immigrants were "feeble-minded," a feature doubtless due to their poor genetic stock.[20]

Thus diminished by academics in America's premier educational institutions, the inferiority of immigrants became a subject of popular culture. In 1916, Madison Grant published *The Passing of the Great Race,* elevating superior Nordic groups above subordinate groups, particularly Jews. In 1920, Lothrop Stoddard wrote *The Rising Tide of Color,* using IQ tests to document the alleged inferiority of nonwhites.[21] In 1923, Carl Brigham published *A Study of American Intelligence,* contending that Nordics were superior to "Alpine and Mediterranean races." In 1926, Clifford Kirkpatrick wrote *Intelligence and Immigration,* stating the futility of educating immigrants: "immigrants of low innate ability cannot by any amount of Americanization be made into intelligent American citizens capable of appropriating and advancing a complex culture."[22] Validated by professors and fueled by ersatz popularizations, throttling foreigners was undertaken by native-born Americans with an enthusiasm that bordered on lynching. When an anxious public responded, it was only a matter of time before anti-immigrant sentiment was codified in law.

EARLY IMMIGRATION STATUTES

Early immigration law was in response to public fear of foreign influence on American culture. The first, the Chinese Exclusion Act of 1882, was directed at Chinese who had immigrated to the United States, primarily to work on westward expansion of the railroad, but who later set up small businesses, often laundries.[23] Although numbering only 100,000, Chinese worked for low wages, causing American citizens to fear their competition—to say nothing of alien customs. The enactment of the Exclusion Act entirely stopped further immigration of Chinese to the United States.[24] Five years later, the Act was amended prohibiting any readmission of Chinese who had immigrated to the United States, even those who had property and families here. As a result, some 20,000 Chinese Americans who were abroad when the Act took effect were not allowed back in to the United States, leaving them bereft of livelihood and family.[25] By World War I, the list of "excludables" included idiots, lunatics, people with tuberculosis, polygamists, political radicals, and "practically all persons born in Asia."[26] Provisions of the Chinese Exclusion Act remained in effect until after World War II.

The first comprehensive immigration act was signed by President Harding in 1921. The law put in place a national-origins quota system whereby the number of visas granted to various nations reflected their portion of the American population. Congress also limited the number of immigrants from the eastern hemisphere to 150,000 annually. By contrast, there was no limit on the number of immigrants from nations of the western hemisphere. In 1952, the original legislation was amended by the Immigration and Nationality Act, which specified that half of all visas would be allocated to eastern hemisphere immigrants with "urgently needed" skills, the remainder to relatives of U.S. residents. The 1952 amendments also increased the number of exclusions to 31—including mental retardation, drug addiction, prostitution, and contagious disease—and increased to 18 the grounds for deportation.[27]

The 1965 amendments to the Immigration and Nationality Act eliminated the national-origins quota system in favor of a schedule of preferences regarding the familial relationship of an immigrant to a U.S. resident. In emphasizing family reunification, the 1965 Act specified six criteria for obtaining a visa, four of which clearly favored relatives of U.S. residents. In addition, the Act limited the number of immigrants to 270,000 with no more than 20,000 from any one nation.[28] Subsequent events were to compound immigration policy and exhaust the provisions of the 1965 amendments. After the Vietnam War, there were over 411,000 Vietnamese who applied for refugee status under the 1980 Refugee Act.

In 1980, 473,000 Cubans came to Miami as refugees during the Mariel Boatlift.[29] Each of these events strained the annual quotas for immigration.

Through the 1980s, the origins of immigrants shifted dramatically. Before passage of the 1965 amendments, most immigrants came from Europe; by 1990, the source of most immigration to the United States was the third world. This transition is illustrated in Table 6.1.

The Immigration Act of 1990 altered the 1965 legislation by limiting the number of visas granted relatives living in the United States. In response to the perception that recent immigrants were less skilled than those earlier in the century,[30] the number of visas granted to migrants with desired skills more than doubled. In order to enhance the diversity of the immigrant pool, a new "diversity program" was designated to encourage immigration from ethnic groups that had comprised small percentages of migrants in the past. Finally, the number of visas granted refugees increased steadily to exceed 110,000 per year.[31] Although the 1990 Immigration Act finetuned the 1965 legislation regarding legal immigration, it did little to thwart a continuing tide of undocumented Latino workers entering the United States.

To be sure, much illegal immigration was attributable to circumstances not even remotely connected to the Immigration and Naturalization Service (INS), or the Justice Department, for that matter. The progressive deterioration of the Mexican economy, coupled with the militarization of hostilities in Central America, dislodged tens of thousands of Latinos who came to the United States

TABLE 6.1 Top 10 countries of birth for legal immigrants: 1960 and 1990

	1960			1990	
	Immigrants	%		*Immigrants*	%
Mexico	32,684	12.3	Mexico	56,549	8.6
Germany	31,768	12.0	Philippines	54,907	8.4
Canada	30,990	11.7	Vietnam	48,662	7.4
U.K.	24,643	9.3	Dom. Repub.	32,064	4.9
Italy	14,933	5.6	Korea	29,548	4.5
Cuba	8,283	3.1	China	28,746	4.4
Poland	7,949	3.0	India	28,679	4.4
Ireland	7,687	2.9	Soviet Union	25,350	3.9
Hungary	7,257	2.7	Jamaica	18,828	2.9
Portugal	6,968	2.6	Iran	18,031	2.7
Other	92,236	34.8	Other	314,747	48.0
Total	265,398	100.0	Total	656,111	100.0

SOURCE: Michael Fix and Jeffrey Passel, *Immigration and Immigrants: Setting the Record Straight* (Washington, DC: Urban Institute, 1994), p. 25.

illegally. Although the number of illegal aliens was unknown, it was becoming an unavoidable problem. For 1986, the Border Patrol reported 1.8 million apprehensions. Estimates of the number of undocumented workers in the United States ranged from 3 to 4 million to 5 to 10 million.[32]

THE IMMIGRATION REFORM AND CONTROL ACT

Attempts to curtail the large numbers of illegal entrants to the United States led to the Immigration Reform and Control Act (IRCA) of 1986. In many respects, IRCA was in response to the rising number of immigrants from the third world.[33] Since 1980, immigration policy provided the designation of refugee status for immigrants fleeing a "well-founded fear of persecution," and American military adventures in Southeast Asia and Central America generated hundreds of thousands of asylees (asylum seekers). Simple geography impeded a massive and direct influx of refugees from Southeast Asia to the United States, many of whom became housed in refugee centers near the region, such as Hong Kong. Central America was another matter. U.S.-prompted escalation of military action against guerrilla insurgencies in Guatemala and El Salvador, coupled with American support of "contra"-revolutionaries in Nicaragua, dislocated many working-class and indigenous Central Americans who easily blended into the stream of poor Mexicans traveling *al Norte* for reasons of economic opportunity. Management of the growing Central American asylum problem proved enormously difficult for the Reagan administration, which was prosecuting a war against a perceived Communist threat in the region. The vehicle for such maneuvers were the pro-U.S. oligarchies in Guatemala and El Salvador, and anti-Sandanista insurgents in Nicaragua, all of whom on occasion acted ruthlessly against indigenous populations, slaughtering tens of thousands. In response to military threats against civilians in disputed territories, the Reagan administration turned a deaf ear, even when there was compelling evidence that government troops planned and executed massacres of the populations of entire villages, such as El Mozote, El Salvador.[34] Many of the Central Americans who fled to the United States sought political asylum, which the Reagan administration was unwilling to grant; to do so would be to tacitly recognize that the atrocities were committed with the assistance and approval of the United States. Yet the magnitude of the problem was unavoidable. By the late 1980s, over 2,000 Central Americans were crossing the border into Texas weekly in search of asylum.[35] The consequence of economic and military destabilization of Latin America for illegal immigration to the United States was a deluge of undocumented persons, most of whom were from Central America, as illustrated in the Table 6.2.

In order to stem the flow of illegal aliens into the United States, the IRCA contained two broad provisions. The primary feature was the introduction of *sanctions* against employers who hired undocumented workers. The assumptions behind sanctions were (1) that stiff penalties against employers would dissuade them from hiring the undocumented and (2) that the subsequent decline in jobs

TABLE 6.2 Countries of origin of the resident undocumented population, October 1992

Region/Country	Number	Percent
Central America	1,991,000	62
Mexico	1,002,000	31
El Salvador	298,000	9
Guatemala	121,000	4
Other countries	570,000	18
Europe and Canada	421,000	13
Canada	104,000	3
Poland	102,000	3
Other countries	215,000	7
Asia	340,000	11
South America	205,000	6
Africa	125,000	4
Oceania	15,000	—
Total	3,200,000	100

SOURCE: Michael Fix and Jeffrey Passel, *Immigration and Immigrants: Setting the Record Straight* (Washington, DC: Urban Institute, 1994), p. 24.

would dry up the immigrant flow, particularly Latinos who were coming to the United States for economic reasons. The employer sanctions provision was consistent with the agency responsible for executing IRCA, the INS. Since its inception, the INS has emphasized interdiction and deportation of aliens. Thus, enforcement of penalties against employers was consistent with its "law and order" culture.

IRCA's employer sanctions provisions departed from traditional immigration policy in two ways. Rather than mandating that the INS distinguish between valid and illegal work applicants, IRCA assigned this responsibility to employers. The INS generated a form for work applicants, the I-9, but employers were responsible for determining the legality of their employees. When Latino advocacy groups feared that reserving such responsibility for employers invited massive discrimination against legal Latinos (employers would try to avoid penalties by refusing to hire anyone appearing to be Latino, even legal residents), lawmakers included a clause deactivating those sanctions if widespread discrimination in fact occurred. As a gesture to employers, IRCA called for a one-year period during which the INS would educate employers about their obligation in determining the legal status of applicants as well as the penalties for hiring aliens, which ranged from $250 to $2000 per illegal worker.

The *amnesty* provisions of IRCA varied with an immigrant's status in the labor market. Illegals who had lived continuously in the United States since January 1, 1982, were allowed to apply for amnesty during a twelve-month window, between May 5, 1987, and May 4, 1988. Those qualified obtained temporary resident status for 18 months and had one year to satisfy basic requirements in order to receive permanent residency status. Amnesty would be denied applicants who were felons, were HIV positive, or who had benefited from a federally funded welfare program during the previous five years. For purposes of outreach and assistance in processing amnesty applications, IRCA allowed the INS to contract with private Qualified Designated Entities (QDEs), usually nonprofit social service agencies.

This basic amnesty offer was complemented by special provisions for two populations. Under the Special Agricultural Workers (SAW) program, laborers who had worked with perishable crops for 90 days in the year ending May 1, 1986, were eligible for amnesty. Under the Replenishment Agricultural Workers (RAW) program, between 1990 and 1993, agricultural laborers who had worked with perishable crops for 90 days in each of these years and who had been admitted by the Department of Agriculture could also apply for amnesty. In this manner, IRCA outlined an amnesty fast track for applicants who had worked with perishable crops, an obvious concession to agricultural interests. Thus configured, the IRCA amnesty provisions augmented a small, but expanding, social service function within the INS.

IRCA was to prove a less than qualified success. Because of the focus on employer education, most of the additional staff employed through new IRCA appropriations for the INS were diverted from enforcement. As a result, by 1989 only 16,000, or 0.2 percent, of American employers had been visited by the INS to determine the accuracy of their employment practices.[36] Only 3,500 fines had been issued by INS enforcement agents, and the average fine had been cut in half after negotiation with employers.[37] Such limited and weak penalties were unlikely to dampen employers' enthusiasm for hiring undocumented workers. Regarding general amnesty, 1.8 million aliens applied, a somewhat low number given earlier projections. On the other hand, the SAW program short-cut to amnesty yielded numbers of applicants far higher than what had been projected. California received 700,000 applicants for SAW program amnesty, when researchers had anticipated the number of qualifying farmworkers at only 100,000. Altogether, SAW applications exceeded projections by about 50 percent.[38] The processing of applicants for general amnesty encountered legal challenges that liberalized the program signficiantly. Eventually, the rejection rate of applicants seeking permanent residency status was only one in 10,000.[39] Ultimately however, IRCA would be judged by the extent to which it dissuaded undocumented persons from entering the United States. Here again, IRCA was to disappoint. Assuming a conservative scenario by placing the number of undocumented persons in the United States in June 1986 at 4 million, by June 1989, the number had fallen to 2.4 million; but by October 1992 it had risen to 3.2 million, approximating the rate of increase prior to the enactment of IRCA.[40] "It is already clear that [IRCA] did not stop the flow of illegal aliens into the United States," concluded George Borjas in an assessment shared by many immigration analysts; "there are good reasons to be skeptical about the law's long run effectiveness."[41]

"BIRDS OF PASSAGE"

Among IRCA's several flaws, the greatest concerned undocumented workers who were in the United States temporarily and who were not necessarily interested in permanent residency status. Compounding this, the ambiguous requirements of the SAW program were successfully challenged in court, making it a back door to amnesty for those not meeting the criteria for the general amnesty program. Finally, amnesty was a one-shot offer. The deadline for filing for amnesty was May 4, 1988; late applicants need not apply.

In these respects, IRCA reflected a longstanding American ambivalence about foreigners in the United States who worked for limited periods, then returned home. Historically, the nation's military exploits had benefited from the assistance of foreigners, as in the case of mercenaries who fought alongside American troops during the Revolutionary War. During the Civil War, 40,000 French Canadians fought for the Union Army in exchange for a bounty.[42] The labor shortage precipitated by American entry into World War II led to the legal entry of hundreds of thousands of Mexican workers from 1942 to 1964 under the Bracero Program. At the height of the program in 1956, the United States authorized the entry of 445,000 "braceros" to work in the Southwest.[43]

Despite the contributions that foreigners have made during wartime, the immigrant who works in the United States for a brief period and then returns home is generally treated with a great deal of skepticism. In the history of immigration, such temporary workers have been called "birds of passage," a quaint term that lacks the gravity that would more accurately reflect their quite substantial numbers. That Americans would disparage birds of passage is perhaps understandable given a pervasive jingoism. Walter Nugent observed:

> The birds of passage inflamed opinion in a special way. America was believed to be the haven for Europe's oppressed; immigrants were expected to stay once they arrived. To leave again implied that the migrant came only for money; was too crass to appreciate America as a noble experiment in democracy; and spurned American good will and helping hands.[44]

Dismissed as ungrateful opportunists, birds of passage rarely receive the attention they warrant in the immigration debate. Yet, the data available suggest that temporary alien workers constitute a large stream of the migrant flow. During the early European migrations to America, the number of returning migrants ranged from 10 percent before 1860 to 46 percent between 1908 to 1914. During 1908, several ethnic groups—Southern Italians, Croatians and Slovenians, and Slovaks—experienced more members *leaving* the United States than were arriving.[45]

The temporariness of immigrants' residence varied from ethnic group to ethnic group. Thus, while about half of all Italian immigrants returned to Italy, only about 5 percent of Jews left the United States.[46] Evidently, Italians viewed their residence in America as temporary, the opportunity to earn better wages that would reestablish them back home. Jews, on the other hand, had made an irrevocable commitment to the New World, probably as a response to the pogroms that regularly terrorized their communities in Eastern Europe. Further encouraging repatriation, by the early twentieth century trans-Atlantic travel had become faster, less expensive, and safer than it had been 50 years before, making the return home more feasible. As enhanced opportunity matched accelerating mobility, increasing numbers of migrants returned to their native lands, many remigrating to America when desirable conditions returned.

An unavoidable question is posed by birds of passage: If increasing numbers of migrants came to America during the Industrial era only to return home, how many *more* immigrants would be expected to be birds of passage during a more dynamic post-Industrial era? Take the example of the experience of Latino immigrants to the United States. In examining the migration of Mexican workers to the United States, Alexander Moto sketched a portrait of contemporary birds of passage:

> [G]rowing labor circulation developed into a network tying particular labor source areas in Mexico to specific sites in the United States. Now nearly a century old, this circulation has been institutionalized in the social and economic structure of the sending and receiving areas, and it persists despite the predominance of wage labor in Mexico.
>
> This circulatory flow . . . is substantially illegal in terms of U.S. immigration laws, though it is widely tolerated and even relied on. It is substantially concentrated in the U.S. Southwest, and half of migrants go just to one state, California, though there are enclaves of Mexican migrants in other states. Between certain sending towns in Mexico and their corresponding receiving towns or areas in the United States, the migration occurs point-to-point, following patterns established generations before.[47]

Undoubtedly, passage of NAFTA will accelerate this circulatory flow as Mexican birds of passage seek employment opportunities in the United States only to return to Mexico.

IMMIGRATION AND SOCIAL WELFARE

Few aspects of immigration are more disputed than its influence on social welfare. In considering the matter, it is useful to separate indirect from direct consequences. Regarding indirect consequences, immigrants can influence social welfare by displacing native workers from the labor market, in which case Americans become more dependent on welfare programs. Regarding direct consequences, immigrants may have a weak attachment to the labor market—in which case *they* become beneficiaries of welfare. With the contraction of public resources for social programs during the 1980s—a period of substantial immigration—researchers began mounting studies of the social costs of immigrants. By the early 1990s, sufficient research had been conducted to allow immigration analysts some confidence in conclusions about the relationship between migrants and welfare.

Researchers across the ideological spectrum have concluded that if immigrants displace natives from jobs, the effect is negligible. So concluded Julian Simon, writing under the imprimatur of the conservative Cato Institute.

> The effect [of immigrants' employment] upon natives' unemployment is much less than common belief has it, and native unemployment may even be lessened rather than increased due to immigrants. Immigrants not only take jobs, they make jobs. They open new businesses that employ natives as well as other immigrants and themselves. And they do so in important numbers.[48]

In a more discriminating analysis, George Borjas differentiates among immigrant groups that have arrived during different periods, following his thesis that more recent third-world immigrants are less skilled than earlier European immigrants. Although immigrants from either circumstance enter the United States decidedly disadvantaged with regard to their labor force prospects, eventually their experience mirrors that of natives. Borjas concluded,

> After thirty years in the United States, the labor force participation rate of immigrants is as high as, if not higher than, that of natives. In fact, the impact of assimilation is so strong that immigrants in earlier waves eventually have labor force participation rates that are 4 to 6 percentage points higher than those of natives.[49]

Researchers from the liberal Urban Institute reviewed the labor market research as it relates to immigration and concluded that "there is no strong evidence that immigration reduces overall availability of jobs or wages," stated Michael Fix and Jeffrey Passel. "Immigrants contribute substantially to the U.S. economy. They create more jobs than they themselves fill."[50] If there is a negative influence on the employment of natives, it is with regard to Americans working in immigrant enclaves and those who have poorer work skills. Even then, the effect is small. What job displacement that does occur with the arrival of immigrants in a labor market tends to happen to older immigrants.[51] Thus, rather than take jobs from Americans, immigrants' labor market influence has been one of creating employment opportunity.

The influence of immigrants on welfare programs is more complex than that regarding employment. There are several different welfare programs that immigrants may receive benefits from (AFDC, Food Stamps, Supplemental Security Income, Medicaid); welfare programs are financed in varying degrees by different governmental jurisdictions (federal, state, and local); finally, it is important to differentiate among types of immigrants (legal residents, undocumented aliens, and refugees). To compound matters, it is essential to approximate the contribution that immigrants make by paying taxes, of which there are several: the sales tax, the property tax, Social Security withholding, among others. After examining the immigrant welfare experience in several nations, Julian Simon found that American "immigrants contribute more to the public coffers than they take from them."[52] Borjas, by contrast, noted that immigrants are "only slightly more likely to receive welfare than native households."[53] He observes that, on the one hand, immigrants' tentative attachment to the labor force pushes them toward welfare programs; but, on the other hand, most welfare programs cannot be accessed by illegal immigrants. On balance, Borjas concluded that research fails to affirm "the conjecture that immigrant households are generally more welfare-prone than native households."[54]

Fix and Passel concur that "immigrants generate significantly more in taxes paid than they cost in services received."[55] Beyond this generalization, they offer important clarifications. First, when refugees are removed from the analysis, immigrants are much less likely to be recipients of welfare than are natives. Second, the tax-contribution/welfare-burden ratio varies with different levels of government. Thus, legal immigrants who pay withholding and income taxes represent a positive revenue flow for the federal government, whereas illegal immigrants who tend to use state-financed welfare programs represent a negative cash flow for state and local governments. Where illegal immigrants are concentrated in specific states, as is the case for California, or in metropolitan areas, such as Los Angeles, the impact is more pronounced. This disparity in cost to different levels of government helps explain the enthusiasm the California voters showed toward Proposition 187. The proposition would terminate health, education, and welfare benefits, the costs of which are disproportionately paid by state government, to illegal immigrants residing in California.[56]

Still, the drain that immigrants represent on the government treasury is less than what is often alleged. The immigrant welfare burden to the states is mitigated somewhat by the tendency of older immigrants to rely on the federally funded Supplemental Security Income program.[57] For that matter, the immigrant welfare burden to the federal government is mitigated by the millions of dollars undocumented workers contribute to Social Security with no intention of collecting benefits. Exactly how much is contributed to Social Security is unknown, but the amount is certainly significant. During the 1970s, when Woolworth's marketed a cheap wallet by inserting a phoney Social Security card, within a few months 33,000 people were paying into the bogus account, presumably most of them being undocumented workers.[58]

In contrast to public perception, immigrants do not increase unemployment by taking jobs held by Americans, nor do they drain increasingly scarce public revenues through welfare programs. Quite the contrary—the evidence demonstrates that immigrants create more jobs than they take, and they contribute more in taxes than they consume in social program benefits. There are exceptions to this general pattern—some job displacement has probably occurred among poor African Americans in Miami due to the influx of Latinos;[59] and in all likelihood,

California has incurred disproportionate social program costs due to illegal aliens.[60] The prudent response would be to treat them as discreet events warranting "compensatory assistance."[61] Considering the substantial contributions that immigrants make to our culture, maligning them as a group is contrary to public interest.

THE NEXT IMMIGRATION POLICY AGENDA

The myth that the United States was a "welfare magnate" to immigrants who, when not on welfare programs, stole jobs from Americans permeates official pronouncements on immigration reform. Nowhere is this more evident than in the 1994 report of the U.S. Commission on Immigration Reform. Mandated by the Immigration Act of 1990, *U.S. Immigration Policy: Restoring Credibility* was the product of a nine-member panel chaired by former Congresswoman Barbara Jordan. Citing the failure of immigration policy to control illegal immigration, the Commission declared, "The immediate need is more effective prevention and deterrence of unlawful immigration."[62] Toward that end, seven objectives were advanced:

1. The border with Mexico would be strengthened by establishing a clear and intimidating presence by the Border Patrol as it is in El Paso in "Operation Hold the Line," costs of which would be covered by the introduction of a "border user fee";
2. Employers would be thwarted from hiring undocumented workers by the deployment of a data system, keyed around each worker's Social Security number, which employers would have to access in acquiring legal employees;
3. Government social welfare benefits would be denied illegal aliens except for emergency aid, public health protection, or Constitutional provisions;
4. Alien criminals would be repatriated to Mexico with assurances that they would not return to the United States;
5. Response to immigration emergencies would be reinforced to counter rapid and unanticipated arrival of migrants, such as Haitians and Cubans in 1994;
6. Attention would be directed toward preventing the dislocation of immigrants from their communities of origin by encouraging economic development in their countries; and
7. The data capacity of the INS would be upgraded as would be its ability to share information with other public agencies.

So stated, the "Jordan Commission" weighed in on the side of law and order. In light of the dual functions that had evolved within the INS as a result of IRCA— police enforcement and social services—the Jordan Commission clearly favored the former, a not altogether surprising development considering that several members of the Jordan Commission were associates of the conservative Federation of

American Immigration Reform (FAIR).[63] Omitted altogether were ambiguous references to inclusionary objections, such as amnesty. In essence, the Commission's recommendations were a de facto admission that IRCA had failed.[64]

Popular though they may be, punitive approaches toward immigration, such as the Jordan Commission report and California's Proposition 187, are inconsistent with future economic and demographic trends. With the passage of NAFTA and the General Agreement on Tariffs and Trade (GATT), the United States should be opening and nurturing its relations with neighboring countries, rather than subverting the benefits promised by these treaties. Already, the economic progress experienced by the South American nations—Argentina, Brazil, Paraguay, and Uruguay—that belong to Mercosur, the South American common market, suggests that increasing American nativism will be at the expense of our economic welfare.[65] Demographically, the U.S. labor force is not being replenished fast enough to avoid enormous tax burdens on young workers when current workers retire. As noted in the following chapter, America needs more workers; immigrants present a logical solution to this problem. It follows that a more constructive approach to immigration would put in place those mechanisms whereby immigrants could be selectively encouraged to reside in the United States.

A Rolling Amnesty Date

Among IRCA's shortcomings was the offer of amnesty during one twelve-month period. The purpose of amnesty was to stabilize that population of illegal immigrants who were de facto permanent residents but who had been unable to secure legal authorization to remain in the United States. Approximately 1.8 million immigrants applied for amnesty during the late 1980s.[66] In the decade since the IRCA amnesty offer, many more illegal immigrants have established residence in the United States at least as long as the five-year period suggested by IRCA. Of course, the size of that population is unknown, but it probably exceeds one million.

Public sentiment toward long-term, illegal residents has been decidedly negative. Anti-immigrant groups, such as FAIR, have alleged that the nation is overrun with illegal aliens who are sucking the public sector dry. Issues such as job displacement and welfare dependence have been addressed, but the matter of the immigrant inundation remains. Whereas the nation has experienced different waves of immigration—peak years being 1860, 1890, 1910, and 1990—the percent of the U.S. population that these eras represent varies, although in an unexpected manner. For the peak years of 1860, 1890, and 1910, the number of immigrants was about 10 per 1,000 Americans, but for 1990, the rate of influx was less than 3 per 1,000,[67] as shown in Figure 6.1. During the height of immigration, in 1910, 14.6 percent of Americans were born abroad; by 1980, less than 6 percent were.[68]

Xenophobes may consider current immigration an unnavigable flood, because they have no time to examine the numbers carefully. There *is* a case to be made that the number of immigrants is not disbursed evenly and that some localities bear a disproportionate responsibility for illegal immigrants, but it is unlikely

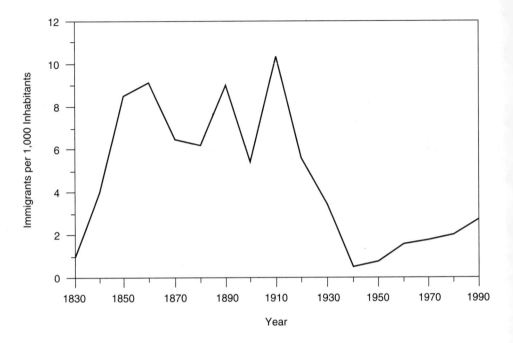

FIGURE 6.1 Change in immigration to the United States

that these represent insuperable numbers. A diminishing labor force makes a compelling case for increasing the number of immigrants, particularly when the social program requirements of a retiring "baby boom" cohort is factored into the equation.

A pragmatic response to permanent, illegal residents would be to designate a "rolling amnesty date." Anyone who can demonstrate continuous residence in the United States for a specified period—say the five years specified in IRCA—would be allowed to apply for amnesty. The processing of applicants would be the same as the general amnesty provisions of IRCA, but with one exception: because of the need for future workers who are healthy and well-trained, amnesty applicants would be entitled to health, education, and job-training benefits as soon as they obtain permanent resident status.

A Guest-Worker Program

As a complement to the continual processing of permanent, illegal residents, it is necessary to regulate temporary workers in the United States. Earl Shorris observed:

> There is still no policy which would permit an orderly entry and exit for those who come to work or shop but not to immigrate. Nor is there any way for people to seek temporary asylum here; to live and work

without fear until conditions at home improve. To distinguish between sojourners and immigrants would be a step in the direction of a truly civil society on the U.S. side of the border.[69]

In the recent past, U.S. immigration policy has addressed directly the circumstances of temporary workers. After World War II, the Bracero Program allowed the entry of Mexican workers until the program was terminated in 1964. Subsequently, 25,000 manual laborers were admitted to the United States under the H-2 Program, established through immigration legislation of 1965.[70] Most recently, the Replenishment Agricultural Worker (RAW) provision of IRCA allowed the entry of field workers between 1990 and 1993.[71] As a series, these programs represent intermittent attempts to regulate undocumented workers who routinely enter the United States only to return home, often to Mexico. Writing of the clandestine entry and exit of Latino workers, Alejandro Portes and Ruben Rumbaut observe that, "The almost routine manner in which thousands of undocumented laborers have come year after year attests to the strength of forces on both sides of the border that sustain this inflow."[72]

Attempts to prohibit the transit of undocumented workers through efforts such as Operation Blockade are futile and impair relations between the United States and Mexico.[73] A more constructive solution would be to follow the suggestion of Ernesto Ruffo, the governor of Baja California, Mexico, and reestablish a guest worker program.[74] One such model is the Replacement Agricultural Worker provision of IRCA, which has the desirable feature of being coupled with amnesty; field workers allowed entry via authorization of the Department of Agriculture and who have worked for a specified period are eligible to apply for temporary residency status and eventually permanent residency.[75]

Negotiate a NAFTA Side-Agreement on Immigrant Labor

A rolling amnesty date and a guest-worker program should serve as a more comprehensive initiative that would regulate migrant labor in North America. The obvious context for such an agreement would be NAFTA. As proposed by Maria Jimenez of the American Friends Service Committee's Immigration Law Enforcement Monitoring Project, a NAFTA side-agreement on migrant labor would include "worker rights, labor standards, and labor mobility."[76]

The scope of negotiations around such a side-agreement should be sufficiently broad to incorporate the factors that drive migrant labor: disparate economic opportunity. Accordingly, a primary issue has been the proliferation of hundreds of *maquiladora* (low-wage assembly) plants along the U.S.–Mexico border. Despite the low wages, typically $.98/hour,[77] employment opportunity is so limited in the interior of Mexico that *maquiladora* plants have lured tens of thousands of Mexicans north. A secondary issue is the substantial remittances that migrant workers send to families in their communities of origin. If poor economic opportunity in disadvantaged communities encourages workers to migrate to the United States, a second feature of a side-agreement should endeavor to enhance the economic viability of those communities. Because migrant workers send significant "remittances" back home, the most direct way to revitalize the communities that are most distressed would be for the federal government to contribute to migrants' remittances as a form of foreign aid.[78]

By incorporating migrant labor within NAFTA, the United States would be following a precedent adopted by the European Economic Community (EEC). In order to regulate the flow of workers within member nations, the EEC has forged a "social charter" specifying the rights of workers, including the portability of worker benefits.[79] A similar provision in NAFTA would serve as a long-range investment in a portion of the continent's labor force that will become increasingly important as regional trading syndicates evolve commensurate with global capitalism.

Unhappily and inaccurately, much of the immigration debate has assumed that immigrants are deficits—unwelcome trespassers who abuse the goodwill and beneficence of America. The resultant immigrant-bashing reflects a churlishness of public sentiment that is as inconsistent with the nation's past as it is our future. In San Diego County, children who are American citizens but living in Tecate, Mexico, are intimidated from attending elementary school in the United States.[80] In 1994, California voters passed Proposition 187, which denies health, education, and welfare benefits for undocumented immigrants, a reversal of that state's history of cultural diversity and tolerance.[81] Much to their credit, farsighted Democrats (led by President Clinton) and Republicans (Jack Kemp and William Bennett) opposed its passage.[82] Immediately after the passage of Proposition 187, a federal district judge enjoined the State of California from implementing its provisions on the grounds that a state did not have the authority to abridge Constitutional protections, in this case the equal protection provisions of the 14th Amendment.[83] Immediately, health providers to California's migrant population noted a decrease in patients visiting clinics. Dr. Juan Ruiz of a Los Angeles health clinic feared that the failure of a large number of immigrants to obtain health care could jeopardize public health. "Disease could be really advanced if people wait until the last minute to come to us," he observed. "That could put the entire community at risk."[84]

Anti-immigrant sentiment was not isolated to California. In evaluating options in financing welfare reform, the Clinton administration's panel of advisors narrowly rejected wholesale denial of social benefits to immigrants who were political refugees and retirement-aged.[85] But, after the 1994 midterm elections, leaders of a Republican-controlled 104th Congress indicated they would go further. Alleging that federal social welfare programs were "a deluxe retirement system for elderly people from the third world," the Heritage Foundation's Robert Rector endorsed a Republican plan to deny public assistance benefits to immigrants. The GOP proposal called for saving $22 billion over five years by denying welfare for legal immigrants, most of whom are refugees.[86]

Public scapegoating notwithstanding, the empirical record demonstrates that this negative caricature contradicts fact: Instead of displacing natives from jobs, immigrants invigorate the economy, in the process increasing employment opportunity; rather than inordinate dependence on social program resources, immigrants pay more in taxes than they consume in program benefits, thus contributing social capital. The anecdotal evidence further affirms immigrants as assets. A *Wall Street Journal* reporter chronicled how a run-down, formerly Scandinavian part of Brooklyn is being reclaimed as a "new Chinatown."[87] Not far away, a journalist writing for the *Washington Post* discovered another neighborhood in the process of reclamation:

> At the very top of Eighth Avenue in Brooklyn's Sunset Park, where six years ago only vacant storefronts stood, are a Buddhist temple, a Chinese business center, a Chinese beauty shop and an Italian laundromat. On the next block are a Middle Eastern grocery and a mosque, and down the street are a Chinese market, a Hispanic delicatessen, a dim sum restaurant and offices, cafes, and small clothing and jewelry stores in a crowded, bustling jumble that stretches at least 20 blocks.
>
> This was a dying neighborhood, slowly abandoned in the late 1960s by European immigrants who settled here at the turn of the century and built the two-story frame houses and brownstones that line surrounding streets. But then more newcomers arrived; first, Puerto Ricans, then Dominicans and, in the past five years thousands of Asians and Arabs.
>
> Today, along the once neglected corridor, storefront buildings sell for half a million dollars, twice what they fetched in the late 1980s. Crime in Sunset Part has declined sharply. Hundreds of brownstones and frame houses have been refurbished.[88]

It would be difficult to conceive of a more effective urban restoration program than that undertaken by the immigrants in Sunset Park.

And immigrant assets are not confined to the multicultural East Coast. David Hayes-Bautista and his colleagues at UCLA have examined specific attributes of Latinos in California. Their findings? Latinos rank above Anglos, Asians, and blacks in their labor force participation; Latinos have a lower infant mortality than blacks and Anglos; Latinos have the lowest rate of low-birthweight babies.[89] Similarly, a nationwide health study revealed that Latinos were less likely than Anglos to die of most chronic diseases: cancer, heart disease, and pulmonary illnesses *"despite poverty, poor access to medical care and a lack of health insurance."*[90]

In light of such evidence, negative portrayals of immigrants are not only wrong, but they run counter to the nation's interest. By denying immigrants rights and opportunities, Americans are writing off precisely what the country needs to retain its standing in the global economy: young, ambitious workers who adhere to the work ethic and maintain strong families. Rather than diminish immigrants and deny them opportunities, we should celebrate them and invest in their futures. "We should keep our borders open, welcome the new immigrants, allow them to keep their language and culture, and enrich ourselves in the process," suggests Alan Wolfe; "since diversity and pluralism will not only generate new sources of economic growth, but they will also contribute to the social mosaic that makes our country distinct."[91]

NOTES

1. Jim Sagel, *Dancing to Pay the Light Bill* (Santa Fe: Red Crane, 1992), p. 10.
2. Richard Serrano, "El Paso Blockade Holding Fast on Illegal Crossings," *Los Angeles Times* (April 14, 1994), p. A-1.
3. Christine Spolar, "The Anti-Immigrant Mood in California Borders on Ugly," *Washington Post Weekly* (June 20-26, 1994), p. 14.
4. Gebe Martinez and Doreen Carvajal, "Prop. 187 Creators Come Under Close Scrutiny," *Los Angeles Times* (September 4, 1994), p. A-1.
5. Alan Wolfe aptly observes that recent usage of the term "African American" is an attempt to add Blacks to the European legacy of ethnicity, though at considerable cost to the history of slavery. See "The Return of the Melting Pot," *New Republic* (December 31, 1990), p. 28.
6. Alan Miller, "Data Sheds Heat, Little Light, on Immigration Debate," *Los Angeles Times* (November 21, 1993), p. A-1.
7. Russell Jacoby, *Dogmatic Wisdom* (New York: Doubleday, 1994), p. 150.
8. Walter Nugent, *Crossings* (Bloomington, IN: University of Indiana Press, 1992).
9. Alan Kraut, *The Huddled Masses: The Immigrant in American Society, 1880-1921* (Arlington Heights, IL: Harlan Davidson, 1982), p. 48.
10. Kraut, *The Huddled Masses*, pp. 52-54.
11. Kraut, *The Huddled Masses*, p. 53.
12. Kraut, *The Huddled Masses*, pp. 20-21.
13. George Borjas, *Friends and Strangers* (New York: Basic Books, 1990), p. 6.
14. Russell Jacoby, *The Last Intellectuals* (New York: Basic Books, 1987), p. 151.
15. Kraut, *The Huddled Masses*, p. 99.
16. Kraut, *The Huddled Masses*, pp. 162-65.
17. Graham Sumner, quoted in Don Martindale, *The Nature and Type of Sociological Theory* (Boston: Houghton Mifflin, 1960), pp. 166-67.
18. Jacoby, *The Last Intellectuals*, p. 137.
19. Edward Alsworth Ross, quoted in Kraut, *The Huddled Masses*, pp. 152-53.
20. Thomas Toch, *In the Name of Excellence* (New York: Oxford University Press, 1991), pp. 43-44.
21. Kraut, *The Huddled Masses*, p. 153.
22. Alejandro Portes and Ruben Rumbaut, *Immigrant America* (Berkeley, CA: University of California Press, 1990), pp. 185-86.
23. Technically, the Aliens Act of 1798 was the first federal immigration law, but it expired after two years and seems to have been inconsequential.
24. Kraut, *The Huddled Masses*, p. 25.
25. Kraut, *The Huddled Masses*, p. 161.
26. Borjas, *Friends and Strangers*, p. 27.
27. Borjas, *Friends and Strangers*, pp. 28-29.
28. Borjas, *Friends and Strangers*, pp. 29-31.
29. Borjas, *Friends and Strangers*, p. 33.

30. Borjas, *Friends and Strangers,* Chapter 7.
31. U.S. Commission on Immigration Reform, *U.S. Immigration Policy: Restoring Credibility* (Washington, DC: author, 1994), p. 34.
32. Borjas, *Friends and Strangers,* p. 65.
33. David Reimers, *Still the Golden Door* (New York: Columbia University Press, 1985).
34. Mark Danner, "The Truth of El Mozote," *New Yorker* 69 (December 6, 1993).
35. Jason Juffras, *Impact of the Immigration Reform and Control Act on the Immigration and Naturalization Service* (Santa Monica, CA: RAND Corporation, 1991), p. 46.
36. Borjas, *Friends and Strangers,* p. 75.
37. Juffras, *Impact of Immigration Reform and Control Act,* p. 25.
38. Juffras, *Impact of Immigration Reform and Control Act,* p. 59.
39. Juffras, *Impact of Immigration Reform and Control Act,* p. 60.
40. Michael Fix and Jeffrey Passel, *Immigration and Immigrants* (Washington, DC: Urban Institute, 1994), p. 23.
41. Borjas, *Friends and Strangers,* p. 74.
42. Kraut, *The Huddled Masses,* p. 24.
43. Reimers, *Still the Golden Door,* pp. 43, 46.
44. Nugent, *Crossings,* pp. 158-59.
45. Nugent, *Crossings,* pp. 157, 160.
46. Nugent, *Crossings,* p. 160.
47. Alexander Moto, *The Roots of Mexican Labor Migration* (Westport, CT: Praeger, 1994), p. 204.
48. Julian Simon, *The Economic Consequences of Immigration* (Oxford, UK: Basil Blackwell, 1989), pp. 223, 252.
49. Borjas, *Friends and Strangers,* p. 138.
50. Michael Fix and Jeffrey Passel, *Immigration and Immigrants: Setting the Record Straight* (Washington, DC: Urban Institute, 1994), p. 47. See also Michael Fix and Jeffrey Passel, "Setting the Record Straight: What Are the Costs to the Public?" *Public Welfare* (Spring 1994), pp. 6-15.
51. Fix and Passel, *Immigration and Immigrants,* pp. 49-51.
52. Simon, *The Economic Consequences,* p. 128.
53. Borjas, *Friends and Strangers,* p. 153.
54. Borjas, *Friends and Strangers,* p. 157.
55. Fix and Passel, *Immigration and Immigrants,* p. 57.
56. Paul Feldman and Patrick McDonnell, "Prop. 187 Sponsors Swept Up in National Whirlwind," *Los Angeles Times* (November 14, 1994), p. A-1.
57. Jennifer Dixon, "Increasing Number of Immigrants Learn to Unlock Door to SSI Vault," *San Diego Union-Tribune* (May 7, 1993), p. A-10.
58. Ted Conover, *Coyotes* (New York: Vintage, 1987), p. 207.
59. Peter Schuck, "The New Immigration and the Old Civil Rights," *The American Prospect* (Fall 1993), p. 106.
60. Pete Wilson, "Immigration: Is It Time to Really Say No?" *San Diego Union-Tribune* (August 22, 1993), p. G-4.
61. Jagdish Bhagwati, "Behind the Green Card," *New Republic* (May 14, 1990), p. 39.
62. *U.S. Immigration Policy,* p. 3.
63. Interview with Maria Jimenez, October 20, 1994.

64. Stuart Silverstein, "7 Years Later, Many Scoff at Immigration Act, *Los Angeles Times* (August 28, 1993), p. A-1.
65. William Long, "Look Out, NAFTA! Latin Trade Bloc is Growing," *Los Angeles Times* (January 24, 1995), p. H-2.
66. Juffras, *Impact of Immigration Reform and Control Act*, p. 58.
67. Julian Simon, "The Case for Greatly Increased Immigration," in Robert Emmet Long (ed.), *Immigration to the United States* (New York: W.W. Wilson, 1992), pp. 161–62.
68. Simon, "The Case for Greatly Increased Immigration," p. 162.
69. Earl Shorris, "Borderline Cases," in Robert Emmet Long, *Immigration to the United States* (New York: W.W. Wilson, 1992), p. 85.
70. Alejandro Portes and Ruben Rumbaut, *Immigrant America* (Berkeley, CA: University of California Press, 1990), p. 235.
71. Borjas, *Friends and Strangers*, p. 73.
72. Portes and Rumbaut, *Immigrant America*, p. 235.
73. Jonathan Fried, *Operation Blockade: A City Divided* (Houston: American Friends Service Committee, 1994).
74. Ed Mendel, "Baja Governor Suggests a Guest-Worker Program," *San Diego Union-Tribune* (May 24, 1994), p. A-1.
75. Borjas, *Friends and Strangers*, p. 73.
76. Maria Jimenez, "Labor Mobility and the North American Free Trade Agreement," *Immigration Newsletter*, Vol. 19, No. 4, pp. 5–6.
77. Jimenez, "Labor Mobility," p. 4.
78. This suggestion was introduced by Linda Wong as part of a C-Span conference on immigration in Atlanta, Georgia (August 18, 1994); for details, see Beth Asch (ed.), *Emigration and Its Effects on the Sending Country* (Santa Monica, CA: RAND, 1994), pp. 13–14.
79. See Commission of the European Communities, *The Community Charter of Fundamental Social Rights for Workers* (Brussels, 1990); *Proposal for a Council Recommendation on the Convergence of Social Protection Objectives and Policies* (Brussels, 1991).
80. Leonel Sanchez, "Residency Crackdown Forces 325 from School," *San Diego Union-Tribune* (February 11, 1994), p. A-1.
81. Kevin Starr, "California Reverts to Its Scapegoating Ways," *Los Angeles Times* (September 26, 1993), p. M-1; Ronald Brownstein and Richard Simon, "Hospitality Turns into Hostility," *Los Angeles Times* (November 14, 1993), p. A-1.
82. James Bornemeier, "Kemp, Bennett Warn of GOP Rift on Prop 187," *Los Angeles Times* (November 22, 1994), p. A-1.
83. Paul Feldman and James Rainey, "U.S. Judge Extends Ban on Prop. 187," *Los Angeles Times* (November 23, 1994), p. B-1.
84. Patrick McDonnell, "Health Clinics Report Declines after Prop. 187," *Los Angeles Times* (November 26, 1994), p. A-1.
85. William Claiborne, "Noncitizens Need Not Apply," *Washington Post Weekly* (December 27–January 2, 1994), p. 33.
86. "Legal Immigrants' Benefits Targeted," *Idaho Statesman* (November 22, 1994), p. A1.
87. E.S. Browning, "A New Chinatown Grows in Brooklyn," *Wall Street Journal* (May 31, 1994).
88. Malcolm Caldwell, "Huddled Masses, Yearning to Buy a Brownstone, *Washington Post Weekly* (September 27–October 3, 1993), p. 32.

89. David Hayes-Bautista et al., *No Longer a Minority: Latinos and Social Policy in California* (Los Angeles: UCLA Chicano Studies Research Center, 1992).
90. Sheryl Stolberg, "Health Study Ranks Latinos above Anglos," *Los Angeles Times* (November 24, 1993), p. A-1.
91. Alan Wolfe, "The Return of the Melting Pot," *New Republic* (December 31, 1990), p. 28.

chapter 7

Social Security: Showdown at Geezer Gulch

> *The issues of social policy the United States faces today have no European counterpart nor any European model of a viable solution. They are American problems, and we Americans are going to have to think them through by ourselves.*
>
> Daniel Patrick Moynihan[1]

Social Security is the bedrock of the American welfare state. Over the decades, it has been appended to include Disability Insurance, Medicare, and—for a short time—Catastrophic Health Insurance.[2] Meanwhile, the basic Social Security program, Old Age Survivors Insurance, has progressively expanded to become the nation's largest social program. A tribute to its popularity, Social Security weathered the adversity of a hostile Reagan administration, virtually unscathed from cuts and actually strengthened by changes introduced through the 1983 Bipartisan Commission on Social Security Reform. In 1994, President Clinton signed a bill making Social Security a separate cabinet department, the ultimate legislative distinction. Over the decades, Social Security has demonstrated a durability that its creators probably had not imagined, more than any other liberal legislative construct.

Despite its success, Social Security remains the subject of controversy. Liberals have charged that its financing through a mandatory withholding tax is regressive and that benefits are inadequate for the income needs of retirees. Conservatives bridle at compulsory participation in Social Security and the enormous fiscal draw it represents as an entitlement. Left in the lurch are younger workers who wonder if they will receive *their* benefits in an amount comparable to that of their parents. Social policy analysts from both ideological camps have come to question an emerging "generation gap" whereby the nation's commitment to the aged is automatically met through open-ended entitlements, such as Social Security, while discretionary programs for American children are subject to the caprice of annual legislative review. The image of aged "snow birds" wintering in the Southwest in their Winnebagos clashes with the utter depravity experienced by minority youngsters in American inner cities.

A distinguishing feature of the issues surrounding Social Security is that the stakes are so high and the payoff is so long range. Annual appropriations through Social Security already eclipse every other item in the federal budget, and the surpluses now generated in anticipation of retiring baby boomers are so large that they dwarf the annual budgets of even the largest states. What becomes of this surplus will determine the nation's future more than any other factor, with the possible exception of foreign invasion. Yet, few Americans—especially younger workers—have deliberated on the matter. Drafters of the 1983 amendments to Social Security promised solvency well into the twenty-first century, but each new inquiry appears to push up the date that Social Security goes belly-up. The implications of this gamble for young workers are such that they give new meaning to an old policy axiom: The farthest any elected official will plan into the future will not exceed his/her last plausible reelection. In other words, by the time the full consequences of the 1983 amendments to Social Security register with today's young workers, it will be too late for them to do much about it; the legislators who fashioned them will be well beyond reelection—they will all be dead.

THE ORIGINS OF SOCIAL SECURITY

American welfare state mythology portrays Social Security in heroic proportion, a legislative monolith that served as a beacon for decades of social policy. According to this traditional characterization, Social Security became the cornerstone of the American welfare state, borne of the turbulence generated by the Great Depression, advanced by a forward-thinking Franklin Delano Roosevelt, and opposed by a much-antagonized business sector. As in all mythology, this characterization is only partially correct. The circumstances surrounding the origins of Social Security were considerably more ambiguous and interest groups certainly more ambivalent than revisionist accounts now suggest.

Historically, the first governmental insurance for workers can be traced to Germany, where Chancellor Otto von Bismarck introduced a pension program in 1889. The United Kingdom established a similar retirement program in 1911. By the beginning of World War I, all European nations had a public pension program in place.[3] This was not the American experience, however.

The American tradition of voluntarism left the obligation for aid to workers with the private sector. During American industrialization, various nongovernmental organizations responded, but in a way that was irregular and inadequate to meet the needs of workers. Fourteen railroads had established pension programs by 1908. Labor unions, such as the Cigarmakers' Union and the German-American Typographia, provided extensive benefits to worker-members for the period. Immigrant communities created their own fraternal, mutual assistance organizations to aid workers and their families in times of distress. By the turn of the century, commercial insurance companies, such as Prudential, wrote industrial insurance policies in the millions of dollars.[4]

As industrialization accelerated, so did the problems encountered by workers who were disabled, unemployed, or retired. As their numbers increased, they drew the attention of America's captains of industry. *Welfare capitalism*—"industry's attending to the social needs of workers through an assortment of medical and funeral benefits, as well as provisions for recreational, educational, housing, and social services"[5]—became the epitome of ideological correctness among the more conscientious members of the turn-of-the-century business elite. Indeed, what we now consider to be private, employee benefits, were at the time thought of as public welfare, dispensed through the private corporation. In the absence of governmental social programs that did not emerge until the 1930s, beneficent, big business held what little promise there was of ameliorating the social and economic dislocations accompanying immigration and industrialization. To be sure, an evolving group of Charity Organizations and Settlement Houses provided guidance and services to the immigrant poor, but these organizations themselves were often financially dependent on the largesse of industrial corporations.

Business leaders were unabashed about the virtues of welfare capitalism. Speaking before the Chamber of Commerce, corporate titan John D. Rockefeller verged on waxing maternal in his depiction of the engine of capitalism:

> Shall we cling to the conception of industry as an institution, primarily of private interest, which enables certain individuals to accumulate wealth, too often irrespective of the well-being, the health and happiness of those engaged in its production? Or shall we adopt the modern viewpoint and *regard industry as being a form of social service,* quite as much as a revenue process? . . . The soundest industrial policy is that which has constantly in mind the welfare of employees as well as the making of profits, and which, when human considerations demand it, *subordinates profits to welfare.*[6]

There was more to welfare capitalism than rhetoric. Prior to World War I, enlightened business leaders lent their voices to the cause of welfare capitalism, assisting in the development of important philanthropies, such as the Twentieth Century Fund and the Russell Sage Foundation. As early as 1904, the National Civic Federation (NCF) had established its Welfare Department in order to pursue research and development in employee welfare. The executive board of NCF's Welfare Department included the executives of Filene's department store, National Cash Register, General Electric, Studebaker, National Biscuit Company, American Locomotive, H.J. Heinz Company, International Harvester, and R.H. Macy and Company. By 1914, the NCF Welfare Department was able to identify

2,500 American companies that had incorporated employee benefits into their business practices.[7]

Among the advocates of welfare capitalism were academics from prominent American universities, such as Yale, Cornell, Columbia, and Wisconsin. In 1906, professors from major universities formed the American Association for Labor Legislation (AALL) for the purpose of reforming the relations between labor and industry. Under the leadership of Isaac Rubinow, John Andrews, and Adna Weber, AALL was holding national conferences on employment policy within a decade. AALL's proposals for labor reform included social insurance to cover workers who were disabled, unemployed, and retired.[8] As different states experimented with various programs to aid workers no longer participating in the labor force, the research conducted by AALL provided important background material for labor reform legislation. Ironically, many state innovations occurred at the behest of industry. Liberal historian Michael Katz observed:

> Large corporations experimented with social insurance and new labor market policies far more daring than almost any government innovations. Not only were corporations free of the political restraints of government, they were more competent.[9]

By 1929, then, a range of parties had fairly extensive experience with options in aiding workers, including social insurance for retirees. With the abrupt dislocation caused by the Depression, it was only logical for the Roosevelt administration to draw on these experiences in drafting what was to become Social Security. Rarely appreciated in accounts of the crafting of the Social Security Act is the role that business leaders played and the ambivalence of President Roosevelt about social insurance for retired workers. Instrumental in the creation of Social Security was Gerald Swope, a General Electric executive. Swope's vision of social policy was a "corporate welfare state," one that was grounded in "a national system of unemployment, retirement, life insurance, and disability programs and standards." From his position as chairman of Roosevelt's Business Advisory Committee, Swope was well positioned to see that any government retirement program reflected corporate values.[10] Swope could not have been more successful. As it took form, Social Security clearly bore the imprint of the business community: Only workers who had contributed would receive benefits, thus ensuring that no public funds would be required to operate the program. In this manner, the "social security concept" came to refer to a public pension program that was modeled on programs of the private sector. As business historians, Edward Berkowitz and Kim McQuaid observed, Social Security represented nothing less than "the acceptance of approaches to social welfare that private businessmen, not government bureaucrats had created."[11] So conceived, the social insurances that were incorporated into the Social Security Act were an acceptable way to divert "welfare for the middle class."[12] Social Security was welfare capitalism triumphant.

If corporate interests were certain about their requirements for a government retirement insurance program, the same cannot be said for President Franklin Roosevelt. In placing social insurance for workers before Congress, FDR displayed a cynicism that bordered on the crass and an uncertainty that approached the feckless. In order to secure the votes of southern legislators, FDR agreed to exempt domestic and agricultural workers—occupational groups not so coincidentally African American—from Social Security.[13] In one of the more glaring examples of institutional racism, the initial Social Security Act meant that an entire generation of African Americans would be forced to work as long as they possibly could, ineligible to retire with benefits from the government pension program.

Programmatically, the major omission of the Social Security Act was a national health program, a feature that FDR feared would subvert the entire legislative package. (Substantial involvement in health care would not be legislated until 1965 with the passage of Medicare and Medicaid.) Yet, Roosevelt's trepidations about the fate of his major domestic policy initiative extended far beyond health reform. At the last minute, FDR had second thoughts about even including Social Security in the Act, fearing that conservative business interests would sabotage what was otherwise an initiative to assist distressed workers. On learning of the president's misgivings, White House aides scrambled, executing an adroit media maneuver, leaving FDR with little choice but to include Social Security in the Social Security Act.[14]

So qualified, the Social Security Act was a much-diluted initiative compared to that advocated by the president's more progressive Committee on Economic Security. Given the hair-raising few months preceding its passage, however, New Dealers such as Harry Hopkins and Frances Perkins were undoubtedly relieved when FDR signed the legislation on August 14, 1935. Liberal academics would prove less charitable, referring to the Social Security Act as "a modest beginning program of social assurances."[15]

AN EXPANDING ENTITLEMENT

In its initial form, Social Security intended to award minimal benefits to workers who had reached age 65 beginning January 1, 1942. Benefits were assessed by a 1 percent tax on the first $3,000 in income assessed on individual workers as well as employers, so that the maximum contribution by a worker would not exceed $30 per year. Between 1937 and 1942, the program would accrue sufficient reserves to pay benefits. Single workers could expect to receive $22 per month, married workers $36, benefits that represented about 40 percent of what they had contributed to the program. Thus, the "replacement rate"—the percent of earnings represented by benefits—was less than half what workers had earned.[16] Workers who received very low benefits from Social Security might be eligible for Old Age Assistance (now part of Supplemental Security Income), a public assistance program for the aged poor included in the Social Security Act.

Shortly after Social Security became law, a citizen's advisory council was created to review the provisions of the 1935 Act. The 1939 recommendations of the council shaped Social Security for the next three decades. Prominent among the council's suggestions was the conversion of Social Security financing from being based on a reserve to a "pay-as-you-go" arrangement; benefits would be accounted for by workers' contributions with a nominal pool set aside for emergencies. In addition, family members of beneficiaries—wives, widows, and children—became eligible for Social Security benefits. The first year of eligibility was moved up to 1942. Low-wage workers were to receive disproportionately higher benefits than had been originally intended.[17] So modified, Social Security grew . . . glacially. By 1950, only 16 percent of retirees were receiving Social Security, whereas 22 percent received Old Age Assistance.[18] At the time, the withholding tax had risen to only 1.5 percent, still levied on the first $3,000 in income.[19]

The council report of 1950 altered Social Security in subtle, but significant, ways: (1) The replacement rate was increased along with other changes in benefit computation, the result of which was a 77-percent increase in benefits; (2) More groups were made eligible for Social Security—and, for the first time, Social Security benefits eclipsed Old Age Assistance; (3) Provisions that treated women differently from men were corrected; and (4) A limited form of disability insurance was implemented, a precursor of federal Disability Insurance that was incorporated into Social Security in 1956. These changes extended Social Security so that by 1960, 60 percent of workers were covered.[20]

Progressive expansion of Social Security brought millions of Americans under the protective umbrella of what had become the nation's largest income security program. The critical period of growth occurred during the 1960s; by 1970, the program was so large that no politician considering reelection could afford to even consider tampering with Social Security. The growth of Social Security in the post–World War II era was nothing short of spectacular. By 1970, 82 percent of workers were covered; by 1980, the number reached 90 percent. The federal withholding tax had increased accordingly; for 1980, employers and workers each paid 6.13 percent of the first $25,900 in income. (Of federal withholding, 1.05 percent was diverted to Hospital Insurance of the Medicare program that had been introduced in 1965.) Annual expenditures for Social Security and Disability Insurance in 1980 were $120 billion, almost four times what they had been only a decade earlier, a figure that would more than double by 1990.[21]

By the early 1980s, it was evident to Social Security actuaries that exponential growth was straining the fiscal integrity of the program. Although pay-as-you-go had been central to financing the program for almost a half-century, a conspiracy of circumstances raised questions about whether or not Social Security could remain self-financing. Beginning in 1972, Social Security benefits were indexed for inflation and increased 20 percent, guaranteeing a higher level of benefit payment relative to other sectors of the economy, particularly workers making contributions through wages that were not indexed. If workers' wages did not keep up with inflation—a development that began in the mid-1970s and continued through the 1980s—then workers' withholding contributions would be outstripped by Social Security beneficiaries claims that were indexed. Compounding the financing problem, demographers noted that the dependency ratio—the number of workers contributing to Social Security versus the number of retirees claiming benefits—was rapidly diminishing. Not only were there more baby boomers than there had been retirees from the previous generation, but the baby boomers had also been less-procreative, meaning they had raised fewer future workers whose contributions would be the basis for benefits to the baby boomers when they retired. All of these conditions converged as public sentiment swerved to the right, leading to a conservative Reagan presidency and a Republican Senate, which raised doubts about the capacity of government to address social problems.[22]

In response to the crisis facing Social Security, President Reagan established a bipartisan commission under the direction of Alan Greenspan to restore the program to fiscal health. The suggestions of the Greenspan Commission, to be adopted by Congress, promised to keep Social Security solvent well into the twenty-first century. The 1983 amendments to Social Security were, for the most part, incremental adjustments in the program, but the consequence of these changes had radical implications. Modest adjustments in the program included advancing the age of eligibility for benefits, increasing the federal withholding tax, including federal and nonprofit employees in the program, a 6-month delay in benefit increases, and modification in the indexing formula. Altogether, the Commission assured that these changes would generate unprecedented surpluses in anticipation of the retirement of baby boomers. They also spelled the end of pay-as-you-go, placing Social Security financing on a reserve basis.[23] Despite this alteration of funding philosophy, designers of the 1983 amendments were confident that Social Security would continue its wide popularity and broad support as a social insurance.[24]

On the fiftieth anniversary of Social Security, former commissioner Robert Ball commented:

> [Social Security] is built on traditional values and concepts—self-help, mutual aid, insurance, and incentives to work and save. The founding fathers of Social Security planned well, and we are reaping the benefits of their work fifty years later through a program now soundly financed for both the short and the long run.[25]

THE BURGEONING SURPLUS

Others were less sanguine about the soundness of Social Security. The issues surrounding the future of Social Security are summarized concisely by Carolyn Weaver of the American Enterprise Institute. By 1990, the surpluses generated by the 1983 amendments to Social Security were accumulating at a rate of $1.6 billion weekly, and were expected to reach $1 trillion by 1996. By 2030, the surplus should rise to $12 trillion. However, "with the reserves invested entirely in government bonds and the federal government operating in the red," cautioned Weaver, "it is not immediately obvious whether the Social Security surpluses are being saved and invested for future years or spent on current consumption."[26]

The relationship between the Social Security surplus, the federal budget, and the solvency of the program is not as abstruse as it might seem; however, once the various implications are factored in, the result bears more than a slight resemblance to a Rube Goldberg apparatus. In order to spare the next generation of workers extraordinary payroll tax increases as would be necessary if the pay-as-you-go arrangement were to be continued, the 1983 amendments to Social Security promised to generate quite substantial surpluses that would be used to cover the retirement needs of baby boomers. The designers of the 1983 Social Security amendments intended that the resultant surplus and the interest it would generate should assure baby boomers of their Social Security benefits. In this respect, the reserve fund concept that generates surpluses from which future benefits will be paid is more consistent with private retirement insurance after which Social Security was initially modeled than the pay-as-you-go arrangement adopted in 1939.

Unfortunately, the federal government has been operating with enormous deficits since the 1980s, and the deficit exceeds incoming tax revenues, including Social Security taxes. As a result, two things happen. First, the Social Security surplus exists only on paper, it is an IOU that the Social Security Administration secures from the Treasury Department in exchange for withholding tax revenues.[27] For the Social Security Administration, the surplus generates interest that can be used to augment benefits to baby boomers when they retire; for the Treasury Department, on the other hand, the bonds sold to balance the federal deficit, which includes the Social Security surplus, represents a negative flow of interest to bond holders. Second, because Social Security withholding is counted as revenue by the federal government, it offsets the deficit. In other words, the federal deficit would be greater in the amount of the Social Security surplus for a given year.

Thus, the long-term integrity of the Social Security program depends on the socioeconomic health of the economy. An expanding labor market of high-paying jobs, more and younger workers in relation to retirees, and a diminishing deficit portend favorably for the vitality of Social Security; while poorer-paying jobs, fewer and older workers in relation to retirees, and an expanding deficit are unfavorable. Exactly how the many factors affecting Social Security will eventually weigh-in is unknown, but it remains essential to approximate different scenarios' influence. The Social Security Administration does this by charting the cost of the program according to various circumstances relative to revenues. Figure 7.1 illustrates this approach. By holding the tax rate constant at 12.4 percent of taxable payroll, the chart describes the experience of Social Security (Old Age Survivors and Disability Insurance) under three scenarios: Alternative I (optimistic), Alternative II-B (intermediate), and Alternative III (pessimistic). Between 1990 and the early part of the next century, the withholding tax rate exceeds

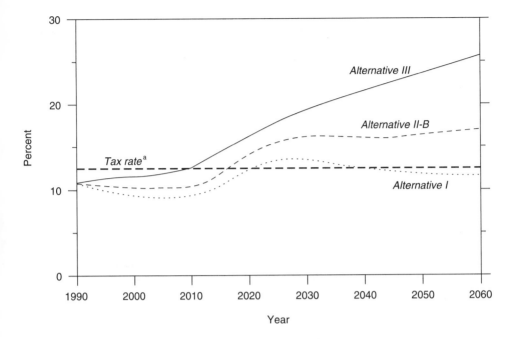

FIGURE 7.1 OASDI cost rate and tax rate, 1990–2060 (as percentage of taxable payroll)

a. Employee and employer rate combined.

SOURCE: 1989 Trustees' Reports, Social Security.

the costs for all of the scenarios, a condition that creates the Social Security surplus. This surplus, plus interest, will be paid out early in the next century to cover retiring baby boomers beginning at different times for each scenario, according to varying social and economic developments. But, by midcentury, the assumptions on which the adequacy of the surplus are based begin to disintegrate. At that point—a condition reached in 2065 for the intermediate and pessimistic scenarios—the surplus is exhausted, and only way to meet continuing benefit demands by retirees will be through higher withholding taxes on workers.[28]

In order to appreciate what the generation of post-baby boom workers is facing, the dependency ratio (the number of workers per beneficiary) becomes important. The aging of the baby boomers compounded by their relatively low birth rate means that the dependency ratio will fall substantially over the next several decades. The trajectory of the falling dependency ratio is depicted in Table 7.1. According to changing demographics, by 2010, the ratio of workers to beneficiaries will fall to 3.0 to 1; and within two decades, by 2030, it will be much less, 2.0 to 1. Assuming that Social Security remains a self-financing social insurance, withholding taxes on workers will begin to skyrocket midcentury

TABLE 7.1 Changing demographics of U.S. workers (1960–2060)

Year	Number of Workers (thousands)	Number of Beneficiaries (thousands)	Workers per Beneficiary	Percentage 65 and Older
1960	72,530	14,262	5.1	9.1
1970	93,090	25,186	3.7	9.7
1980	112,212	35,119	3.2	11.1
1990	130,708	39,618	3.3	12.4
2000	142,124	44,212	3.2	12.7
2010	150,989	50,566	3.0	13.5
2020	151,591	64,129	2.4	17.1
2030	150,613	76,151	2.0	20.9
2040	151,192	79,381	1.9	21.6
2050	150,776	80,780	1.9	21.7
2060	150,606	82,920	1.8	22.5

SOURCE: Carolyn Weaver, "Introduction," in *Social Security's Looming Surpluses* (Washington, DC: American Enterprise Institute, 1990), p. 6.

when the Social Security surplus becomes depleted. In one projection, Peter Peterson has extrapolated the implications of the diminishing dependency ratio for the next generation of workers. By 2040, Peterson's "high-cost scenario" raises Social Security and Medicare taxes to 53.3 percent of workers' payroll, a "low-cost scenario" to 38.2 percent.[29] Given the fiscal demands already placed on the federal budget, the prospect that almost half of all wages would be diverted to one program that benefits retirees is the equivalent of economic euthanasia.

None of this would be necessary, of course, if Social Security continued under a pay-as-you-go arrangement in which current workers pay taxes to cover current retirees. For purposes of simplification, Daniel Patrick Moynihan has proposed regearing Social Security to pay-as-you-go financing through 2012, effectively nullifying the 1983 Social Security amendments. According to Moynihan, combined payroll withholding would be reduced immediately from 15.3 percent to 15.02 percent, then dropped further to 13.1 percent the subsequent year. This would cover benefit payments until 2012 when combined withholding would rise to 19.1 percent.[30] In addition to simplifying the math, Moynihan has argued that his plan is fairer to middle-income workers than the present reserve strategy. This is because Social Security withholding is a regressive tax that is being used to subsidize all federal governmental programs, the amount of subsidization equal to the amount of the deficit deflected each year by Social Security withholding. (Actually, the withholding tax is "doubly regressive" in that it is a flat tax—7.65 percent regardless of income—but the income base against which the tax is assessed is also capped, i.e., limited to the first $60,600 per year.)[31] In other words, Moynihan contends that returning Social Security financing to pay-as-you-go would eliminate the artificial reduction of the deficit that occurs now with the rapidly increasing Social Security surplus. Moreover, if the deficit did not reflect Social Security credits, lawmakers would have to be more honest in making tough decisions about taxes and spending. For example, a more liberal solution to the problem would be to increase the income tax, which would extract more revenue from the wealthy, rather than rely on the regressive withholding tax that disproportionately affects middle- and low-income workers, as is now the case.[32]

THE ENTITLEMENT CRISIS

By the early 1990s, warning flares were going up not only about the solvency of the Social Security program, but social entitlements in general. The first thorough treatment of the rise of entitlement spending by a prominent official was that of Peter Peterson, a former Bell and Howell executive and Nixon White House appointee. Through his position in the Commerce Department, Peterson began to realize that to a substantial degree the productivity lag of the American economy in relation to global competitors could be attributed to the nation's lack of restraint on consumption coupled with a failure to save and invest in productive capacity. In developing his thesis, Peterson challenged orthodoxy from both the Right and the Left. He blamed "happy-time Republicans" for frittering away the revenue windfalls of the Reagan tax cuts on Savings and Loan misadventures, arguing that they should have been pumped into capital producing investment initiatives. At the same time, Peterson identified liberal social entitlement programs that were indexed for inflation as also responsible for fueling consumption to the detriment of savings. The burden of the consequences of this generation's fiscal profligacy, Peterson argued, would fall on the next generation of workers who would have "to pay as much as one-third to one-half of their paychecks before the middle of the next century to finance our own public retirement and health-care programs."[33] As early as 1982, Peterson had recruited a small army of public officials as the Bipartisan Budget Appeal to examine the implications of high-consumption, low-investment economics for the federal budget.

Peterson's crusade against what he perceived to be irresponsible economic policy would probably have been dismissed as so much polemic from a conservative policy institute with which he was associated, had he not received unexpected assistance from the freshman senator from Nebraska, Bob Kerrey. A Vietnam War Medal of Honor awardee, Kerrey's political ambitions were reflected in his vaulting from governor of Nebraska to U.S. Senator, then candidate for president during the 1992 primaries. Kerrey's reputation as a maverick Democrat was carved in stone because of a spectacular vote during the 1994 budget debate. Stunned by defeat of the 1993 economic stimulus package, the Clinton administration frantically cut deals to rescue its budget proposal, the defeat of which would have surely crippled the White House. With each Democratic vote becoming increasingly essential, Kerrey held out to the end, publicly faulting the

Clinton proposal for its failure to contain entitlement spending. In private, Kerrey was less charitable, describing it as "incremental bullshit."[34] In a speech from the Senate floor, Kerrey actually chastised the president for fielding such a timid plan. In relenting to support it, Kerrey insisted on the creation of a special Bipartisan Commission on Entitlement and Tax Reform. To salvage his presidency, Clinton agreed. Among the members of the Commission was Peter Peterson.

The bleak assessment portrayed in the Entitlement Commission's initial report can be traced to the unfathomable deficit that emerged during the first Reagan term, and the attempt to contain it during the second: the Balanced Budget and Emergency Deficit Control Act of 1985, otherwise known by its prime sponsors: Gramm-Rudman-Hollings. Although certain provisions of Gramm-Rudman-Hollings were ruled unconstitutional, its focus remained: In order to reduce the deficit, program spending would be limited, any increases accounted for by higher taxes or decreases in other program expenditures. By the time George Bush assumed the presidency, the tension within the federal budget process was palpable. Entitlement programs strained to meet their mandated obligations while discretionary programs bore more and more of the budget cuts dictated by Gramm-Rudman-Hollings. The resolution of this problem was the 1990 Budget Enforcement Act in which Bush agreed—fatefully—to raise taxes in exchange for a scheme in which three categories of expenditures were designated: defense, international, and domestic programs. Through 1995, programs in each category would be held constant, balanced by higher taxes or within-category cuts, any "overages" made up by across-the-board cuts of programs within the respective category. Any within-category savings, particularly in defense, would be credited toward the deficit.[35]

Constrained by these circumstances, the Entitlement Commission's report projected dire straights for future budgets if entitlements continued to spiral out of control:

> In 2012, unless appropriate policy changes are made in the interim, projected outlays for entitlements and interest on the national debt will consume all tax revenues collected by the federal government.
>
> In 2030, unless appropriate policy changes are made in the interim, projected spending for Medicare, Medicaid, and Federal employee retirement programs alone will consume all tax revenues collected by the Federal Government.[36]

The relationship between entitlement spending and other major components of the federal budget is depicted in Figure 7.2.

Under current assumptions, discretionary spending—including such diverse programs as student loans, space exploration, health research, highway construction, and defense—is virtually squeezed out of the budget by 2010. Of secondary interest is the significant increase in "net interest" payments after their small reduction approximate to 2000, reflecting in part the diminishing offset of the federal deficit by the Social Security surplus.

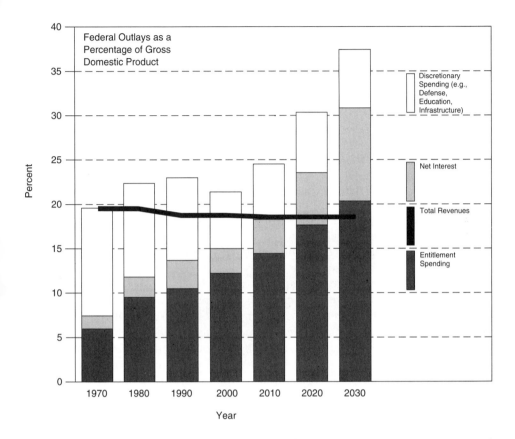

FIGURE 7.2 Current trends are not sustainable

SOURCE: Bipartisan Commission on Entitlement and Tax Reform, *Interim Report to the President* (Washington, DC, 1994), p. 7.

Policy changes that would rebalance the relationship between entitlement and discretionary spending have come from several quarters. Writing on behalf of the Concord Coalition, co-chaired with former senator and presidential candidate, Paul Tsongas, Peter Peterson has suggested a 24-plank platform, reining in entitlements coupled with strategic tax increases. Regarding entitlements, Peterson would establish a graduated "affluence test" through which benefits could be reduced as much as 85 percent for households with income above $185,000. Similarly, Social Security benefits to the wealthy would be taxed as high as 85 percent. Peterson would accelerate the increase in the retirement age for Social Security. In health care, Peterson's proposal calls for a cap on the tax exclusion value of employer-financed health insurance, the imposition of a 25-percent tax on the insurance value of Medicare, and an aggressive plan to control health care costs. Regarding subsidies to the middle class, the Peterson plan would limit the home mortgage interest deduction as well as subsidies to farmers. With respect to tax policy, upper income tax brackets would be increased and a 5-percent consumption tax would be instituted, exempting food, housing, and education. Peterson would also increase taxes on gasoline, tobacco, and alcohol. In order to enhance productivity, Peterson called for a tax credit for corporate research and development, tax incentives for worker retraining, and the indexing of capital gains. Out of concern for equity, Peterson would redistribute resources to the poor, including expanding the Earned Income Tax Credit and providing health insurance to the uninsured.

According to Peterson, his plan would generate sufficient savings that would exceed the budget deficit in 2000 by $29 billion and in 2004 by $98 billion.[37] So structured, Peterson's scheme is generally bipartisan, targeting public social programs, middle-class tax expenditures, and corporate benefits. To his credit, Peterson makes the case that the middle class must share much of the burden for deficit reduction, a reality dodged by most elected officials. "Middle-class sacrifice has become the true 'third rail' of American politics," he observed. "Everyone is at pains to avoid touching it. Many conservatives like to scapegoat the poor. Many liberals like to scapegoat the rich."[38]

Perhaps the most extensive comparative analysis of entitlement program options has been prepared by the Congressional Budget Office (CBO). In response to the rising clamor for entitlement reform, the CBO extrapolated the consequences of three strategies: (1) subject entitlement benefits not already taxed to the income tax, which would affect approximately 85 percent of social insurance benefits; (2) reduce benefits for middle- and higher-income beneficiaries according to a graduated scale that would tax up to 85 percent of benefits for families with annual incomes exceeding $40,000; and (3) deny benefits to upper-income recipients by a phase-out applied to individuals whose nonentitlement income exceeds $100,000 and couples above $120,000. Of particular interest is the second option, since this was modeled after proposals similar to those of Peterson and the Concord Coalition. In denying benefits to wealthy families, the third option is premised on a means test, albeit at a high-income level. Savings according to the three strategies are depicted in Table 7.2. In each of the scenarios, more than 80 percent of savings are derived from Social Security and Medicare. Beyond that, they vary considerably in their implications. The first option, counting entitlement benefits as taxable income, generates the most revenue and is also the easiest to implement since it would utilize existing procedures within the Internal Revenue Service (IRS). The second, reducing or denying benefits to upper income beneficiaries, requires the creation of a new agency or expansion of an existing one, such as the IRS. The third option, lopping off benefits at a fixed percentage of income, would be the most regressive approach (because it leaves existing regressive taxes that penalize the poor unchanged)—even though denying benefits to the wealthy is the most progressive (because it would be targeted at the rich). By contrast, the benefit reduction option is midway between the others with regard to progressivity, but it would be the most expensive to administer.[39]

TABLE 7.2 Estimated gains in revenues and reductions in spending under three policy options to cut net entitlement costs, fiscal years 1995–1999 (in billions of dollars)

		Policy Option	
Year	Include Benefits as Taxable Income	Cut Benefits to Middle- and High-Income Recipients	Deny Benefits to Upper-Income Recipients
1995	18.0	9.4	4.1
1996	52.6	45.4	10.1
1997	57.0	42.2	9.3
1998	62.3	44.9	10.0
1999	68.1	47.9	10.7
Total 1995–99	258.0	189.9	44.2

SOURCE: Congressional Budget Office, *Reducing Entitlement Spending* (Washington, DC, 1994), p. xiii.

Unlike Peterson's proposal for structural changes throughout the economy, only the first two CBO entitlement reforms—including entitlement benefits as taxable income and reducing entitlement benefits to middle- and upper-income families—would significantly affect the deficit. Between 1996 and 1999, the budget deficit is expected to increase from $176 billion to $231 billion per year.[40] For the years 1996 through 1999, including entitlement benefits in the income tax accounts for no more than 30 percent of the deficit, reducing benefits for middle- and upper-income families accounts for about 21 percent of the deficit. Clearly, major reductions in entitlement benefits alone will not solve the deficit problem.

The response to the doomsday forecast of entitlement spending—of which Social Security is a primary component—consisted largely of head-in-sand posturing. Clearly, a defensive pose served the reelection interests of the 20 Congressional representatives who served as members of the bipartisan Entitlement Commission. No sooner had the Commission released its preliminary report outlining the magnitude of the problem (but avoiding any recommendations) than the National Committee to Preserve Social Security and Medicare raised a panic among its 6 million members with an editorial harangue warning that "nearly half of commission members already have shown antisenior colors."[41] Widely credited with torpedoing Catastrophic Health Insurance in 1989, the National Committee to Preserve Social Security and Medicare was a political force to be reckoned with, even if its methods were odious.

For some time, financial analysts from both ends of the ideological continuum had warned that retirees must be willing to make sacrifices for the economic well-being of the nation. Conservative columnist Robert Samuelson proposed options such as a one-year suspension of the cost-of-living increase and increasing the retirement age.[42] Liberal columnist Hobart Rowen preferred options other than targeting the cost-of-living increase because it fell more heavily on the poor, but concurred that Social Security and Medicare beneficiaries with higher incomes should bear a larger portion of program costs.[43] Ironically, even wealthier retirees were willing to acknowledge the drain of their benefits on the federal budget. A December 1994 poll revealed that 63 percent of Americans above age 65 agreed that wealthier recipients of Social Security should pay a higher tax on their benefits.[44]

Given the choice between accepting the challenge presented by entitlement spending and appeasing constituent lobbies, elected officials chose the latter. The Entitlement Commission quickly bogged down in finger-pointing at those who suggested even minor changes in entitlements. Lobbyists for labor and the elderly were particularly critical of attempts to reduce the budgetary expansion of social programs. "There is no crisis in the Social Security retirement program," said the secretary-treasurer of the AFL-CIO. At best, Commission co-chair Bob Kerrey could count no more than four or five votes in favor of entitlement reform.[45]

Meanwhile, the political parties fell over each other in courting the elderly vote. On the eve of the 1994 election, the Democratic party aired campaign ads accusing Republicans of economic proposals that, if enacted, would eventually require reductions in Social Security.[46] Through the "Contract with America," Republicans had actually promised to *raise* the income limit of Social Security recipients, which would be taxed. After the 1994 midterm election, incoming House Speaker Newt Gingrich acknowledged that some elements of the Contract might affect programs serving the elderly, such as Social Security and Medicare, then conveniently postponed them "six to eight years"—well after he would be held accountable.[47] Protecting his left flank, President Clinton used his 1995 State of the Union address to reassure retirees that his administration would not reduce programs for the elderly, citing Social Security specifically. Unaccountable to future generations, elected officials remained conveniently oblivious of the economic damage to be inflicted from spiraling entitlement spending.

THE NEXT AGENDA FOR SOCIAL SECURITY

Any serious initiative to reconcile the expansion of entitlements with a deficit-ridden budget must address program finance and economic productivity. Typically, these are treated separately. The CBO, as an example, publishes annually a volume of options for reducing the deficit. For 1994, the CBO proposed four options regarding Social Security: (1) reducing the replacement rate, (2) eliminating benefits for children of retirees aged 62 to 64, (3) increasing the benefit computation period by three years, and (4) accounting for veterans' benefits in determining Social Security benefits.[48] Investment of the savings derived from these changes, however, is not featured in the CBO analysis.

On the other hand, proposals to enhance American productivity often neglect the commanding presence of social entitlements in the budget. Writing for the Progressive Policy Institute, Rob Shapiro has proposed a "cut-and-invest" strategy to replace the "tax-and-spend" orientation associated with liberal Democrats. Detailing an idea with which Bill Clinton flirted as a presidential candidate, Shapiro suggests dividing the federal budget into two accounts: one for "public economic investments," the other for everything else. Except during recessionary periods, the noninvestment category would have to operate according to a balanced budget. Finally, the Shapiro plan would limit federal spending to growth of the private economy, except during a recession. Rather than target social program entitlements, Shapiro's plan focuses on eliminating subsidies that artificially protect select industries, particularly agriculture, resource extraction, and transportation, among others. Over a 5-year period, elimination of subsidies would generate about $114 billion in savings. In order to enhance American competitiveness, Shapiro lists three priorities for public investment: (1) human capital, (2) basic research and development, and (3) physical infrastructure. Using these priorities, investments in competitiveness would increase progressively from 5.8 percent in 1994 to 24.6 percent in 1998.[49] Unlike the Peterson proposal that relies on entitlement trimming, Shapiro's emphasizes public investment to accelerate economic performance. Recognizing that the United States has traditionally underinvested in human capital through social programs, Shapiro would leave entitlements intact and stimulate the economy so that social program obligations could be honored.

Deficiencies in the CBO and Shapiro analyses could be corrected by reforming entitlement spending in such a way that savings can be diverted to investment directly. Specifically, savings in the restructuring of Social Security should be channeled to a research and development fund. In so doing, entitlement spending for the aged will contribute to the nation's economic capacity, relieving the next generation of the full burden of supporting the retiring baby boomers, while assuring younger workers that they will receive the Social Security and Medicare benefits to which they are entitled.

Lift the Cap on Taxable Income

Since its inception, the Social Security withholding tax has been levied on only a portion of a worker's income. The cap on taxable income (initially set at $3,000 and now $60,600) limits the exposure of wages to the Federal Insurance Contribution Act (FICA) withholding tax. Presumably, the rationale for this was that individuals with higher incomes would invest part of their above-cap income in private funds for purposes of retirement security. Regardless, what this means is that the typical college professor is paying in withholding taxes at the same rate each year as Donald Trump.

Since the withholding tax is matched by employers, it would be necessary to limit removing the cap to only the worker's contribution in order to avoid placing an unfair burden on employers. While removal of the cap would increase FICA taxes paid by upper-income workers, it could lower contributions of lower-wage workers. Michael Graetz has speculated that "elimination of the wage ceiling would permit a revenue neutral reduction of about 2 percent in the payroll tax rate."[50]

Make the Withholding Tax Progressive

Since the inception of the Social Security Act, the withholding tax has been regressive. In 1994, the withholding tax was a flat 6.2 percent paid by both employees and employers. To some extent the regressivity of FICA has been offset by the benefit computation formula that awards higher benefits to poorer workers. For workers eligible for Social Security in 1990, for example, low-wage workers will have benefits calculated according to a replacement rate of 58.2 percent, while maximum earners will receive benefits computed at a 24.5 percent replacement rate.[51]

A fairer method of taxation would be to make FICA progressive—say, instituting rates of 4 percent for low-wage workers, 6 percent for middle-income workers, and 8 percent for those earning high incomes. Under a progressive scheme such as this, minimum-wage workers would receive a substantial reduction in their withholding, middle-income workers a slight reduction, and upper-income contributors a modest increase. A side benefit of lowering the withholding tax for lower-wage workers is that this would encourage employers to hire more employees since their FICA tax would decrease, as well.[52] Ideally, the tax rates would be set at rates that would be revenue positive.

Allow Workers to Designate a Portion of Withholding

Current options for retirement investing create a disadvantage for lower-income workers who are dependent on limited returns through Social Security, relative to higher earners who can maximize their investments through private retirement funds. This could be corrected by allowing workers to designate a portion of their withholding contribution up to a limited amount, say 25 percent, to a Generational Investment Fund. Workers exercising this option would be supplementing their Individual Development Account (see Chapter 3) through an investment strategy that would almost certainly appreciate more rapidly than their base Social Security benefits. As significantly, the contributions so diverted would form a capitalization pool that could enhance the productive capacity of the nation's economy.[53]

Create a Generational Investment Fund

Revenues generated by the withholding designation would be diverted to an investment fund that would be used to promote competitiveness. Shapiro includes in his "cut-and-invest" plan the designation of a Commission on National Competitiveness and Industry Subsidies to target investments to enhance competitiveness. Four criteria determine the designation of public investment projects:

> First, all public investment should be targeted to elements common to all economic enterprise, not to those specific to one industry or firm. In order to qualify, the training should be *general,* the research should be *basic* and the infrastructure should be *primary.*

Second, federal funding in these areas should be steady and reliable, so as to discourage frantic competition for support and subsequent project bottlenecks.

Third, the government can encourage sound investment analysis by applying strict planning and review requirements to all state and local infrastructure or training programs seeking federal support.

Fourth and most important, public-investment decisions should incorporate a crucial element of private-market discipline: *those who receive support for a project should bear part of the project's cost.*[54]

Investment decisions should be made by a panel representing beneficiaries of Social Security, workers paying withholding taxes, business, labor, and government.

Failure to restructure Social Security so that it contributes to economic revitalization through investment, as opposed to accelerating consumption as is now the case, probably spells the end of the program as we know it. A cataclysmic scenario will evolve if no action is taken to shore up the program for the seismic shock of mid-twenty-first century when the surplus and interest are exhausted for retiring baby boomers. At the point future workers are faced with double-digit FICA contributions, they will be sympathetic to politicians who suggest that the program be means-tested. At the latest, 2040, this scenario has the Republican presidential candidate intoning that Social Security was a creation of a recession-prone industrial America, a thing of the past. Since doubling or tripling withholding taxes will, by that time, be the only remedy to insolvency—under pay-as-you-go or building another surplus—the conservative presidential candidate will suggest that the program be merged with a means-tested program, such as Supplemental Security Income, so that benefits can be targeted to the elderly poor. The Democratic presidential candidate will invoke the social insurance legacy of Social Security, reminding the public that it has been the most effective social program in the nation's history, and ask voters to gird themselves for a substantial sacrifice in payroll taxes to maintain the program. Reporters covering the demise of Social Security will note that the stability of the program became uncertain as long ago as 1989 when Catastrophic Health Insurance was terminated by Congress.

Another scenario is more gradual, but no less consequential. Here, the federal budget is increasingly consumed by entitlement spending, putting enormous fiscal pressure on discretionary programs. Older lawmakers of the mid-twenty-first century will recall the budget convulsions that began to rack Congress in the late 1990s. In retrospect, the 1990 Budget Enforcement Act had proven as ingenious for Republicans as it was Draconian for Democrats. For liberals, the long-run consequences of holding discretionary programs in check while entitlements continued to grow were perverse: Eventually social programs had been pitted against each other in a Darwinian scramble for diminishing resources. First to go were a handful of discretionary programs that had been sacrificed to entitlements, but the process had not stopped there. Eventually, entitlements were pitted against each other. When that had happened, the more politically popular and indexed entitlements for the aged, particularly Social Security and Medicare, crowded out the more stigmatized and un-indexed programs for poor families, like Aid to Families with Dependent Children program. Daniel Patrick Moynihan had understood the ramifications clearly: "The United States has now become the first society in history in which a person is more likely to be worse off if young rather than old."[55]

By 2040, however, that statement will be a half-century old, and social program advocates will acknowledge that the remaining means-tested programs have all the viability of the late-Senator Moynihan. Eventually, liberal welfare advocates acknowledge publicly what they had whispered among each other in private: The only way to salvage the few remaining programs for poor children will be to cashier the social insurance programs for the elderly. Reluctantly, liberal social program advocates agree to meet with fiscal conservatives in Congress to ease the decommissioning of Social Security.

Escaping everyone's notice, Daniel Patrick Moynihan has turned in his grave.

NOTES

1. Daniel Patrick Moynihan, *Came the Revolution* (San Diego: Harcourt Brace Jovanovich, 1988), p. 291.
2. Medicaid was introduced with Medicare in 1965 as an amendment to the Social Security Act. Because Medicaid is a public assistance program—unlike Medicare, which is a health insurance program funded in part through the federal withholding tax—it is considered in more detail in the chapter on health care.
3. Howard Karger, "The Challenge of Financing Social Security in the United States," (unpublished manuscript), p. 2.
4. Roy Lubove, *The Struggle for Social Security* (Cambridge, MA: Harvard University Press, 1968), ch. I.
5. Neil Gilbert, *Capitalism and the Welfare State* (New Haven: Yale University Press, 1983), p. 3.
6. Original emphasis, quoted in Norman Furniss and Timothy Tilton, *The Case for the Welfare State* (Bloomington: Indiana University Press, 1977), p. 156.
7. Edward Berkowitz and Kim McQuaid, *Creating the Welfare State* (New York: Praeger, 1980), pp. 18–20.
8. Roy Lubove, *The Struggle for Social Security,* pp. 147–48.
9. Michael Katz, *In the Shadow of the Poorhouse: A Social History of Welfare in America* (New York: Basic Books, 1986), p. 186.
10. Berkowitz and McQuaid, *Creating the Welfare State,* p. 83.
11. Berkowitz and McQuaid, *Creating the Welfare State,* p. 103.
12. Michael Katz, *In the Shadow of the Poorhouse* (New York: Basic Books, 1986), p. 235.
13. John Hope Franklin, *From Slavery to Freedom: A History of Negro Americans* (New York: Knopf, 1980), p. 396; Katz, *In the Shadow,* p. 244.
14. Kenneth Davis, *FDR: The New Deal Years* (New York: Random House, 1986), pp. 454–55.

15. June Axinn and Herman Levin, *Social Welfare: A History of the American Response to Need,* 2d ed. (New York: Harper and Row, 1982), p. 198. Social Security, as noted by one liberal analyst, was "a *conservative* program" (original emphasis): Diana DiNitto, *Social Welfare: Politics and Public Policy* (Boston: Allyn and Bacon, 1995), p. 105.
16. Howard Karger and David Stoesz, *American Social Welfare Policy,* 2d ed. (White Plains, NY: Longman, 1994), p. 239.
17. Robert Ball, "The Original Understanding on Social Security," in Theodore Marmor and Jerry Mashaw (eds.), *Social Security: Beyond the Rhetoric of Crisis* (Princeton: Princeton University Press, 1988), pp. 25-26.
18. Ball, "The Original Understanding," pp. 27, 29.
19. Committee on Ways and Means, U.S. House of Representatives, *Overview of Entitlement Programs* (Washington, DC: USGPO, 1993), p. 79.
20. Ball, "The Original Understanding," pp. 28, 31.
21. Committee on Ways and Means, U.S. House of Representatives, *Overview of Entitlement Programs,* (Washington, DC: USGPO, 1994), pp. 5, 76.
22. James Tobin, "The Future of Social Security," in Theodore Marmor and Jerry Mashaw (eds.), *Social Security: Beyond the Rhetoric of Crisis* (Princeton: Princeton University Press, 1988), pp. 47-54.
23. *Overview of Entitlement Programs,* 1993, pp. 33-34.
24. Fay Cook and Edith Barrett, *Support for the American Welfare State* (New York: Columbia University Press, 1992).
25. Ball, "The Original Understanding," p. 39.
26. Carolyn Weaver, "Introduction," in *Social Security's Looming Surpluses* (Washington, DC: American Enterprise Institute, 1990), p. 1.
27. Patrick Dattalo, "Social Security's Surpluses: An Update," *Social Work* (July 1992), p. 377.
28. Weaver, "Introduction," pp. 7-8.
29. Peter Peterson, *Facing-Up* (New York: Touchstone, 1994), Chart 5.10.
30. Howard Karger, "The Challenge of Financing Social Security in the United States," in James Midgley and Martin Tracy (eds.), *Challenges to Social Security: An International Exploration* (New York: Greenwood, 1995), p. 26.
31. Beginning in 1995, the withholding income cap will increase with the average index.
32. Weaver, "Introduction," pp. 11-12.
33. Peter Peterson and Neil Howe, *On Borrowed Time* (San Francisco: Institute for Contemporary Studies, 1988), p. 11.
34. Bob Woodward, *The Agenda* (New York: Simon and Schuster, 1994), pp. 286-87.
35. David Stoesz and Howard Karger, *Reconstructing the American Welfare State* (Savage, MD: Rowman and Littlefield, 1992), pp. 66-67.
36. Bipartisan Commission on Entitlement and Tax Reform, *Interim Report to the President* (Washington, DC: author, August 1994), p. 6.
37. Peterson, *Facing Up,* Chapter 10.
38. Peter Peterson, "What I Really Say about Balancing the Budget," *The American Prospect* 19 (Fall 1994), p. 15.
39. *Reducing Entitlement Spending,* (Washington, DC: Congressional Budget Office, 1994), pp. xvii-xviii.
40. Congressional Budget Office, *The Economic and Budget Outlook* (Washington, DC: author, 1994), p. xiii.
41. Paulette Thomas, "Bipartisan Panel Outlines Evils of Entitlements, But Hint of Benefit Cuts Spurs Stiff Opposition," *Wall Street Journal* (August 6, 1994), p. A-12.

42. Robert Samuelson, "Guess Who'll Balance the Budget," *Los Angeles Times* (November 13, 1994), p. M-5.
43. Hobart Rowen, "Seniors, Too, Must Sacrifice," *Washington Post Weekly* (February 15-21, 1993), p. 5.
44. Robert Hershey, Jr., "Speaking the Unspeakable to Retirees," *New York Times* (January 1, 1995), p. F-3.
45. Robert Pear, "Plans to Cut Entitlements Draw Fire Immediately," *Idaho Statesman* (December 10, 1994), p. A-3; Robert Jackson, "Seniors' Benefits Unfair to Young, Tax Group Says," *Los Angeles Times* (December 31, 1994), p. A-4; Eric Pianin, "Want to Save Money? Simple: Cut Social Security," *Washington Post Weekly* (July 11-17, 1994), p. 15; David Broder, "Cold Feet on the Reform Committee," *San Diego Union-Tribune* (August 7, 1994), p. G-2.
46. Christopher Georges, "Democrats and Republicans Lock Horns Over Who Will Defend Social Security," *Wall Street Journal* (November 1, 1994), p. A-18.
47. Adam Clymer, "Gingrich Sees No Need to Review Social Security until 6-to-8 Years," *San Diego Union-Tribune* (January 3, 1994), p. A-4.
48. Congressional Budget Office, *Reducing the Deficit: Spending and Revenue Options* (Washington, DC: author, 1994), pp. 262-64.
49. Robert Shapiro, "Cut-and-Invest to Compete and Win," (Washington, DC: Progressive Policy Institute, 1994).
50. Michael Graetz, "Retirement Security Policy," in Theodore Marmor and Jerry Mashaw (eds.), *Social Security* (Princeton: Princeton University Press, 1988), p. 100.
51. *Overview of Entitlement Programs,* 1994, p. 16.
52. Thanks to Scott Moeller for this observation.
53. This is a modification of the restructuring of the Chilean pension system that has generated substantial funds for capitalization. See Dominique Hachette and Rolf Luders, *Privatization in Chile* (San Francisco, CA: Institute for Contemporary Studies, 1993), pp. 52-55.
54. Shapiro, "Cut-and-Invest to Compete and Win," p. 29.
55. Moynihan, quoted in Peter Peterson, *On Borrowed Time: How the Growth of Entitlement Spending Threatens America's Future* (San Francisco: Institute for Contemporary Studies, 1988), p. 2.

chapter 8

Paradigm Lost

> *Americans pick a President every fours years and for the next four years we pick him apart.*
>
> Adlai Stevenson[1]

Much of the Clinton domestic policy record is a product of the political and economic forces that have buffeted the nation during the past two decades. This is paradoxical in that Bill Clinton constructed his presidential candidacy largely in counterpoint to the very dynamics that are proving so problematic. Three forces propelled his campaign for the presidency and later served to sabotage his first two years in office.

    First, special interests increasingly clogged the arteries of democracy. As political analyst Jonathan Rauch pointed out, since the 1970s Washington has experienced a veritable explosion in the number of lobbying organizations. By 1992, the nation's capital boasted 92,000 lobbyists, a proliferation that not so coincidentally was matched by a rapid increase in the number of advocacy organizations, the number of attorneys employed, and the amount of legislation—all impeding the work of Congress.[2] The nation's Capital had gradually become less the center of government by the people and more the province of elites whose power and influence was connected to the special interests they represented. The consequence of Washington becoming a bastion of elites has been pointed out by Kevin Phillips: a significant expansion of a "parasite structure" populated from "the ranks of lawyers and interest-group representatives out to influence Uncle Sam, interpret his actions or pick his pockets for themselves or their clients."[3] No better illustration of the evolution of interest-group politics can be found than that of Willis Gradison. A ten-term Congressman, Gradison

(R. Ohio) resigned his seat on January 31, 1993, to take over the Health Insurance Association of America—just in time to mount the media campaign that scuttled Clinton's Health Security Act. Gradison's skirmish, among the first in the health care reform debate, was prelude to the $100 million in special-interest money spent to influence health care in 1994. But in many respects, Gradison was only exceptional because of his visibility among the thousands of policy hit-men stalking Washington. (After leaving office, 60 percent of Congressmen take positions with Washington lobbying organizations.)[4] The health care reform debate demonstrated to many Americans that special interests had confounded the essential functions of the federal government.

Second, working families failed to gain ground economically. As income stagnated for middle-income male workers, many families dispatched "mom" to the labor force to match increasing costs of living. Although this checked the slide in family income, it posed additional problems (supervising children after school), to say nothing of additional expenses (child care). Even then gains were marginal, as shown in Table 8.1.

Young families with children were particularly disadvantaged. Between 1973 and 1990, the median income of families under 30 declined 28.6 percent.[5] As baby boomers looked back a generation, they realized that not only had their parents benefited from government programs, such as the GI Bill, but that the boomers themselves were barely making it in the middle class due to the high cost of housing and college tuition.[6]

Third, the fiscal resources of the federal government were rapidly being exhausted by the deficit and entitlement spending. A cumulative total of all federal debt since the founding of the nation reveals that more than three-fourths, or $3,549 billion, was incurred during the 12 years of the Reagan and Bush administrations. While the debt plunged to unfathomable depths, the cost of interest on it coupled with entitlement spending grew to malignant proportions. In 1960, debt interest and entitlement spending accounted for 34.0 percent of federal outlays; by 1990, they consumed 66.9 percent of federal appropriations, almost doubling.[7] In 1994, the Bipartisan Commission on Entitlement and Tax Reform projected that by the year 2013, interest on the debt and entitlement spending would consume 100 percent of federal outlays.[8] Although federal lawmakers bickered about how to *reduce* the deficit, there was general agreement that *contributing* to federal debt was out of the question. Such consensus

TABLE 8.1 Changes in family earnings

	Poorest 25%	Median	Richest 25%
1963–1973	38%	38%	38%
1973–1992	−7%	2%	10%

SOURCE: Paul Richter, "It Just *Seems* Like We're Worse Off," *Los Angeles Times* (January 26, 1994), p. A-25.

was evident in the Deficit Reduction Act and the unwillingness of Congress to authorize additional social programs.

The expansion of interest-group politics, the stagnation of middle-class family income, and the ballooning of debt and entitlement spending pushed voter patience to the breaking point. Under such circumstances, it is understandable that struggling families would eventually look to government as contributing to their difficulties by the taxes it imposed on them, not to mention resent the unconditional benefits of welfare programs that granted assistance to nonworkers and their families. These, of course, were the conditions that were so masterfully exploited by the Reagan and Bush administrations. As liberals would discover, the traditional Democratic response to the problems faced by middle-income families—higher taxes on upper- and middle-income families for programs to benefit workers, minorities, and the poor—was decreasingly tenable.

THE "NEW DEMOCRATS"

Since 1980, the Democratic party has struggled to adjust to the new political reality. The conservative triumphs of the 1980s were catastrophic for Democrats. The unqualified and unapologetic liberalism of Walter Mondale was trounced as easily as the tepid and at-arms-length liberalism of Michael Dukakis. Clearly, the Democratic machine needed to be regeared if it was to compete in the new American polity. In 1985, a handful of "neoliberal" Democrats stepped into the breach between their party and the electorate, and committed themselves to returning the Democratic party to the American mainstream. Among the leaders of the neoliberals were the governor of Arkansas, Bill Clinton, and a senator from Tennessee, Al Gore.

Clinton and Gore contended that the nation was entering an era that required a new approach in domestic policy. Accordingly, they organized the Democratic Leadership Council (DLC) and deployed a neoliberal think tank, the Progressive Policy Institute (PPI), to divert the Democratic party away from the liberal precepts that it had advocated for decades toward a formulation that was at once post-conservative and post-liberal. The DLC-PPI message resonated with Democrats who had strayed from the fold and had supported Republicans during the 1980s. In 1991, Clinton secured the Democratic nomination and designated Gore as his running mate; the following year the Democratic ticket captured the White House. As late as a year before, few pundits would have expected a Democratic southern governor to win the presidency, particularly so soon after the Carter presidential fiasco—especially a governor from what some called a third-world state like Arkansas.

Clinton's victory was as much a reflection of his understanding of history as his political tenacity. To guide America into the twenty-first century, Clinton vowed "CHANGE," a theme that he had invoked in various versions during the campaign: He was a "new Democrat"; he advocated a "New Covenant" in domestic policy; the nation needed "a third way" in public philosophy. Anticipating a

Democratic Congress, Clinton fashioned an ambitious agenda for his presidency; although his first 100 days might not be as liberal as FDR's or LBJ's, it would be no less consequential. To chronicle its achievements, Clinton agreed to allow *Washington Post* journalist Bob Woodward into the White House to record its innermost workings. Clinton recognized that America was at a turning point and that his presidency would be instrumental in shaping a new generation of public policy. Before an interfaith breakfast audience, Clinton said:

> I am convinced that we are in a period of historic significance [and] profound change here in this country and throughout the world, and that no one is wise enough to see to the end of all of it, that we have to be guided by a few basic principles and an absolute conviction that we can recreate a common good for America.[9]

Anticipating the millennium, Clinton fully intended to have his administration's accomplishments registered for posterity.

An avid reader, Clinton recognized his presidency as the reversal of fortune suggested by Arthur Schlesinger, Jr., who had prophesied that a liberal president would emerge one generation after the last major progressive era in American politics, Lyndon Johnson's "Great Society." Having observed that revolutions in public policy occurred at 30-year intervals—FDR's New Deal introduced by the 1935 Social Security Act; LBJ's War on Poverty declared by a flurry of legislation in 1965—Schlesinger all but begged: Who would be the liberal president in 1995? Even before the White House had been won, the president-elect had the answer: Bill Clinton would be the man of the hour. Although Clinton had yet to settle on a moniker for his presidency, he recognized it would be pivotal and anticipated it with an eagerness that bordered on arrogance.

WHITE HOUSE FOLLIES

As president, Clinton had to staff his administration beginning with the White House. While an interim group eased the transition between the outgoing Bush and incoming Clinton administrations, a closeted group of advisors—Vernon Jordan and Warren Christopher—would review candidates for cabinet positions, referring a select few for background checks, or "vetting." At the same time, the president-elect and his staff would forge an agenda to present to Congress. Much of this would have to be done during the interlude between election day and the inauguration, little more than six weeks. The nexus of these tasks would form the inner circle of the White House: Hillary Rodham Clinton, the First Lady and children's advocate; Vice President Al Gore; George Stephanopoulos from the election campaign; and Mack McLarty, a boyhood chum of Clinton and the executive of an Arkansas gas company. The Clinton team looked to the Reagan presidency as a model for a new administration coming to Washington with an ambitious agenda. Using data on candidates for presidential appointments generated by a consulting firm, the Reagan team had moved into the White House and "hit the ground running." Preparation by the Reagan transition team was widely credited with the success of Reagan's first year in office.

But the Clinton transition was not as fortunate. As Elizabeth Drew noted, "astonishingly, there was no real plan for what the new administration would do after it got to Washington." As one seasoned Washington observer recounted to her: [The Clinton team] "hit the ground barely standing."[10] Primary among the problems encountered by Clinton was the youthfulness of his staff and their inexperience in the sophisticated, clandestine, and often predacious nature of Washington politics. From their failure to obtain security clearances for administration officials, to inadequately vetting senior candidates for Cabinet positions, to the lazy pace of making subordinate appointments, the White House staff quickly distinguished itself for its lack of savvy. When a $200 haircut on the L.A. airport tarmac was coupled with the ineptitude of mishandling the Zoe Baird and Kimba Wood Attorney General nominations, it began to look like amateur hour in the White House. Compounding a credibility gap that was to emerge around the White House, Clinton's affinity for aides who had been fellow Rhodes Scholars—Stephanopoulos, Robert Reich (Secretary of Labor), Ira Magaziner (organizer of the administration's health care reform initiative)—contradicted his image as a populist. Instead of cultivating an outside-the-beltway cadre of advisors who had a grounding in mainstream America, Clinton selected an elite group of erudite liberals to guide his presidency.

Rather than marking the first months of his presidency with a series of major policy successes, the Clinton White House anguished over more minor affairs. The issue of gays serving in the military, the failed nomination of Lani Guinier (nominated as Assistant Attorney General for Civil Rights), and the uncertainty over policy toward Bosnia characterized Clinton as indecisive. On matters where decisions were clear and forthright—signing the parental leave bill, canceling the prohibition on abortion counseling, and authorizing fetal tissue research—Clinton acted like a traditional liberal. Instead of asserting himself as a "new Democrat" forging a "third way" in public policy, Clinton became portrayed by conservative critics as a traditional, liberal Democrat—and a not particularly effective one at that.[11] Symbolically, the White House had still not settled on a phrase to transmit its agenda; if FDR was known for the "New Deal" and LBJ for the "Great Society," what did Bill Clinton stand for?

Much of the ambiguity suffusing the early months of the Clinton presidency could have been dismissed as part of getting acclimated to the White House and Washington, had there not been a revival of "character issues." During the campaign, Clinton had eluded accusations that his opponents had sought to tar him with. He avoided the draft by studying at Oxford University; he tried marijuana, but stopped short of inhaling; he had sexual indiscretions in the past. At best, Clinton was successful at portraying these as evidence of his fallibility; at worst, they validated opponents' caricature of the president as "slick Willie." Thus, while the campaign flap over Jennifer Flowers could be dismissed as a "bimbo eruption," the formal allegations of Paula Jones, bracketed by Arkansas

State Troopers' charges that they had helped Clinton arrange sexual liaisons, confirmed to many that the president was fundamentally flawed. Compounding alleged sexual improprieties, the possibility that the Clintons had manipulated their influence to channel funds from a defunct real estate deal, Whitewater, for campaign purposes, indicated that the character deficit was not limited to illicit sex nor was it specific to the president. The Whitewater imbroglio and accusations that Hillary Rodham Clinton had misused influence to make a windfall investment in cattle futures expanded the moral inquiry beyond the president to the First Lady.

THE CLINTON RECORD

The "character issue" had a corrosive effect on the Clinton presidency. With only 43 percent of the vote, Clinton's mandate fell far short of a majority. In part, this could be attributed to Ross Perot's winning 19 percent of the vote, and Perot showed no inclination to pipe down and wait for the next election to spout his nostrums. Hobbled by the legacy of the Reagan deficit and confronted with an unruly Democratic Congress, Clinton would have to toe a very thin line, indeed, to accomplish his legislative objectives. Among the few resources at his disposal to induce Congress to do his bidding was an ability to command a higher moral ground, to insist that sacrifice was necessary for the public good. In this respect, Clinton had to portray his presidency as one based on foresight and principle. He was a pilgrim leading the nation out of a stagnating Industrial era into a more promising and, at the same time, uncertain postindustrial future. Given the slender electoral margins, success was, to a large extent, contingent on the sheer will of the president reinforced by Americans' abiding faith in him and his mission. It was unlikely that voters would enthusiastically embrace tax increases and benefit reductions for a leader who was perceived to be a philanderer and charlatan. To the extent that the character issue compromised the presidency, Clinton was in a bind—unable to correct the past, the only way he could convince the people of his ultimate concern for their prosperity was a positive legislative track record that eclipsed the negativism of the morals charges. "Clinton was in a race against himself," wrote Elizabeth Drew; "If the productive Clinton could stay ahead of the Clinton about whom people had questions, he would be successful. Therefore, it was of utmost importance to him—and his wife—to keep moving their program."[12] The Clintons had run hard to win the White House; they would have to run harder to keep it.

A roadblock soon encountered by the Clinton White House was the deficit. During the campaign, candidate Clinton had relegated it to secondary status, preferring to elaborate on the virtues of his "new Democrat" ideas: national service, microenterprise, charter schools, welfare reform, a police corps, among others.[13] These initiatives not only differentiated him from the "old (liberal) Democrats," but Clinton also used them to illustrate what he meant by making "investments" in the American people. Without such investments, the prospects of working families would lag, and the future of the Democratic party would remain anchored to the "tax and spend" liberalism that had been so effectively exploited by conservative Republicans. Clinton's ability to place his investment agenda before Congress was ill-fated, however. Initially, many of the investments were frontloaded into the 1993 economic stimulus package. But a Republican filibuster in the Senate caught the new White House by surprise, and the initiative failed.

The backup strategy was to insert the investments into the 1994 budget, but problems arose here as well. A full menu of Clinton's investments exceeded the parameters dictated by tax and deficit reduction requirements. Although Clinton was willing to raise taxes on the wealthy, he could not raise the funds needed for fully funding investments without increasing taxes on the middle class. This contradicted his campaign pledge of a middle-class tax cut. On the other hand, Perot's candidacy had made it clear that deficit reduction was a primary concern for a substantial number of voters. In an attempt to appeal to the Perot camp, then, some of the revenue exacted from tax increases and program cuts would have to be diverted to deficit reduction. Looming in the background were Wall Street financiers who feared that a budget scenario featuring sharp increases in taxes would fuel more government spending, leaving the budget deficit virtually untouched, a situation that would jolt interest rates upward, thereby jeopardizing the nascent economic recovery.

Clinton consulted with Alan Greenspan, chair of the Federal Reserve, who confirmed the risk that a too ambitious budget posed for the economic recovery. Greenspan also pointed out that a more modest White House budget proposal had benefits: In the short run, it would contribute to lower interest rates, which would stimulate consumer activity through spending and loan refinancing. In the long run, such a strategy would reduce the deficit, bolster economic recovery, and in so doing leave the White House in a stronger position to fund investments later.

Greenspan's approach to the 1994 budget left Clinton in a conundrum: He could meet his campaign promises to fund investments, possibly subverting the economic recovery; or he could ride the recovery, hoping that a healthy economy would be convincing to voters for the Congressional election of 1994 and ultimately his reelection campaign of 1996. His reelection for a second term would provide the opportunity to move confidently with social investments. For the "new Democrats" in the White House, however, this was a bargain with the devil. The consultants who had engineered the campaign were vociferous in their support of investments; the economic analysts nearer to Wall Street opted for ensuring economic recovery and delaying investments. Clinton, always one to ruminate over complex options, deliberated long over the matter. The tension within the White House increased until it was palpable. Clinton was jammed into a corner by forces that were not of his making, and they were sabotaging his presidency just as it was beginning. Bob Woodward captured the president's frustration of the moment:

> "Where are all the Democrats?" Cinton bellowed. "I hope you're all aware we're all Eisenhower Republicans," he said, his voice dripping with sarcasm. "We're Eisenhower Republicans here, and we are fighting

the Reagan Republicans. We stand for lower deficits and free trade and the bond market. Isn't that great?"

The room was silent once more.

He erupted again, his voice severe and loud, "I don't have a goddam Democratic budget until 1996. None of the investments, none of the things I campaigned on."[14]

Regardless of the contradiction it posed, Clinton was realizing the inevitability of a budget that emphasized deficit reduction and economic recovery over investments in new programs.

Shortly after entering the White House, Clinton had set out his domestic policy agenda. The first 100 days of his administration were to see a wide range of proposals put before Congress: an economic stimulus package, a budget that reduced the deficit while funding new investments, campaign reform, a national service bill, welfare reform, and health care reform.[15] By the end of the 103rd Congress, however, the Clinton agenda was in tatters. The economic stimulus package had been extinguished by filibuster; the budget plan downplayed investments in "new Democrat" initiatives, favoring deficit reduction and economic recovery; campaign and health care reform were killed; and national service was enacted, though in modest format. The only major initiative that Clinton was to omit from his review was NAFTA, the North American Free Trade Agreement, which he saw through to enactment over the angry protests of liberal labor advocates.

SMALL CHANGE

Of course, there was more—much more—to the Clinton presidency than the handful of proposals that captured public attention. The president accurately portrayed his legislative record as among the most successful of recent presidents.[16] After the 1994 Republican electoral sweep, the liberal editors of the *American Prospect* restated what Clinton had accomplished during the 103rd Congress:

1. Increased the Earned Income Tax Credit,
2. Raised the highest income tax bracket for the rich,
3. Enacted gun control through the Brady Bill,
4. Signed the "motor-voter" bill,
5. Enacted the Family and Medical Leave Act,
6. Passed the crime bill, including prevention programs,
7. Targeted Chapter One education aid to poor children,
8. Signed a child immunization act,
9. Enacted educational reform through *Goals 2000,*
10. Signed the national service bill,
11. Passed an apprenticeship program for teenagers,
12. Signed a bill ensuring access to abortion clinics,

13. Reformed federal government procurement practices,
14. Reduced the federal deficit by half,
15. Increased Head Start funding by 20 percent,
16. Increased funding for WIC and Food Stamps,
17. Doubled aid to the homeless,
18. Increased funding for low-income housing,
19. Increased funding for Legal Services to the poor,
20. Doubled funding for dislocated workers,
21. Increased funding for AIDS public health services.[17]

Still, the White House failed in making its legislative accomplishments coherent, and when major chunks fell by the wayside, Clinton became vulnerable to one of the charges he had used so effectively during the campaign—contributing to gridlock in Washington. A review of the major areas of domestic policy pursued by the Clinton White House revealed that the whole seemed to be less than the sum of the parts.

Health

The most prominent failure of the Clinton presidency was the demise of health care reform. The Health Security Act was so complex that subsequent autopsies suggested any number of fatal flaws. The plan was conceived by a large number of experts who operated, at least initially, outside of public view. Rather than buying-in health care interests—except for the academic experts—the White House froze them out. Once the plan became public, the health industry lobby reacted strongly, as should have been expected. Yet the administration had not organized an effective counteroffensive. The most damning evidence of White House ineptitude in health care reform was not that the Health Security Act was shot down by one of the large health interest groups, such as the American Medical Association or the American Hospital Association, but that it was so easily scored by a relatively minor interest group representing small health insurers, the Health Insurance Association of America (HIAA). The "Harry and Louise" ads fielded by HIAA were remarkable in that they were targeted at isolated media markets and that their content was so disputable. In its failure to respond aggressively, the White House suggested that its health care reform proposal was more vulnerable than anyone had suspected. Subsequently, Congressional representatives proceeded to take it apart, piece by piece, health alliances giving way to the basic benefit package falling off before global budgets, so that the only remaining "non-negotiable" component was universal coverage. By the time the president blinked on universal coverage, suggesting that 95 percent might meet the goal, debris of the health care reform proposal already littered Capitol Hill.

By insisting on an all-or-nothing strategy early in the health care reform process, the administration decided not to isolate subparts that might be salvaged in the event the entire package was threatened. Yet, this very strategy had been successful in the last significant wave of health care reform during the Great Society. In the mid-1960s when it became evident that there was not the Congressional support for a universal health care program, health care advocates settled on caring for the old and poor through Medicare and Medicaid. Had the Clinton White House planned accordingly, a fall-back option could have ensured universal care for all children or all workers—both admirable objectives. Approaching the end of the 103rd Congress, however, there was too little time left to retrieve these aspects of health care reform so the Clinton initiative was not just a partial failure—meaning, of course, that it would have been partially successful—but a complete and utter defeat.

Welfare

Welfare reform was a "no-brainer" for Clinton. He had won high praise from a frustrated public during the campaign when he pushed issues such as hounding "dead-beat dads" for child support, preparing employable welfare recipients for participation in the job market, and limiting receipt of welfare to two years. On the occasions when President Clinton spoke out about the damaging consequences of teen pregnancy, the insidious affects of drugs, and the chaos attendant with the violence so prevalent in poor communities, he came across as authentic and convincing as a moral crusader. This was perhaps in part due to his experience as governor of Arkansas: He had overseen the implementation of one of the more successful welfare-to-work programs.

Yet, out of concern for other, more pressing initiatives such as health care reform, welfare reform was shelved. This drove neoliberal intellectuals, such as Mickey Kaus, an editor of the *New Republic,* apoplectic. Why, they anguished, would an administration with such a flimsy electoral mandate continue to postpone the most resonant issue on its agenda? But, that is precisely what the Clinton White House did. Arguably its most bankable domestic proposal, welfare reform, was squandered out of preference for other initiatives, until there was insufficient time to launch it during the 103rd Congress. While the Clinton White House focused on other proposals, Congressional Republicans refined their more punitive counterproposal. As a result, when the 104th Congress revisits welfare reform, it will be the Republican version that will be forwarded to the White House for a presidential signature, not Clinton's. Replacing a positive Clintonesque portrait of poor mothers trying to extricate themselves from welfare dependence by enrolling in training and job-placement programs is a negative Gingrichian caricature of poor mothers as indolent sots whose children should be placed in orphanages if the mothers cannot find employment or secure charitable assistance.

Urban Policy

In urban affairs, the Clinton administration enjoyed more success, though indirectly. This was by design insofar as Clinton wished to distinguish himself as a "new Democrat" not beholden to traditional liberal interest groups, such as racial minorities and the poor who populated major American cities. The urgency of aid to distressed cities was underscored by a stream of media accounts of drive-by shootings, then punctuated by the Los Angeles riot that followed the not-guilty verdict in the trial of police officers accused of beating Rodney King. Initially, urban aid was incorporated in the ill-fated economic stimulus package. When this bill expired, urban aid was resurrected and inserted in other legislation, the designation of "empowerment zones" incorporated in the 1994 budget proposal and gang prevention programs, such as "midnight basketball," featured in the 1994 crime bill. In a maneuver that proved embarrassing to the White House, conservative House Republicans intercepted the crime bill, temporarily holding it up with a procedural technicality, objecting to the cost of social "pork" programs.

As in the case of welfare reform, the 104th Congress did not bode well for urban policy. Immediately after the conservative victories of the 1994 midterm elections, new Republican leadership in Congress announced it would reevaluate and attempt to excise social "pork" from Clinton's domestic legislation. As president, Clinton will be able to veto any Republican proposals that he deems harmful to American cities; but the loss of Democratic leadership in Congress will mean that no new initiatives can be expected that might halt the precipitous drop in the quality of life in poor, urban neighborhoods. As a result, most of the new urban assistance programs that were passed during the 103rd Congress will, in all likelihood, be short-lived. The half-life of crime prevention programs before a Republican 104th Congress will not be long—something on par with the life span of a German tourist in Miami.

Education

Several important education proposals advanced by the Clinton White House were passed by the 103rd Congress, marking it the most successful area of domestic policy for the president. In addition to school-to-work transition legislation, reauthorization of the Elementary and Secondary Education Act, and a bill intending to reduce violence in schools, the administration saw its *Goals 2000* proposal become law. Meritorious though it was, White House boasts of *Goals 2000* might have been qualified. Foremost, the educational reform initiative had its origins in the Bush White House, known then as *America 2000,* so much of the groundwork had been done prior to Clinton assuming the presidency. Programmatically, *Goals 2000* is likely to succumb by the very goals it advocates. To aspire to objectives such as eliminating illiteracy, making every child ready to learn upon entry to elementary school, and elevating American students to first place with regard to their command of science and math in international ratings, is laudatory rhetoric; but as public policy, it borders on deception. Few educators would predict that *Goals 2000* would be more than a yardstick for measuring the disappointing performance of American schools.

The Clinton administration could well have made a distinctive contribution to the momentum in educational reform—on a par with Terrel Bell's *A Nation at Risk* and George Bush's *America 2000*—had it presented a bold plan to salvage the nation's poorest schools. Ample evidence warranted such an initiative. Jonathan Kozol's *Savage Inequalities* graphically described the literal collapse of many American schools. Several educators undertook heroic missions to save poor students from an inferior public education, among them James Comer, Marva Collins, and Jaime Escalante. Poignantly, it was a former welfare mother and later state legislator, "Polly" Williams, who conceived of a radical solution to urban educational blight: vouchers for poor Milwaukee school children. In light of such ventures, the Clinton record on education is modest at best.

Immigration

Surely the "sleeper" in domestic policy, the immigration issue sprung onto the national agenda when the anti-illegal immigrant proposition, California's Proposition 187, passed by a substantial margin in 1994. Prior to the 1994 midterm elections, the Clinton administration was content to await the pronouncements of the Jordan Commission. Largely in response to fallout from the failed Immigration Reform and Control Act, the Jordan Commission took a decidedly conservative approach to containing the problem of illegal immigration. In so doing, the Jordan Commission addressed the fiscal problems that certain states had experienced, particularly California, Texas, and Florida. In waiting for the Jordan Commission report, the Clinton White House delayed presenting its immigration proposal, a decision which was to prove fatal.

The 1994 midterm elections were a nightmare for progressive advocates of immigration reform. Not only did Proposition 187 pass in California, but Republicans won majorities in the Senate and House of Representatives, giving them control of the federal legislative process. Only a week after the election, California Governor Pete Wilson was speaking before a standing-room-only crowd at the conservative Heritage Foundation in Washington, DC, promoting Proposition 187 as national law. Announcing his support of the idea was Newt Gingrich, incoming Speaker of the House. In contrast to crypto-conservative features of Proposition 187, the pronouncements of the Jordan Commission seemed liberal. In procrastinating the presentation of its immigration proposal, the Clinton administration had become a virtual nonparticipant in the immigration debate. The president did not state his objection to Proposition 187 until late in the 1994 Congressional election, while he was campaigning in California. The Republican sweep of the 1994 Congressional elections drove the immigration debate further to the Right, most evident when the incoming Republican leadership of the 104th Congress announced intentions to deny social welfare benefits to legal immigrants who were refugees. Behind the curve, the Clinton White House could do little but watch a tidal wave of immigrant-bashing bills build in the 104th Congress.

Social Security

Recognizing the influence of elderly advocacy groups, the Clinton administration opted to rely on the 1983 amendments as a basis for its position on Social Security, even though an increasing number of prominent Americans were skeptical about the long-term viability of the program. Although doubt about the solvency of Social Security was initially expressed by conservative policy analysts (in order to raise the more general issue of entitlement spending), Congressional Democrats were also joining the chorus. To the considerable embarrassment of the White House, Nebraska Democrat Robert Kerrey chastised President Clinton from the Senate floor about the fiscal timidity of his proposed budget. Kerrey's concession for his vote in favor of the president's budget was the designation of a commission to examine entitlement spending.

Even though deliberations of the Bipartisan Commission on Entitlement and Tax Reform degenerated into acrimony and name-calling, the issue of entitlement spending will surely feature prominently in the 104th Congress. Conservative Republicans have been eager to contain federal expenditures for open-ended social entitlements through such measures as a balanced budget amendment to the Constitution; their Congressional majorities will provide them with a virtually unprecedented opportunity to craft legislation toward that end. Radical overhaul of social entitlements by Congressional Republicans is unlikely, however, considering the influence of elderly interest groups, such as the American Association of Retired Persons. Instead, conservative entitlement reform will probably be restricted to the means-tested programs, such as Aid to Families with Dependent Children, Food Stamps, Medicaid, and Supplemental Security Income. Here, conservative options in welfare reform proposals will include a stringent work-test for employable recipients, time-limiting benefits, reserving programmatic authority to the states, changing federal funding to a block grant to state government, and possibly capping expenditures. The total effect of such changes will, in all likelihood, be a restructuring and further defunding of welfare programs. To a significant extent, the Clinton administration would not be faced with such Draconian reforms had it pursued welfare reform during the 103rd Congress.

Had the administration moved more assertively to address the problem posed by unconditional entitlement spending, it might have reinforced the more vulnerable welfare programs. Coupled with a welfare reform proposal, the Clinton White House probably could have reinforced faith in programs that serve the poor as well as social insurances for retirees. Having done neither, President Clinton is on the defensive with regard to both—means-tested entitlements for the poor and social insurance entitlements for retirees. But, when the dust settles, it will probably be the former that are sacrificed for the latter. An axiom of public policy holds that "poverty programs are poor programs"—not only are the benefits of means-tested programs low, but they are politically unpopular. Exactly how unpopular is a depth that will be plumbed by the 104th Congress.

SEISMIC SHOCK: THE 1994 MIDTERM ELECTIONS

As the forgoing suggests, whatever promise lay with the early months of the Clinton presidency was aborted by the Republican landslide of 1994. That a transformation in American politics was in the offing was no surprise to public opinion pollsters; the storm clouds had been gathering for some time. Evidence that Americans were losing faith in government continued to fall, as indicated in Table 8.2.

Disillusionment with government coincided with increasing public sentiment that opportunity for the middle class was diminishing. As Table 8.3 indicates, Americans were not optimistic about their current circumstance and perceived it to be decidedly worse than a decade or so earlier. Such perceptions, sampled on the eve of the 1994 election, were forbidding for Democrats in Washington. A shift in political affiliation was in the wind, and the direction clearly favored the Right.

The sheer magnitude of the political transformation represented by Republican majorities in the Senate and the House was astonishing. In gaining control of the means of legislation, conservatives not only monopolized the legislative process, but also asserted dominance in major agencies assisting federal lawmakers: the Government Accounting Office and the Congressional Budget Office, among others. But the extent of the Republican victories betrayed a much more extensive change, one of public philosophy. During the 1980s, many liberal intellectuals found succor in public opinion research that indicated public sentiment on a range of issues—reproductive freedom, welfare assistance, aid to the cities—remained liberal. The Reagan, then Bush, administrations, they contended, were anomalies—political artifices constructed of the machinations of conservative wealth and ideology. Despite the aberrant pronouncements from a Republican White House, liberals maintained a faith in the fundamentally progressive orientation of the public during the 1980s. If the 1994 midterm elections demonstrated anything, it was that this liberal assumption was, in retrospect, a chimera.

No one could have been more euphoric about the outcome of this election than Newt Gingrich, the Republic representative from Georgia. Since his election to Congress in 1979, Gingrich had been on a one-man mission to reverse the image of the Republican party that seemed to have been indelibly stained by Watergate. Toward that end, Gingrich resorted to any variety of pranks and smears, by sheer tenacity moving his way upward in the Republican hierarchy in the House of Representatives. By the 1992 election, Gingrich had a widely, if

TABLE 8.2 How much of the time can you trust the government to do what's right?

	1964	1984	1994
Always or most of the time	76%	44%	19%
Only sometime	22%	53%	72%
Never*		1%	9%

*Volunteered response
SOURCE: Kevin Phillips, "Fat City," *Time* (September 26, 1994), p. 49.

TABLE 8.3 Do you think things are becoming better for the middle class?

Yes	8%
No	57%
Staying the same	34%

Compared with 10 or 20 years ago, do you think there are more opportunities for the average American to get ahead today?

More	25%
Less	49%
Not much difference	24%

SOURCE: Kevin Phillips, "Fat City," *Time* (September 26, 1994), p. 52.

not highly, regarded reputation as a lounge-lizard ideologue and a ruthless politico.[18] By the 1994 election, Gingrich had mobilized a new constituency composed of working-class rednecks and middle-class Puritans, a "bubba-iosie,"[19] and was poised to challenge the control of Congress that the Democratic party had exercised, in varying degrees, for 40 years.

The scaffold that Gingrich constructed to lynch liberal Democrats was his "Contract with America," a summation of 10 bills that a Republican Congress would pass during its first 100 days:

1. Instituting a balanced budget amendment and line-item veto, in order to restore fiscal accountability in Washington.
2. Stopping violent criminals through more prisons, stiffer sentences, and imposition of the death penalty.
3. Introducing welfare reform that emphasizes work and dissuades young women from having children out of wedlock.
4. Protecting children by restoring parental control over education, aggressively pursuing child support, and eliminating child pornography.
5. Offering a middle-class tax cut so that working families could buy a home and send their kids to college.
6. Reinforcing national defense by increasing funding for national security.
7. Raising the limit on earnings for Social Security recipients as a way to reduce age discrimination and encourage the aged to work.
8. Rolling back government regulations that stifle small business and discourage job creation.
9. Reforming the legal profession to stop frivolous and excessive legal suits.

10. Establishing term limits for Congressional officeholders to discourage career politicians.[20]

In order to attract media to the Contract, Gingrich choreographed a ceremony on the Capitol steps in which 350 Republican aspirants to elected office signed on.

The Clinton White House was swift to respond. President Clinton relabeled the Contract as the "Contract *on* America," insinuating it was a clandestine attempt to undermine the nation's political economy. Appearing before a number of audiences on behalf of beleaguered Democratic candidates, Clinton denounced the Contract as a return to the flawed logic of Reaganomics. If enacted, Clinton suggested it would increase the federal deficit and necessitate a 20-percent cut in Social Security benefits. Major economists concurred, noting that even in its brief outline, the tax cuts indicated in the Contract would increase the deficit substantially or require major cuts in social programs.[21]

Whether voters were attracted to the Contract with America or simply fed up with incumbent Democrats, Gingrich claimed credit for the 1994 Republican electoral triumph. In characteristic style, he slammed the president and First Lady in a post-election day diatribe as "counter-culture McGovernicks" presiding over a White House staff of "left-wing elitists."[22] Indeed, it seemed that if Gingrich had gone to Washington for half a chance to sling mud, he would go to hell for a whole one. But Gingrich was more a mastermind than rhetorical vitriol might suggest. The extent to which his objectives sabotaged Clinton's could not be overemphasized. For Gingrich, the 1994 midterm election had made "the 104th a transforming Congress, one that sets the agenda for a 1996 election that will cement a new majority that finally replaces the New Deal–Great Society era."[23] Shortly after assuming the gavel as Speaker of the House of Representatives, Gingrich targeted the welfare state as a primary source of sinister influences in American culture:

> The decay of the welfare state . . . has reduced citizens to clients, subordinated them to bureaucrats and subjected them to rules that are anti-work, anti-family, anti-opportunity and anti-property. The welfare state must be replaced, not reformed.[24]

By contrast, Clinton's objectives had been considerably more modest. During the 103rd Congress, he had expected to put in place the foundation for the social investments that would be delivered by the 104th, and in fact had made concessions in his budget proposals toward that end, delaying his human services agenda until late in his first term at the earliest. Through the 1994 midterm elections, Gingrich had obviously outmaneuvered the Clinton White House. Instead of using the 104th Congress to sanction his "new Democrat" social agenda, the president would have to be on his guard that Republicans might well take down the Social Security Act and the American welfare state with it.

BEYOND THE POLITICS OF RETRENCHMENT

By the end of 1994, the promise of the "new Democrats" lay shredded on the cutting room floor, a casualty of the intransigence of old-guard Democratic liberals who insisted on unconditional entitlement spending and the onslaught of arch-conservatives eager to return to Reaganism. In the aftermath of the 1994 midterm elections, Democrats watched haplessly as Republicans began to orchestrate the Congress for a return to the first principles of the Reagan era: higher defense spending, lower taxes, cuts in welfare spending, and a traditionalist social agenda. A demoralized White House struggled to reassert leadership over a divided and defeated Democratic party.[25]

The conservative Congressional conquest notwithstanding, the fundamental question remains: To what extent has the Clinton presidency to date prepared the nation for the postindustrial requirements of the twenty-first century? Has domestic policy in the Clinton White House facilitated America's adjustment to the future or anchored it in the past? The four dynamics introduced in Chapter 1 provide a means for answering these questions.

From Commonweal to Commerce

Clearly, the administration has recognized the imperatives of global capitalism in shaping its domestic policy agenda. Among its most convincing victories was passage of NAFTA, legislation ardently opposed by the pro-labor Democratic old guard. In urban policy, Clinton attempted to have it both ways. On the one hand, the White House pushed an integrationist policy modeled after the *Gautreaux* experiment in Chicago that emphasized housing vouchers, on the other, using a community development strategy in designating empowerment zones for urban revitalization. Considering that empowerment zones are a modified version of "urban enterprise zones" promoted by the conservative Heritage Foundation during the 1980s, the Clinton imprint on urban policy clearly favors mainstreaming the poor through the marketplace.

Within health and welfare, the report is more mixed. The Health Security Act clearly minimized the role of government, electing to focus on various private sector institutions to extend health care to all. While health reform failed, it is usually attributed to the allegation that the Health Security Act, market-oriented as it was, proved too dependent on the federal government. In other words, in health care reform Clinton evidently erred by not moving far enough to the Right. Traditional liberals held out for the possibility that the public was more progressive than the White House or Congress, hoping that Californians would enact health care reform modeled on the Canadian single-payer health system, only to have their hopes dashed when voters defeated that initiative by a substantial margin. By the early 1990s, health care had become so commodified that an even marginal role for government seemed implausible.

In education and welfare, the Clinton administration was more ambivalent about orienting policy around commerce. The school choice movement provided an opportunity for the White House to endorse an incipient educational market, but it chose not to. Although its welfare reform efforts were postponed for the 104th Congress, the Clinton preference—for a two-year time limit after which a JOBS graduate must find work or risk losing benefits—indirectly favors the labor market. Otherwise, the White House has proposed no bold plans to privatize welfare.

From Dualism to Hypermobility

Among Clinton's first accomplishments in office was signing the Family Leave Act, allowing parents—most important, female workers—to take time off from work to care for a family member. With passage of school-to-work legislation, the Clinton administration facilitated the transition of secondary students into the job market. In convincing Congress to reauthorize the Elementary and Secondary Education Act, the White House continued federal funding of poor school districts. And, as noted above, in endorsing the *Gautreaux* plan, the Clinton administration contributed to the upward mobility of poor African Americans. In each of these instances, the Clinton White House opted for initiatives to enhance upward mobility through various social institutions, such as employment, education, and housing. In doing so, the Clinton White House moved deliberately to diminish the social and economic forces that create and maintain the underclass.

Thus, it is in ironic counterpoint that the White House also indicated its willingness to suspend federal social programs for legal and illegal immigrants. The administration's attempt to use the Jordan Commission to explore options in immigration policy—options which are clearly conservative—were eclipsed by the landslide passage of California's Proposition 187, which would deny health, education, and welfare assistance to illegal immigrants, to say nothing of Republican plans to curtail social program benefits for refugees who are legal immigrants. If Clinton's reluctance to speak strongly against immigrant-bashing is an indirect way to telegraph White House intentions to reduce programs for immigrants, the result will reinforce the alien underclass in America.

From Bureaucracy to Restructuring

After twelve years of Republican administrations in which federal employment had increased, the Clinton administration was in a strong position to restructure the national government. Many states, including Arkansas, had engaged in ambitious experiments to restructure education, health, and welfare. The severe budget cuts in aid to the cities during the 1980s had made many of the nation's mayors magicians in municipal finance. Yet, Clinton was able to make little of these openings. During the first two years of the Clinton presidency, the only orchestrated event suggestive of restructuring government was the National

Performance Review undertaken by Vice President Gore, modeled on precepts proposed by David Osborne and Ted Gaebler in *Reinventing Government*.[26] To his credit, Gore made the most of the opportunity, at one point using forklifts to demonstrate the sheer mass of unnecessary federal regulations. The National Performance Review, Gore claimed, identified $108 billion in savings by the federal government over five years.[27]

Within specific areas of social policy, however, the administration moved cautiously. Its Health Security Act was portrayed as unnecessarily bureaucratic, an accusation that stuck despite arguable accuracy. In education, the Clinton White House demurred from taking on the teachers' lobby by advocating school choice, even though this had been pioneered in poor inner-city districts. In social policy for the poor, the administration failed to moved aggressively on dismantling the welfare bureaucracy, despite its unpopularity among clients, welfare workers, and taxpayers.

If politicians ever pay a price for ambivalence in public affairs, Bill Clinton paid that penalty with the 1994 elections. Despite a vibrant economy, low interest rates, peace at home, and an expanding job market, the Democratic party was staggered by voters' rejection of their leadership, and their election of a Republican Congress for the first time in forty years. Speaking for many, William Raspberry explained the Democratic losses of 1994 this way: "Government doesn't work. It costs more (and becomes more intrusive) with every passing year, but hardly anywhere can it be said that it is performing better."[28] In preferring incremental strategies that seemed to batten bloated bureaucracies, the White House fueled voter resentment about the cost and unresponsiveness of government, thereby sowing the seeds for the voter purge of Democrats in 1994.

From Entitlements to Human Capital

If the Clinton White House failed to take advantage of opportunities to restructure government, it actually worked to reinforce the status quo of entitlement programs, at the expense of opting for strategic targets of human capital. In elevating Social Security to cabinet-level status, the administration further reinforced the outflow of public dollars for retirees. When Congressional Democrats—and Republicans, of course—objected to uncontrolled entitlement spending, it took the public humiliation by Senator Bob Kerrey before the White House agreed to examine the issue. Thus, a debate of enormous import was not only delayed, but White House indifference to the problem suggested it was unconcerned about long-run public interest.

Had Clinton enjoined the issue early, the White House could have assumed a commanding presence in discussing the virtues versus the demerits of various entitlements: social program benefits for retirees and the poor, of course, but also crop subsidies for farmers, tax expenditures for the middle class, and redundant retirement benefits for veterans. Tardy to take the initiative, the administration fell behind the curve while the Bipartisan Commission on Entitlements and Tax Reform assumed the charge. In its lapse, the Clinton administration not only lost the opportunity to recast the problem as one warranting major investments in human capital, but, as a consequence of the 1994 election, it may well have set the context for a conservative evisceration of entitlements for the poor.

Of the dynamics shaping a postindustrial future, the need to redouble targeted investments in human capital is most fundamental, yet it is often diminished to the point of caricature. President Reagan derided traditional Democrats as "tax and spend" liberals because of their preference for unconditional, open-ended entitlement programs. The antidote suggested by supply-side conservatives was a "slash-and-binge" approach to public finance, aggravating the conditions of the poor while S&L financiers fed at the federal trough and the deficit ballooned. After the excesses of the Reagan and Bush presidencies, the Clinton administration was well positioned to propose a "trim-and-invest" strategy coupling entitlement pruning with investments in human capital. But, as in other matters, White House procrastination would subvert this as well; instead of setting a new course in federal fiscal policy, a Republican 104th Congress shows every inclination of returning to "slash-and-binge." It is unlikely the American economy can afford a decade of federal financial waste on a scale of the 1980s and remain competitive internationally.

In all this, the Clinton administration understood—at least, at one time—that ideas are fundamental. Since passage of the Social Security Act in 1935, the welfare state had served as an organizing principle for American domestic policy. Yet, as events unfolded beginning in the late 1970s, the validity of the welfare state came open to question. At the end of the second Reagan term, none other than Senator Ted Kennedy recognized the tentativeness of traditional Democratic liberalism. "We now stand between two Americas, the one we have known and the one toward which we are heading," Kennedy said to the Woman's National Democratic Club. "The New Deal will live in American history forever as a supreme example of government responsiveness to the times. But it is no answer to the problems of today."[29]

In response to Democratic presidential election humiliations of 1980 and 1984, Clinton, Gore, and other neoliberal Democrats founded the Democratic Leadership Council (DLC) in 1985 to goad the party toward the political center. The defeat of Michael Dukakis by George Bush in 1988 underscored the DLC initiative; the election of Clinton and Gore in 1992 validated the DLC thesis. During the 1992 presidential campaign, Clinton spoke convincingly about the need for the nation to forge a new path in public policy—one that avoided the unfocused spending associated with big-government liberalism as well as the excesses of supply-side, laissez-faire conservatism. To fill in the political canvas, he invoked a constellation of new ideas: national service, microenterprise, charter schools, a police corps, among others—ideas that would guide America into the twenty-first century. During the campaign and shortly after assuming the presidency, Clinton spoke eloquently about how static economic opportunity had become for middle-income families that played by the rules. The "new Democrat" agenda proposed by the Clinton White House would restart the dead economic battery of bourgeois family economics; the nation's families would be the prime beneficiaries of "CHANGE."

The optimism of the "new Democrats" who moved into the White House is hard to imagine. After a dozen years of conservative presidency, the backlog of social legislation was substantial. Blessed by executive talent and a Democratic Congress, President Clinton expected to move so many initiatives through Congress that his first hundred days would parallel those of FDR and LBJ. Authorized by the president, *Washington Post* writer Bob Woodward chronicled the events that followed—but it revealed more of White House naïveté and ineptitude than anything else. Beset by staff inexperience and a cranky Congress, Clinton careened through the first two years, claiming hair-breadth victories that were followed by embarrassing defeats. Fatally, the White House learning curve jerked up, then down, during a 103rd Congress controlled by Democrats. The inability of the Clinton White House to enact its agenda despite largely favorable circumstances in Congress exposed the Democratic party to voters' wrath in the 1994 election. The Republican Congressional election sweep in 1994 confirmed the depth of public doubt about the Clinton presidency. The morning after the election, Democrats were stunned. "The first thing to understand is that this was an earthquake," fumed DLC director Al From.

> The New Deal Era is over. It was a grand and glorious era for Democrats, but it is over. The nails are in the coffin of New Deal liberalism, and it is dead and buried. It was a great ideology while it lasted—it was the ideology that built the middle class of America—but the policies that built the middle class can no longer earn their support. And we have lost them.[30]

Never long on harmony, the Democratic party was splintering into unorchestrated cacophony. In a postmortem of the 1994 election, columnist Nicholas von Hoffman observed that the Democrats "have no organizational web to stay in touch with this quasi-constituency of theirs."[31] Prominent inside the Washington beltway, the DLC had deployed organizations in several states, but such organizing was nascent and unable to resist the Republican electoral tide.

In many respects, the shortcomings of the Clinton presidency can be attributed to the failure of the White House to cultivate the policy *intelligence* essential to accomplish the paradigm shift in domestic policy. Clearly, Clinton understood the historic circumstance before him, hence his references to a "new covenant" and a "third way." Toward that end, the DLC had created a think tank to incubate new ideas, the Progressive Policy Institute (PPI). As envisioned by its president, Will Marshall, PPI would replicate the astonishing accomplishments of the conservative Heritage Foundation by generating innovative concepts in public policy and placing creative thinkers throughout the incoming Clinton administration. The success of the Heritage Foundation during the Reagan and Bush presidencies was nothing short of legendary in Washington intellectual circles. Having been established as recently as 1973 from a $250,000 grant from the Coors family, the Heritage Foundation was so central to conservative thought that, by the eve of the Reagan inauguration, it was poised to transfer over three dozen policy analysts into top positions in the incoming administration.[32] As From and Marshall saw it, Heritage had provided the intellectual staffing for the Reagan revolution in the same way that PPI would for the Clinton administration.

But this was not to be. The Clinton White House selected only a handful of DLC and PPI staff for appointments in the new administration. PPI continued to generate monographs on policy options and offer seminars to decision makers, all on a modest $3.5 million budget—a fraction of the revenues invested in the conservative policy institutes around the nation. During the 1980s, conservative policy institutes, such as Heritage, the American Enterprise Institute (AEI), the Hoover Institution, and the Cato Institute boasted a battery of scholars who generated policy analyses by the dozens. The conservative think tanks made savvy use of the print and electronic media, distributing at no charge op-ed pieces and videos to newspapers and TV stations that served the major metropolitan media markets. For backup, they had recruited a network of hundreds of university researchers across the nation. In the face of such opposition, PPI was often outgunned. By the 1994 election, PPI had been in operation only five years, while the conservative opposition—Heritage, AEI, Hoover, and Cato—benefited from decades of experience massaging public policy. Most troubling, Clinton, a former head of the DLC, did little to cite PPI as the intellectual fount of his domestic policy agenda. Then, to compound matters, when the Clinton administration moved in a traditionally liberal direction, the DLC and PPI questioned White House judgment, creating a distance that proved awkward to bridge. With the 1994 election approaching ominously, Marshall conceded that the marriage between the White House and PPI had deteriorated to "one of convenience."[33]

This failure to nurture the intellectual base for "new Democrats" cannot be overstated. It goes without saying that societal transformation is inevitable, and that prudent nations prepare accordingly—they place themselves on the right side of history. Great thinkers are known for their foresight in explaining moments that are fraught with intransigent and antiquated institutions on the one hand, and with social turbulence and instability on the other. Karl Marx recognized as much when he suggested that the critical question introduced by the Industrial Revolution was, Who controls "the means of production?" With the subsequent rise of civil authority to ameliorate the dislocations attendant with industrial capitalism, Max Weber rephrased the question as, Who controls "the means of administration?" In the information-insatiable service sector of the postindustrial era, the fundamental question is, Who controls "the means of analysis?"[34]

In this respect, conservatives have incisively understood the requisites for leveraging public policy in the postindustrial context, and they have exploited this capacity masterfully. Indeed, it is unthinkable that any significant policy initiative, regardless of its ideological origin, would escape the review of analysts from conservative policy institutes who would make public their imprint through the op-ed pages of major newspapers and weekend TV news programs. Liberals, on the other hand, are decidedly behind the curve, the institutional consequences of which are enormous. Conservatives have honed their policy craft and seasoned a cadre of analysts who served in upper administrations within the Reagan and Bush administrations. Now, these intellectuals are updating their public philosophy in anticipation of the next Republican president. Democrats, on the other hand, have only begun to field a full squad of new thinkers through PPI. As a result, White House pronouncements have too often had a timeworn quality about them and a noticeable liberal tinge. Undoubtedly, this has been reassuring for traditional Democratic liberals who chafed under the conservative agendas of the Reagan/Bush era; but its legislative prospects are dim, consonant with an America long since past. As Clinton belatedly discovered during his first two years in the White House, initiatives that require massive and costly interventions on the part of the federal government are perceived by the public to be suspiciously—and, as the 1994 election revealed, unacceptably—liberal. When voters are slow to make the connection, conservative ideologues are quick to draw the association for them.

The implications of this for domestic policy are troubling, indeed. Having refined their command of the "means of analysis," conservatives stand on the verge of orchestrating a return to the policies of "slash-and-binge," Reagan redux with a vengeance. Having forfeited the promise of the presidency and a Democratic Congress, Clinton is effectively neutralized; any positive definition to emerge from the 104th Congress will be as a result of his using the veto with the same degree of creativity that Republicans used the filibuster during the 103rd. But this will offer little solace to the many American families frustrated by diminishing economic prospects, to say nothing of the minority poor and women who have yet to make up ground lost during the 1980s. In fact, implementation of the much ballyhooed "Contract with America" fashioned by Newt Gingrich for the 1994 election will surely erode, if not wash out altogether, the prospects of the working- and welfare-poor.

It is within the context of American decline that the Clinton presidency most disappoints. Given the heart and mind—if not the genius—required to vault from the political periphery of Arkansas to the White House, the Clinton presidential candidacy offered a promise that resonated with many Americans. Once inaugurated, however, the oft-evoked "CHANGE" turned out to be small change, indeed. Clinton apologists can accurately point out that the enormity of the federal debt, a legacy of the Reagan presidency, precluded major social policy initiatives, and that the series of demonstrations that the White House settled for were optimal given the economic constraints. Yet, this fails to explain the Health Security Act debacle, a political potlatch of unprecedented proportion. Instead of generating a momentum borne of a series of modest initiatives that would form a foundation for a small number of strategically chosen initiatives, much of the early Clinton presidency was consumed with health care reform that seemed ill-conceived, poorly managed, and without a fall-back position—one more example of erratic performance on the part of the White House.

Thus, the president who won the 1992 election verges on the lamentable: A young man of considerable intellect climbs out of rural, working-class America and by dint of tenacity—and against enormous odds—convinces a beleaguered citizenry that he and his ideas are not only timely but also worthy of their confidence. A personification of the Horatio Alger myth, Bill Clinton overcomes the deficits of social status, revisits marital indiscretions, only to encounter accusations about financial improprieties. His insistence on avoiding the hierarchical, and therefore authoritarian, tendencies of White House staff contributes to administrative confusion and leads to questions of his leadership. Soon he loses a close, childhood friend, Vince Foster, to suicide—by most accounts the victim of a ruthlessly predatory Washington environment. Under siege, the White House complains of media failure to portray its successful track record during the 103rd Congress. Neglected altogether are the defamatory statements, literature, and videos generated by the Religious Right that revile the president, accusing him of engaging in sinister machinations, including assassination plots.

Yet, even if his character and management are flawed, Clinton's understanding that this is a historic moment for America seems true: The nation needs a new paradigm for domestic policy. Despite this prescience, persona and policy clash. Although he comprehends the requirements of time and office, Clinton seems ill-matched for the mission. The president is unable to obtain his domestic policy objectives, even as he sees them so clearly before him. The result is a disjuncture of tragic proportion: Bill Clinton, the wrong man at the right time.

This incongruity between the president and his policies is illustrated in a poll taken after the 1995 State of the Union address. Widely anticipated as the most important, if not the last, opportunity to salvage a stumbling presidency, the State of the Union speech was followed closely. For over an hour, President Clinton expressed his willingness to work with Congressional Republicans on issues upon which they agreed, signaled his opposition to specific features of the Contract with America (the balanced budget amendment, repeal of the ban on automatic weapons), and proposed bills to aid working Americans (raising the minimum wage, a middle-class tax cut, and a tax credit for college tuition). Recalling a slogan last heard during the presidential campaign, Clinton organized his proposals around the idea of a "New Covenant": "All Americans have not just a right but a solemn responsibility to rise as far as their God-given talents and determination can take them, and to give something back to their communities and their country in return," he said.

> Our "New Covenant" is a new set of understanding for how we can equip our people to meet the challenges of the new economy, how we can change the way our government works to fit a different time, and above all, how we can repair the damaged bonds in our society and come together behind our common purpose.[35]

Clearly, the president was positioning his administration vis-à-vis the new Republican Congress.

The public was less convinced, however. A nationwide *Los Angeles Times* poll revealed that the president's approval rating actually *dropped* five percentage points after the address. While the vacillation in public opinion lessens the significance of such a drop in public confidence, the poll revealed a more substantial problem. Although respondents expressed support for Clinton's policy objectives, they had serious reservations about *him*. After the speech, only 37 percent of voters indicated they would vote for him if he were to run for reelection in 1996, versus 48 percent who said they would not.[36] Underscoring public skepticism, veteran White House reporter David Broder slammed the speech for Clinton's failure to relay "a real sense of conviction and a clear agenda." Instead of recognizing the gravity of the task at hand—"new times demand new policies"—Broder accused the president of self-indulgence.

> Clinton was again—at just the wrong moment—the loquacious, self-centered youth who somehow slipped into the Oval Office, all charm and "aw shucks" humility one moment, full of braggadocio the next, seeking approval rather than setting a course.[37]

James Pinkerton, one of the New Paradigm enthusiasts in the Bush administration, cited Clinton for being "in full-schmooze mode" and noted, with some smugness, that the real "revolution of ideas" was not coming from the president in his State of the Union address, but from the Speaker of the House in his Contract with America.[38]

To what extent, then, do major policy initiatives within the Democratic and Republican parties presage the emergence of a paradigm that will guide the nation into the next century? Neither Clinton's recently revived "New Covenant" nor Gingrich's "Contract with America" offers much promise. Had Clinton elaborated his "New Covenant" upon entering the White House, it might have provided a way to organize his priorities as a "new Democrat." Having failed to do so, the new, improved covenant has a disingenuous ring, suggestive of the president groping, once again, for better footing on Washington's ever-shifting political shoals. Hammered by the Republican landslide in 1994, the president moved at once in both ideological directions, delivering a $25 billion bonus to the Pentagon, then offering income benefits to working families in his State of the Union address. Such behavior reinforces a negative impression that President Clinton, lacking a clear vision for the nation, typifies the worst of politicians—he is first and foremost an opportunist who happens to be occupying the White House.

The Gingrich incursion is symptomatic of the problems facing Clinton and the Democratic party. Had Clinton moved a Democratic Congress more effectively, Gingrich would have remained a back-bencher, and his influence would have been limited to hurling epithets at liberal Democrats. As an election tactic, the Contract with America was brilliant, highlighting the absence of a comparable plan from the White House. As strategy, however, the Contract is, at best, a rehash of Reaganism; at worst, the provisions of the Contract would accelerate the downward spiral that the nation has experienced since the early 1980s. Of course, not all national indicators are down, but enough have fallen as to leave one questioning the well-being of the nation. The Contract would exacerbate differences between the rich and the poor, Anglos and minorities, men and women, the old and the young. Instead of anticipating the substantial problems facing the next generation, the Contract prefers short-term political gains. Few Americans would knowingly opt for an agenda that would likely double the woes attributed to the economic policies of the Reagan presidency.

If these developments are discouraging, Americans may find some solace in history. The Democratic and Republican parties are political constructs associated with liberal and conservative ideologies that evolved during the Industrial era. With the passing of that era, public philosophy (evident in liberal and conservative ideologies) has begun to dissemble, a process that has now affected the political parties. The resolution of this process will become evident once a new paradigm has emerged—a set of principles upon which political parties have generally agreed that will direct future domestic policy into the postindustrial era. That paradigm remains to be developed.

NOTES

1. Quoted in Thomas Cronin, "How Much Is His Fault?" *New York Times Magazine* (October 16, 1994), p. 56.
2. Jonathan Rauch, *Demosclerosis: The Silent Killer of American Government* (New York: Times Books, 1994), p. 85.
3. Kevin Phillips, "Fat City," *Time* (September 26, 1994), p. 51.
4. Phillips, "Fat City," p. 52.
5. Peter Peterson, *Facing Up: Paying Our Nation's Debt and Saving our Children's Future* (New York: Touchstone, 1994), Chart 2.0.
6. Katherine Newman, *Declining Fortunes: The Withering of the American Dream* (New York: Basic Books, 1993).
7. Peterson, Charts 4.4 and 4.6.
8. Bipartisan Commission on Entitlement and Tax Reform, *Interim Report to the President* (Washington, DC: author, 1994), p. 7.
9. Quoted in Elizabeth Drew, *On the Edge: The Clinton Presidency* (New York: Simon and Schuster, 1994), p. 293.
10. Drew, *On the Edge*, p. 36.
11. Drew, *On the Edge*, p. 123.
12. Drew, *On the Edge*, pp. 395–96.
13. Will Marshall and Martin Schram (eds.), *Mandate for Change* (New York: Berkley Books, 1993).
14. Bob Woodward, *The Agenda* (New York: Simon and Schuster, 1994), p. 165.
15. Drew, *On the Edge*, p. 52.
16. Richard Rothstein, "Friends of Bill? Why Liberals Should Let Up on Clinton," *The American Prospect* (Winter 1995).
17. This list includes most of the legislative accomplishments of the Clinton administration during the 103rd Congress. For a full accounting, see "Clinton's Good Deeds," *The American Prospect* (Winter 1995), p. 34.

18. Other observers have been less charitable in their assessments of Gingrich. John Gregory Dunne wrote that "Newt is the moral equivalent of a bowel movement." See John Gregory Dunne, *Crooning* (New York: Simon and Schuster, 1990), p. 145.
19. Thanks to Mark Lusk and apologies to H.L. Mencken.
20. John Machacek, "Is GOP Contract All It Claims to Be?" *Idaho Statesman* (November 12, 1994), p. 2A.
21. Machacek, "Is GOP Contract All It Claims to Be?" p. 2A.
22. John King, "Demos See Newt Gingrich as Their Possible Salvation," *Idaho Statesman* (November 20, 1994), p. 6A.
23. Paul Gigot, "A Do-Something Congress," *Wall Street Journal* (November 11, 1994), p. A14.
24. Newt Gingrich, "The Challenges We Must Meet to Achieve Our Destiny," *Los Angeles Times* (January 27, 1995), p. B-7.
25. Richard Berke, "Democratic Party Struggles to Restore Its Equilibrium," *New York Times* (November 27, 1994), p. A-1.
26. David Osborne and Ted Gaebler, *Reinventing Government* (Reading, MA: Addison Wesley, 1992).
27. Al Gore, *Creating a Government That Works Better and Costs Less* (New York: Plume, 1993), p. xxvi. Another Clinton appointee has considered reforming government: Alice Rivlin, *Reviving the American Dream* (Washington, DC: Brookings Institution, 1992).
28. William Raspberry, "Gingrich Won't Save Us," *Idaho Statesman* (November 27, 1994), p. 15A.
29. Quoted in David Broder, "Reagan's Policies Are Standard for Would-Be Successors," *Omaha World-Herald* (January 24, 1988), p. 25A.
30. Quoted in Michael Kelly, "You Say You Want a Revolution," *New Yorker* (November 21, 1994), p. 58.
31. Nicholas von Hoffman, "The Democrats: A Party in Search of Itself," *Washington Post Weekly* (November 21–27, 1994), p. 24.
32. David Stoesz, "Packaging the Conservative Revolution," *Social Epistemology*, Vol. 2, No. 2 (1988).
33. Interview with Will Marshall, September 21, 1994.
34. David Stoesz, "The Means of Analysis and the Future of Liberalism," *Social Epistemology*, Vol. 3, No. 3 (1989).
35. Quoted by John Broder and Doyle McManus, "Clinton Urges New Public Spirit, Says Society Is Frayed," *Los Angeles Times* (January 25, 1995), p. A-9.
36. David Lauter, "Clinton's Image Hurts Him More Than His Ideas," *Los Angeles Times* (January 28, 1995), p. A-1, A-14.
37. David Broder, "A Term Paper Isn't an Agenda," *Los Angeles Times* (January 26, 1995), p. B-7.
38. James Pinkerton, "'Raiders of the Lost New Covenant'," *Los Angeles Times* (January 26, 1995), p. B-7.

Index

Aaron, Henry, 11, 26, 65, 81, 82
Abramovitz, Mimi, 82
Adams, J. R., 113
Aid to Families with Dependent Children (AFDC), 7-8, 13, 20, 22, 59-61, 63-66, 68-70, 72, 75-76, 81, 92-93
American Association of Retired Persons (AARP), 14, 36
Anders, George, 54
Anderson, Martin, 57, 81
Applebome, Peter, 145
Asch, Beth, 170
Auletta, Ken, 90, 112
Axinn, June, 111, 193

Backstrom, Charles, 54
Ball, Robert, 179, 193
Baroody, William Jr., 12, 26
Barrett, Edith, 20-21, 27, 193
Bearak, Barry, 112, 114, 115
Berke, Richard, 221
Berkowitz, Edward, 176, 192
Besharov, Douglas, 82, 146
Bhagwati, Jagdish, 169
Bierlein, Louanna, 144-146
Billitier, Bill, 112
Blau, Joel, 101, 115
Bloom, Allan, 131, 145
Bloom, Dan, 83
Bluestone, Barry, 25
Blumenthal, Sidney, 26, 95, 113
Bolger, John, 107, 116
Boo, Katherine, 147
Borjas, George, 157, 160-161, 168-170
Bornemeier, James, 170
Boyer, Ernest, 126, 134, 145, 146
Branch, Taylor, 26, 144
Bratt, L. Erik, 116
Braun, Stephen, 115
Broder, David, 25, 27, 52-54, 99, 114, 194, 219, 221
Brower, Bruce, 146

Brown, Claude, 5, 26
Browning, E. S., 170
Brownstein, Ronald, 53, 82, 83, 170
Burrell, Cassandra, 144
Burt, Martha, 100-101, 115
Bush, George, 6, 15, 21, 45, 69, 92, 97, 129, 184
Butler, Stuart, 27, 91

Caldwell, Malcolm, 170
Carter, Jimmy, 11, 62
Carvajal, Doreen, 168
Chen, Edwin, 53
Child Abuse, 6
Child Abuse Prevention and Treatment Act of 1974, 6. *See also* Hewlett, Sylvia Ann
Chubb, John, 127-128, 138, 145, 146
Cimons, Marlene, 116
Cisneros, Henry, 101, 115
Civil Rights Movement, 10
Claiborne, William, 170
Clinton, Bill, 115
   budget, 103, 200-202, 212
   "Contract with America," 210, 218-219
   crime bill, 109, 205
   Democratic Leadership Council (DLC), 4, 17, 69, 197, 214-216
   education, 130-131, 139, 205-206, 212
   health care, 39-42, 43, 49, 203-204
   Health Security Act (HSA), 40-44, 203, 211, 213
   immigration, 166, 206, 212
   liberal, 4
   NAFTA, 2, 4, 211
   "new Democrat," 1-2, 22, 197, 200, 211, 214-215
   "New Paradigm," 19
   presidency, 1, 6, 22-25, 198-199, 202-203, 217-219
   scandals, 199-200
   social policy, 24-25, 213
   Social Security, 173, 188, 206-207, 213
   urban policy, 102-105, 204-205, 211

Clinton, Bill (continued)
  welfare, 58, 69-70, 72-73, 76, 81, 204, 212-213
  Working Group on Welfare Reform, 69-70, 72, 76
Clinton, Hillary Rodham, 1
  health care, 30, 39-43, 49
  welfare, 74
Cloward, Richard, 11, 26
Clymer, Adam, 55, 194
Cohen, Sidney, 97, 113
Coles, Robert, 142, 147
Collins, Marva, 124-125, 144, 206
Colson, Charles, 114
Comer, James, 124-125, 135, 145, 146, 206
Community Mental Health Centers Act of 1965, 31
Conover, Ted, 169
Conservative Policy Wonks, "ConWonks," 13-14, 26
Cook, Fay, 20-21, 27, 193
Cook, Rhonda, 114
Cooper, Andrew, 115
Cooper, Kenneth, 146
Corbett, Thomas, 80, 84
Cordes, Coleen, 146
Costin, Lela, 26, 146
Cronin, Thomas, 220

Dacy, Sheila, 83
Danner, Mark, 169
Dattalo, Patrick, 193
Davis, Kenneth, 192
Day, K., 113
Denton, Nancy, 87-90, 112, 115
DeParle, Jason, 83
Dickman, Robert, 52
Dilulio, John Jr., 113, 114
DiNitto, Diana, 193
Dionne, E. J. Jr., 19, 25, 27, 116
Dixon, Jennifer, 169
Dolbeare, C., 112
Domestic Policy, 16-17, 20, 22, 195, 218
Drew, Elizabeth, 2, 25, 199-200, 220
Drugs, 97-98
D'Souza, Dinesh, 131, 145
Duerksen, Susan, 52
Duncan, David Ewing, 54
Dunne, John Gregory, 221

Eaton, William, 116
Eckholm, Erik, 54
Edelman, Marian Wright, 117, 144, 146
Edin, Kathryn, 60-61, 82
Edsall, Thomas, 26
Education. See also Silber, John
  alternative schools, 124-127
  America 2000, 129-131, 205
  Apprentice Warranties, 138-140
  charter schools, 129
  desegregation, 120
  "excellence movement," 117-118
  Goals 2000: The Educate America Act, 130-131, 133, 205
  higher education, 131-133
  magnet schools, 129
  national educational plan, 133-134
  policy, 120-122
  Preferred School Choice, 136-138
  ranking, 122-124
  reform, 118-119, 133-139
  School-Based Human Services, 134-136
  school choice, 128-129
  testing, 119
  Universities in the Public Interest, 140, 143
Ellis, Virginia, 84
Ellwood, David, 66, 76, 82, 83
Else, John, 84
Enthoven, Alain, 38-39, 42, 52
Escobar, Gabriel, 113

Falco, Mathea, 113
Family Support Act of 1988, 14
Feldman, Paul, 169, 170
Fix, Michael, 154, 156, 160-161, 169
Fleming, Arthur, 41, 53
Franey, Lynn, 147
Frankel, David, 112
Franklin, John Hope, 147, 192
Frantz, Douglas, 52
Fried, Jonathan, 170
Friedman, Milton and Rose, 4, 25, 137
Fritz, Sara, 54
Fulwood, Sam, 114
Funiciello, Theresa, 79, 81
Furniss, Norman, 192

Gaebler, Ted, 19, 27, 78, 84, 213, 221
Gans, Herbert, 111
Garfinkel, Irving, 76, 83
Gebbie, Kristine, 54
Georges, Christopher, 144
Gerstner, Louis, 144, 145
Gigot, Paul, 221
Gilbert, Neil, 26, 192
Gilder, George, 63, 82
Gingrich, Newt, 2, 10, 74, 188, 204, 208-210, 221
  "Contract with America," 2, 10, 74, 188, 209-210, 217, 219-220
  immigration, 206
  Personal Responsibility Act (PRA), 10, 74-75
  urban policy, 105
  welfare, 74
Ginzberg, Eli, 52
Goldman, John, 147
Gomez, James, 51
Goodman, Michael, 84
Gore, Al, 221
  Democratic Leadership Council (DLC), 4, 17, 197, 214-215
  National Performance Review, 213
Graetz, Michael, 189, 194
Great Society, 10-11, 30, 57
Greenstein, Robert, 112, 113, 115
Greider, William, 113
Gross Domestic Product (GDP), 7-9, 47
Gross National Product (GNP), 14
Gugliotta, Guy, 113-115
Gupta, Udayan, 55

Hachette, Dominique, 194
Hancock, LynNell, 145
Harrington, Michael, 26
Harrison, Bennett, 25
Harrison, Eric, 54
Harvey, Philip, 21, 27
Hayes-Bautista, David, 167, 171
Health Care
  AIDS, 45
  corporation, 33-35

costs, 47-48
Health Maintenance Organizations (HMOs), 30, 35, 44-45, 48-49, 50-51
Health Security Act (HSA), 40-44, 49-50, 211
Magaziner, Ira, 30, 39-41, 49-50, 199
"managed competition," 38-40. *See also* Enthoven, Alain; Kronick, Richard
Mitchell Plan, 43-44
prevention, 45-46
reform, 29-30, 36-39, 49-50, 52-53
"single-payer," 37-38. *See also* Himmelstein, David; Woolhandler, Steffie
state approaches/experiments, 44-45, 48. *See also* Medicaid, Medicare
types of systems, 29-30
Hecht, Brian, 146
Henig, Jeffrey, 144-146
Hersh, Richard, 141, 147
Hershey, Robert Jr., 194
Hewlett, Sylvia Ann, 6, 26, 135, 146
Hill, Edward, 95, 113
Hill, Retha, 146
Hilzenrath, David, 55
Himmelstein, David, 37, 52
Holmes, Steven, 114
Hombs, Mary Ellen, 114
Homelessness, 99-102, 114-115. *See also* Snyder, Mitch; Cisneros, Henry
Honan, William, 147
Howe, Irving, 11, 26
Howe, Neil, 193
Hoyt, Kenneth, 146

Immigration
amnesty, 156-157, 163-164
"birds of passage," 158-159
Bureau of Immigration, 150
Chinese Exclusion Act of 1882, 153
education, 119, 152-153
European, 150-154
guest worker program, 164-165
illegal, 154-155
Immigration Act of 1990, 154
Immigration and Nationality Act, 153-154
Immigration and Naturalization Service (INS), 154, 156-157
Immigration Reform and Control Act (IRCA) of 1986, 155-158, 162-163
"Jordan Commission," 162-163, 206, 212
NAFTA, 165-166
Proposition, 149, 161, 166, 187, 206, 212
Social Darwinism, 151-152
social welfare, 159-162
third world, 154-155
Isikoff, Michael, 113

Jackson, Robert, 54, 194
Jacoby, Russell, 132, 144, 146, 168
Jaschik, Scott, 146
Jenks, Christopher, 82, 100-101, 113, 114
Jimenez, Maria, 165, 169, 170
Johnson, Lyndon, 10
Jordan, May, 146
Juffras, Jason, 169, 170

Kantrowitz, Barbara, 113
Karger, Howard, 26, 27, 51, 52, 82, 111, 112, 146, 192, 193

Kasarda, John, 87-89, 92, 111, 112
Katz, Michael, 176, 192
Kaus, Mickey, 18, 27, 82, 83, 204
Kelly, Michael, 221
Kemp, Jack, 15, 22, 91, 166
Kennedy, John F., 10
Kimball, Roger, 131, 146
King, John, 221
Klein, Joe, 116
Kolderie, Ted, 129, 145
Kozol, Jonathan, 99-100, 114, 115, 118, 124, 144, 206
Kraut, Alan, 168
Kronick, Richard, 38-39, 52

LaFraniere, Sharon, 114
Lauter, David, 52, 53, 115, 221
Lazare, E., 112
Leo, John, 115
Leonard, Paul, 112, 113, 115
Lerman, Robert, 145
Levin, Herman, 111, 193
Lipsky, Michael, 78, 84
Long, William, 170
Longman, Phillip, 52
Lubove, Roy, 192
Luders, Rolf, 194
Lusk, Mark, 83, 221
Lynn, Laurence Jr., 82

Machacek, John, 221
Maraniss, David, 115
Marmor, Theodore, 21, 27, 193, 194
Marshall, Jonathan, 113
Marshall, Will, 17, 19, 27, 73, 82, 215-216, 220, 221
Mashaw, Jerry, 21, 27, 193, 194
Martindale, Don, 168
Martinez, Gebe, 168
Massey, Douglas, 87-90, 112, 115
Mathews, Jay, 84, 145
McCall, Nathan, 85, 111, 147
McCart, Linda, 83
McDonnell, Patrick, 169, 170
McManus, Doyle, 221
McMullan, Michael, 55
McQuaid, Kim, 176, 192
Mead, Lawrence, 63, 82
Medicaid, 10-11, 29-31, 33, 35, 46, 59-61. *See also* AFDC, SSI
Medicare, 29-32, 35, 36, 173
   Catastrophic Health Insurance (CHI), 36, 173, 191
   Diagnostic Related Group (DRG), 32
   Prospective Payment System (PPS), 32
Medoff, Peter, 116
Mencimer, Stephanie, 82
Mencken, H. L., 25, 221
Mendel, Ed, 170
Merl, Jean, 145
Midgley, James, 193
Miller, Alan, 54, 168
Mishel, Lawrence, 112
Moe, Terry, 128, 138, 145, 146
Moeller, Scott, 194
Mofitt, Robert, 112
Monto, Alexander, 159, 169
Morgan, Dan, 54
Morganthau, Tom, 82
Moskos, Charles, 145

Moynihan, Daniel Patrick, 5, 12, 14, 26, 42, 72, 90, 94, 111-113, 122, 173, 182, 192, 194
Murphy, Dean, 114
Murray, Charles, 63, 68, 82
Myrdal, Gunnar, 111, 116

Navarrette, Ruben Jr., 147
Navarro, Vincente, 52
Nelson, Jack, 53
Neoconservatives, 12
Neoliberalism, 15-16, 197. *See also* Peters, Charles
New Deal, 6, 10-11, 85
"New Federalism," 44
Newman, Katherine, 26, 220
New Paradigm, 6, 18-20, 27. *See also* Kaus, Mickey; Osborne, David; Pinkerton, James
Newton, Jim, 114
Nicklin, Julie, 147
Nies, Joseph, 83
Nixon, Richard, 8, 10-11, 58
North American Free Trade Agreement (NAFTA), 2, 4, 16, 23, 159, 165-166, 211
Nugent, Walter, 158, 168, 169

Offner, Paul, 72-73, 82, 83
Omnibus Budget Reconciliation Act (OBRA) of 1981, 13, 64, 92-93
O'Neill, D., 146
O'Rorke, P. J., 57, 81
Osborne, David, 18, 19, 27, 54, 78, 84, 213, 221
Ostrow, Ronald, 112
"Overclass," 94-96

Passel, Jeffrey, 154, 156, 160-161, 169
Passell, Peter, 145
Pasternak, Judy, 115
Pear, Robert, 53, 194
Pearlstein, Steven, 27, 52
Peters, Charles, 16, 27, 29, 51
Peterson, Paul, 113
Peterson, Peter, 182-186, 193, 194, 220
Phillips, Kevin, 15, 25, 27, 82, 93, 95, 112, 113, 195, 209, 220
Pianin, Eric, 194
Pines, Burton, 13, 26
Pinkerton, James, 18, 27, 221
Piven, Frances Fox, 11, 26, 82
Portes, Alejandro, 165, 168, 170
Poverty, 57-59, 61-62, 75
Powell, Ronald, 116
Powell, Stewart, 53
Priest, Dana, 52-54
Pritchard, Colin, 26
Putka, Gary, 145

Quadagno, Jill, 26

Rahwim, Salome, 84
Rainey, James, 170
Raspberry, William, 213, 221
Rauch, Jonathan, 195, 220
Ravitch, Diane, 144
Reagan, Ronald
  budget, 14
  domestic affairs, 14
  education, 121-122
  health care, 36, 45
  immigration, 155, 166
  presidency, 11, 199
  Social Security, 173, 179
  social services, 9, 13-15, 99
  urban policy, 90-92, 94-95, 97
  welfare, 15, 20-21, 57-58, 62-64
Reich, Robert, 118, 144, 199
Reimers, David, 169
Relman, Arnold, 37, 52
Rich, Spencer, 53, 54
Richardson, Elliot, 41, 53
Richter, Paul, 52, 53, 115, 196
Risen, James, 82
Rivlin, Alice, 221
Roan, Shari, 52
Robins, Leonard, 54
Rodriguez, Marcelo, 115
Rohrlich, Ted, 115
Rose, Robert, 84
Rosenbaum, David, 112, 115
Rosenstiel, Thomas, 147
Ross, Edward Alsworth, 152, 168
Ross, Michael, 116
Rothstein, Richard, 220
Rowe, Jonathan, 84
Rowen, Hobart, 187, 194
Rumbaut, Ruben, 165, 168, 170
Rusk, David, 108, 110, 116
Ryan, William, 11, 26

Sagel, Jim, 168
Sahagun, Louis, 113
Samuelson, Robert, 187, 194
Sanchez, Leonel, 170
Savage, David, 115
Savings and Loan (S&L) scandal, 94-96
Sawicky, Max, 19-20, 27
Schiller, Zachary, 51
Schlesinger, Arthur Jr., 3-4, 25, 198
Schorr, Lisbeth, 144
Schram, Martin, 82, 220
Schuck, Peter, 169
Seib, Gerald, 53
Serrano, Richard, 114, 168
Sexton, Joe, 113
Sapiro, Isaac, 51
Shapiro, Robert, 188-190, 194
Sharpe, Rochelle, 146
Sherman, Arloc, 46, 54
Sherraden, Michael, 77, 84
Shogan, Robert, 53
Shogren, Elizabeth, 82, 115, 116, 145
Shorris, Earl, 164, 170
Silber, John, 142
Silverstein, Stuart, 170
Simon, Julian, 160-161, 169, 170
Simon, Richard, 170
Sklar, Holly, 116
Sleeper, Jim, 115
Smith, James, 26
Snyder, Mitch, 99-101, 114
Social Policy
  conceptualizations of, left and right, 2-3
  "Pendulum Theory," 3-4. *See also* Schlesinger, Arthur Jr.
  post WWII, 10, 24
  "Tide Metaphor," 4-5. *See also* Friedman, Milton and Rose, 4, 25
Social Security, 7, 14, 16, 20, 31, 63, 173-174, 176-179, 206-207

INDEX

Congressional Budget Office (CBO), 137, 186-189, 208
Disability Insurance, 173, 178, 180-181
Old Age Survivors Insurance, 173, 180-181
  origins of, 174-177
  reforms, 178-180, 185-186, 188-189
  surplus, 179-183
  withholding tax, 189-191. *See also* Medicare; Social Security Act of 1935
Social Security Act of 1935, 6-7, 10, 57, 176-178
  Federal Emergency Relief Administration (FERA), 6-7
  Hopkins, Harry (director of FERA), 6-8, 77, 85
  Public Assistance Programs, 7, 11, 14, 20. *See also* AFDC and SSI
  reform, 186-188
  "social entitlements," 7-8, 183-189, 192, 207, 213-221
  Social Insurance Programs, 7, 11, 20. *See also* Social Security; Unemployment Compensation
Sosin, Michael, 114
Specht, Harry, 26
Spechter, Michael, 112
Special interests, 195-196
Spolar, Christine, 168
Stark, Steven, 53
Starr, Kevin, 170
Starr, Mark, 147
Starr, Paul, 35, 52
Stecklow, Steve, 145
Steinmetz, Greg, 54
Stoesz, David, 26, 27, 51, 52, 82, 111, 112, 146, 193, 221
Stolberg, Sheryl, 171
Stout, Hilary, 53
Strawn, Julie, 83
Summer, Laura, 51
Sumner, Graham, 151-152, 168
Supplemental Security Income (SSI), 7, 26, 59, 177
Suskind, Ron, 147
Sykes, Charles, 131, 145

Tamarkin, Civia, 144
Tanouye, Elyse, 54
Taylor, Paul, 145
Tengs, Tammy, 54
Terrell, Paul, 26
"Think Tanks"
  American Enterprise (AEI), 12-13, 216
  Cato Institute, 160, 216
  Empower America, 15
  Heritage Foundation, 9, 13, 166, 215-216
  Hoover Institute, 13, 216
  Progressive Policy Institute (PPI), 17, 197, 215-217. *See also* Marshall, Will
Thomas, Paulette, 193
Tilton, Timothy, 192
Title XX, 8-9, 13
Title XX Social Services Block Grant, 10
Tobin, James, 193
Toner, Robin, 52, 54
Toch, Thomas, 121-122, 144, 145, 168
Tracy, Martin, 193
Trafford, Abigail, 54
Treadwell, David, 112
Trombley, William, 145
Truehart, Charles, 145

Tumulty, Karen, 26, 53
Turque, Bill, 114

"Underclass," 58, 68, 88-90, 92-94, 109, 212
Unemployment Compensation, 7, 63
Urban crime, 93-94
  gang violence, 96-99
Urban Diaspora, 87-90
Urban Enterprise Zone (UEZ), 91, 211
Urban Policy, 85
  Department of Housing and Urban Development (HUD), 86
  federalism of, 90-91
  Housing Act of 1937/1954, 86
  privatization of, 90-91
  public housing dispersement, 106-107
  urban compact, 108-109
  Youth Enterprise Zones (YEZs), 107

Vobejda, Barbara, 83, 113, 147
von Hoffman, Nicholas, 215, 221

Waldman, Steven, 53
Wallace, Amy, 147
War on Poverty, 5, 7, 10-11, 61
  Community Action Program (CAP), 10, 86. *See also* Medicaid
  Economic Opportunity Act of 1964, 10
  Elementary and Secondary Education Act (ESEA), 121
  Head Start, 5, 10-11, 65, 121, 135
  Job Corps, 10-11, 65
  poverty programs and acts of 1960s, 5, 10-11, 26, 86
Weaver, Carolyn, 179-180, 193
Weisberg, Jacob, 52
Welfare
  Child Support Assurance (CSA), 75-77, 80. *See also* Garfinkel, Irving
  Earned Income Tax Credit (EITC), 70
  Family Support Act of 1988, 14, 58, 63-65
  Food Stamps, 20, 59-61, 63
  immigrants, 159-162
  Income Maintenance. *See also* AFDC
  Individual Development Accounts (IDAs), 77-78, 190. *See also* Medicaid, Medicare
  Job Opportunities and Basic Skills (JOBS), 64, 66, 68, 70, 79-80
  Manpower Demonstration Research Corporation (MDRC), 66-68, 73, 81
  state reforms, 66-69, 71-72, 80-81. *See also* SSI
Welfare Bureaucracy Deconstruction, 78-79
welfare fraud, 59-60
welfare policy, 58
welfare reform, 79-81, 207
Whitemire, Richard, 83
Williams, Juan, 113
Wilson, James Q., 113, 114
Wilson, Pete, 169
Wilson, William Julius, 90, 93, 112, 113
Wodarski, John, 112
Wolf, Douglas, 112
Wolfe, Alan, 167, 168, 171
Wolock, Isabel, 112
Wong, Linda, 170
Woodward, Bob, 2, 25, 27, 115, 193, 198, 201, 215, 220
Woolhandler, Steffie, 37, 52

Yen, Marianne, 114

About the Author

David Stoesz (pronounced Stace) is the Samuel S. Wurtzel Chair in Social Work at Virginia Commonwealth University. He has held directive service and administrative appointments in public welfare and mental health. His primary research interests include the rise of for-profit health and human service firms, the role of think tanks in the social policy process, social welfare theory, and a post-industrial formulation for health and human services. Dr. Stoesz is the coauthor of *American Social Welfare Policy, Reconstructing the American Welfare State,* and *The Politics of Child Abuse in America.* He lives in Richmond, Virginia.